SURVEY OF ADVANCED SALES

7TH EDITION

DEARBORN™
A **Kaplan Professional** Company

This publication is designed to provide accurate and authoritative information in regard to the subject matter covered. It is sold with the understanding that the publisher is not engaged in rendering legal, accounting, or other professional service. If legal advice or other expert assistance is required, the services of a competent professional person should be sought.

This text is updated periodically to reflect changes in laws and regulations. To verify that you have the most recent update, you may call DEARBORN at 1-800-423-4723.

©1969, 1981, 1985, 1987, 1991, 1996, 2000 by Dearborn Financial Publishing, Inc.®
Published by Dearborn Financial Institute, Inc.

Printed in the United States of America

First printing, April 2000

Library of Congress Cataloging-in-Publication Data

Survey of advanced sales. -- 7th ed.
   p. cm.
  ISBN 0-7931-3830-2
  1. Insurance agents.   2. Finance, Personal.   3. Investments.

HG8091 .S87 2000
368'.0068'8—dc21   00-025089

Table of Contents

Acknowledgments

he publisher would like to acknowledge the following individuals for their thoughts, input and contributions toward the revision of this text. James W. Eckel, J.D., CFP, CLU, who specializes in insurance and financial planning for individuals and small business owners, and John A. Oliver, MBA, CLU, ChFC.

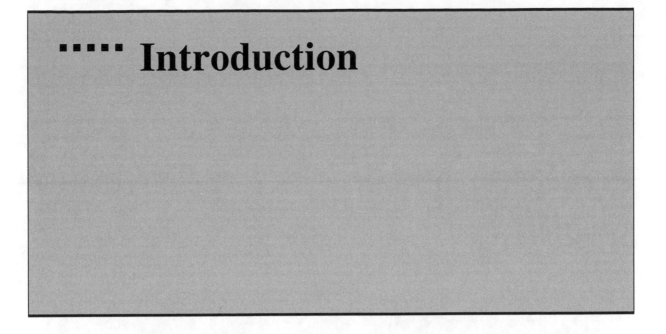

Introduction

elcome to *Survey of Advanced Sales*. This course presents an overview of a number of exciting and expanding areas in which the financial services professional has tremendous opportunities today: business insurance, retirement and disability plans and estate and investment planning.

Taking advantage of opportunities in today's increasingly competitive market requires detailed and up-to-date knowledge, as well as hard work and dedication to serving the needs of prospects and clients. Recent tax law changes, as well as changes in the marketplace, have resulted in an expansion of the ways in which the insurance industry can serve the needs of individuals and businesses.

The information in this course is designed to help you recognize these opportunities and to devise solutions for particular problems you may encounter. We have endeavored to present this information in clear and concise language with numerous examples and illustrations. A new format also aims to convey the material in an orderly, progressive fashion. The course is now broken into four sections: planning for individuals, business entities, planning opportunities with business entities and transfer planning for individuals and business entities.

Survey of Advanced Sales strives to arm you with the necessary knowledge to aid you in your quest for greater success and professionalism. As always, we value your commitment to Dearborn and hope that through our other products and services we can continue to meet your training and licensing needs.

Suzanne C. Bibko, J.D.
Legal Editor

Section One

Planning for Individuals

1
Investment Planning

Individuals pursue many different financial objectives depending upon their particular circumstances. An increasingly complex array of financial resources can be utilized to attempt to achieve these objectives. This chapter is an introduction to investment planning, including the concept of net worth, measures of return on investment and the possible impact of inflation and/or deflation. An evaluation procedure is suggested to answer the question "Should this particular financial resource be owned by this particular individual?" The key to this evaluation procedure is establishing the individual's objectives. We conclude with a listing of some of the most commonly sought objectives.

In today's highly competitive marketplace, there is an increasingly complex—and often confusing—array of investment possibilities available to the individual. Once an individual's income has increased beyond providing the necessities of life, thoughts increasingly turn to how to use discretionary income to meet other goals.

Life insurance and annuity products can provide security for the individual and his or her family, business and property. Through these vehicles, we can make sure that the value of a business is not lost at death through forced liquidation. Such products can help guarantee that there will be adequate funds available for a comfortable retirement. Life insurance will also minimize estate shrinkage and ensure that estate assets are distributed as the estate owner would have desired.

Today's financial advisors and life agents are dealing with a more sophisticated public. Increasingly, consumers want to make insurance purchasing decisions as a part of a complete investment strategy. You should endorse this approach since it will actually make your task easier. With very few exceptions, a sound investment strategy will include one or more plans of life insurance. Many financial experts agree that life insurance is the foundation upon which other financial and investment vehicles are based.

Let's take a brief look at the topic of investment planning. By necessity, this discussion is limited in scope, focusing on general principles and practices.

■ ■ ■ ■ ■

■ FINANCIAL OBJECTIVES

Broadly stated, financial objectives that individuals pursue involve the accumulation, conservation and/or distribution of wealth. In everyday language, those objectives pertain simply to people's needs and desires to save or invest successfully, to build estates, to reduce or defer taxes, to avoid financial losses, to be able to obtain or distribute earnings and/or principal as they prefer, etc. At the other extreme, of course, objectives may include the desire to experience the challenges and thrills of near-gambling risks or sheer speculation. In addition, the balance between immediate gratification from consumption of financial resources and planning for future objectives is always present. (This is a balance that is necessarily a bit different for each individual.)

All investment vehicles and financial plans should help accomplish an individual's objectives.

■ ASSET ALLOCATION

The concept of asset allocation refers to the dividing of investment funds between stocks, bonds and cash equivalents. This decision is the most important factor in determining an investor's portfolio return. In a recent study, asset allocation policy was responsible for 92 percent of long-term investment performance. On a global scale, the asset allocation decision revolves around three questions:

- What percentage of available funds is to be invested in each country?

- Within each country what percentage of available funds is to be invested in stocks, bonds or cash?

- Within each asset class what percentage of available funds is to be invested in different types of bonds, mutual funds, exchanges—listed stocks vs. NASDAQ, etc.?

Once a portfolio has been put in place, the monitoring of the portfolio becomes of paramount importance. Generally, there are two approaches that very much depend on issues that are specific to each investor, such as risk tolerance, expected returns and asset correlation. The first approach encompasses an allocation derived in advance, put into place, then observed for a number of years. The second approach uses a market timing method, which alters the allocation based on changes in predictions concerning asset returns. Neither approach is a clear and consistent winner over the other. Most major mutual fund companies, investment bankers and security houses publish their own asset allocation models based on their research of current economic and business trends.

■ MEASURES OF NET WORTH

The net worth of any owner of financial resources is the value of the owner's total assets (everything owned) less the value of the owner's total liabilities (everything owed). Knowing one's net worth is important for a number of reasons. For example, it is a major factor in a person's current or potential buying power, in the availability of credit to the individual (both the amount available and the rate charged), in the person's investment earning power and in the analysis and planning of the individual's estate, to name just a few.

So the ability to determine a person's net worth is vitally important. As simple as that determination would seem from the above definition (net worth = assets – liabilities), we will see there are some complexities—particularly in the evaluation of assets and liabilities.

Personal Assets

Assets may be defined as the entire property of all sorts belonging to a person, association, corporation or estate applicable or subject to the payment of his, her or its debts. The discussion here will be limited to the kinds of property (assets) commonly owned by individuals namely, personal assets. Such assets fall into three major categories: (1) cash and near-cash, (2) tangibles and (3) intangibles. (See Ill. 1.1.)

Cash and near-cash. This category includes money and any assets that can be used as money or almost instantly converted to money. Checking and NOW (negotiated order of withdrawal) accounts, traveler's checks, money orders, certified and cashier's checks, bank or savings and loan passbook savings accounts, credit union savings accounts and daily cash money-market drafts are all examples of near-cash assets.

Tangible assets. These are possessions that have physical substance and are themselves the objects of value, such as real estate; oil; meat; grain and other commodities; gold, silver and other precious metals; gems; and works of art and other collectibles.

Intangible assets. These are possessions that represent ownership of (or ownership interests in) things of value, but have little, if any, intrinsic value themselves. They include such assets as stocks, bonds, Treasury bills, certificates of deposit, mortgages, mutual fund shares, real estate investment trusts (REITs) shares, money-market fund shares, patents, copyrights, life insurance and annuity contracts, etc.

Liabilities

An individual's *liabilities* are simply the debts and other financial obligations of that person. They would include such payable or repayable items as personal or commercial loans, financed-purchase loans, mortgage loans, home improvement loans, taxes due, judgments and so on.

People often are, or feel, morally obligated to provide financial support to others—such as people's feelings of financial obligation for the care and education of their children or for the care of their elderly parents. But as important as such moral obligations may be to an individual, they are not liabilities in the legal sense unless the individual is legally obligated to pay them.

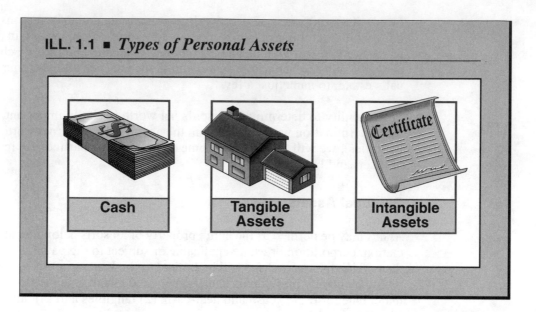

ILL. 1.1 ■ *Types of Personal Assets*

Cash

Tangible Assets

Intangible Assets

Current Value

The value of anything at the time of its evaluation is its *current value*. This generally refers to the value today, but it is also used to mean the actual value at some other specified point in time—at the close of business last year, or on March 31 of next year, for example.

Future Value

As its name implies, *future value* is the amount at which something will be valued at some specified time in the future. This can be a *known* value (such as the maturity value of a bond or endowment) or it can be a *projected* value (such as the value of a fixed-rate savings account or a variable-rate mutual fund) at a known or assumed rate of change or interest.

Future Value

- Investment $\times$ (1+r) n
- $10,000 invested at 8 percent for 3 years = $10,000 $\times$ (1.08) $\times$ (1.08) $\times$ (1.08) = $12,600

OR

- $10,000 $\times$ 1.260 (from chart) = $12,600

Year	4%	8%	12%	16%
1	1.040	1.080	1.120	1.160
3	1.125	**1.260**	1.405	1.561
5	1.217	1.469	1.760	2.100
10	1.480	2.159	3.106	4.411
25	2.665	6.848	17.000	40.874
40	4.801	21.725	93.050	378.721

Present Value

Also called discounted value, *present value* is today's equivalent of a future value, based on a known or assumed rate of change over the period of time involved. In other words, the present value is that amount that, if increased at a known or assumed rate over a given period of time, would equal (1) either a specified future value at the end of that period or (2) the value of a series of specified periodic values (such as, periodic income payments) throughout that period.

Present Value

- Investment $\times 1 / (1+r)$ n
- $10,000 $\times 1 / (1.08) \times 1 / (1.08) \times 1 / (1.08)$
- $((($10,000 $\times .926) \times .926) \times .926)$
- $7,940 invested at 8 percent for 3 years = $10,000

OR

- $10,000 $\times$ .794 (from chart) = $7,940

Year	4%	8%	12%	16%
1	0.962	0.926	0.893	0.862
3	0.888	**0.794**	0.712	0.641
5	0.822	0.681	0.567	0.476
10	0.675	0.463	0.322	0.226
25	0.375	0.146	0.059	0.024
40	0.208	0.046	0.011	0.002

Market Value

The usual definition of *market value* is the price at which both buyers and sellers, dealing at arm's length, are willing to do business. This value is determined chiefly by supply and demand, barring artificial controls (laws, taxes, etc.).

For example, if only a few apples are available one week, and a lot of people want apples, the price would tend to be relatively high. Conversely, if there are a large amount of apples the next week, but relatively few people want them, the price would tend to be lower.

This same principle applies, with varying degrees of complexity, in virtually all marketing situations whether person to person, in the grocery or department stores, at auctions, on organized securities exchanges or in real estate markets.

Replacement Value

Replacement value is the cost to replace the item being valued. This is not the same as market value.

For purposes of illustration, consider any of the big old mansions that represented the ultimate in wealth and luxury 50 to 100 years ago. Because of relatively low demand for such an old home with its outdated electrical and plumbing fixtures, heating equipment and so on—compared with the modern new homes available in the competitive home buyer market—its market value may be relatively low today: $50,000 to $100,000, perhaps.

But now think of the cost of duplicating that old mansion, or replacing it if it were destroyed. That cost undoubtedly would go up into several hundreds of thousands—possibly millions—of dollars. That cost is the *replacement value* of that old mansion.

Replacement value is an important and frequently used method of valuing property for insurance purposes—automobile collision, homeowners, fire and business interruption insurance, to name a few.

Book Value

Book value is the value of something according to the owner's books of account; it rarely equals the current market value. Book value generally is the cost (rather than the current value) of whatever is being valued less any depreciation and any liabilities against it.

The following example better explains book value and shows how it compares to market value. In 1935, a deluxe Ford or Chevrolet could be purchased from Detroit for about $550 to $600. If depreciation (from an accounting standpoint) were taken on that automobile, it would have been reduced to zero book value decades ago. But in terms of market value to antique car enthusiasts, that old car would be worth a few thousand dollars—or many times that amount if it were in mint condition.

Book value is most frequently used with reference to businesses and ownership interests in businesses, especially corporations and shares of stock in corporations. In this context, the book value is often called the *net asset value* of the corporation. For it is the net balance sheet value (usually based on cost, and after depreciation and any depletion allowances) of corporate assets (usually not including intangible assets, such as goodwill and appreciation) after subtracting the full amount of liabilities (claims of creditors, preferred stockholders, etc.). The book value per share of common stock is simply that net asset value divided by the number of outstanding shares of common stock in that corporation.

Appraisals and Other Valuations

The valuation of something by the estimate of an authorized person (usually a recognized expert in the particular field) is called an *appraisal* or an *appraised value*. This method is used, for example, in determining the value of property for tax or loan purposes, or for determining a reasonable price at which to list property for sale.

Forced sale values and *distress sale prices* are determined, not by usual means of valuation, but by whatever buyers (in their mercy) will pay for things that sellers must sell (to pay taxes or other judgments) or on which they will lose more if they don't sell now (perishables that are getting very ripe—or stock that is or is rapidly becoming obsolete). (See Ill. 1.2.)

ILL. 1.2 ■ *Measures of Value*

Current Value—The value of an item at the time of its evaluation.

Future Value—Today's equivalent of a future value, based on a given rate of change over a given period of time.

Present Value—Today's equivalent of a future value based on a given rate of change over a given period of time.

Market Value—The price at which buyers and sellers, dealing at arm's length, are willing to do business.

Replacement Value—The cost to replace the item being valued.

Book value—The value of an item according to the owner's books of account.

Appraised Value—The value of an item based on the estimate of an authorized person.

These and other means of valuation are used in special situations or with respect to certain assets such as stock of a closely held corporation or the value of a lottery ticket in a deceased person's estate.

■ RETURN ON INVESTMENT

The late great social commentator, Will Rogers, once said, "I'm more interested in the return *of* my money than the return *on* my money." Of course, Rogers spoke these words during the Great Depression, and while the phrase is still applicable today, in this discussion we will concentrate on asset growth as opposed to asset loss.

When we speak of *return on investment,* the term *return* is being used in a broad sense. It includes virtually all results of investment—earnings and capital growth, tangible and intangible, gross and net. Consequently, this discussion will be broken down into five segments:

1. gross return—earnings

2. gross return—capital growth

3. investment costs

4. net return—earnings

5. net return—capital growth

Gross Return—Earnings

Gross return earnings encompass many kinds of returns including interest, dividends, rents, royalties and other cash flow stemming from investments, before any costs relative to the investments are deducted.

Interest

By far the most common kind of earnings return on investment is *interest*. Interest is the payment for the borrowed use of commodities, especially money, and thus is often described as *the rental payment* for borrowed funds. Savings accounts and certificates—bills, notes, bonds and mortgages—for example, all represent borrowing by, and loans to, the issuers of those accounts or instruments. And all pay for the use of what is borrowed in some form of interest. Interest can be *simple, compound* or *discount* (or *accrual*).

Simple interest is interest computed on the original principal only. For example, assume you lend a friend $5,000 at 9 percent *simple interest* (annual rate) for six months. At the end of six months, the friend would owe you *simple interest* of $225 [(6/12 × .09) × $5,000] plus the principal of $5,000. Moreover, your friend would owe you no more than that, even if the interest and principal were not repaid to you on time, but were held for another month or so—unless a new or extended loan was provided for originally, or was negotiated on or by the due date.

Compound interest is the interest upon principal that is being increased or augmented periodically by the interest paid on the previous amount of principal. It is interest computed periodically on the sum of original principal and accrued interest. Periodic compounding may be daily, weekly, monthly, semiannually or annually.

For example, assume the above loan was at *compound* (rather than *simple*) interest—$5,000 for six months at 9 percent compounded monthly. At the end of six months, your friend would owe you the $5,000 principal plus compound interest of $229.26:

First month	$5,000			×	($\frac{1}{12}$	×	.09)	=	$ 37.50
Second month	$5,000	+	$37.50	×	($\frac{1}{12}$	×	.09)	=	$ 37.78
Third month	$5,037.50	+	$37.78	×	($\frac{1}{12}$	×	.09)	=	$ 38.06
Fourth month	$5,075.28	+	$38.06	×	($\frac{1}{12}$	×	.09)	=	$ 38.35
Fifth month	$5,113.34	+	$38.35	×	($\frac{1}{12}$	×	.09)	=	$ 38.64
Sixth month	$5,151.69	+	$38.64	×	($\frac{1}{12}$	×	.09)	=	$ 38.93
									$229.26

Thus, *compound* interest for six months at the same rate produces $4.26 more earnings on the $5,000 principal than does *simple* interest. This may not seem too great a difference over a short period, but note the ever-increasing amount of interest added each successive month of compounding—then think how much more significant this would be over a number of years. To illustrate, in 93 months (7¾ years) the interest would make the total amount repayable more than double ($10,017.52). In a total of just 12¼ years, the total amount due would be more than *triple* the amount of the original loan at 9 percent compounded monthly.

Useful tools in determining the compound effect of investment return are the Rules of 72 and 115. Use the Rule of 72 to find either the rate of return or number of years it would take to double an initial sum. For example, an investment of $100,000 earning a 12 percent rate of return would double to $200,000 in six years. The Rule of 115 will find the same information to triple an initial sum. For instance, an initial investment of $250,000 earning 10 percent would be worth about $750,000 in 11½ years.

Discount (or *accrual*) is the form of interest realized on a loan (bill, note, bond, etc.) when an amount or percentage (for interest earnings) is deducted from the total repayable value of the loan to determine the loan amount that actually changes hands initially. Then the reduced amount is really the principal actually loaned initially; the repayable amount is the total face, maturity or scheduled value; and the difference is interest on the initial amount.

Two terms used to describe the interest rate period are *exact interest* (which means interest computed on the basis of 365 days to the year) and *ordinary interest* (which means interest computed on the basis of 360 days to the year—12 months of 30 days each). These terms simply modify the interest rate periods in the three foregoing forms of interest. They do not alter the definitions or descriptions.

Dividends

Just as interest is the earnings on lender (loan) investments, so dividends generally are the distributed earnings on owner (equity) investments. The word *distributed* is important because there are some earnings on owner investments that are not always distributed, as will be discussed later.

Dividends, in general, may be defined as portions of a corporation's net profits that have been officially declared by the board of directors for distribution on its outstanding issues of stock to its stockholders. The total to be distributed is divided by the number of outstanding shares to determine the dividend per share. Each shareholder receives a distribution equal to that dividend per share times the number of shares he or she owns. Obviously, each declaration of dividends will vary in amount influenced by the profit results of the company although a company prefers to pay an equal or larger dividend with each successive dividend declaration.

Dividends are usually distributed in *cash* on a *regular* periodic basis, such as quarterly or annually. But sometimes dividend distributions are made in *stock, bonds, property* or *script* (promissory notes). Sometimes *extra* or *special* or *interim* dividends may be distributed, as when the company realizes unusual profits. Sometimes stockholders are given the *option* of receiving cash or stock dividends. Then there are *liquidation* dividends that, unlike other dividends that represent the distribution of earnings, represent the return of capital to the owners—as distributions of funds arising from the operation of wasting assets (for example, from depreciation allowances), or as distributions to owners of a corporation's net assets when the company is winding up its affairs.

There are also *insurance policy* dividends from participating life insurance contracts, which are really not dividends in the above sense. They are really distributions of the excess of the premium paid for coverage at the beginning of a period (usually a year) over the actual premium needed as determined at the end of the period. This excess arises from such sources as savings in actual to expected claims (in life insurance, more favorable than expected mortality), savings in actual to expected expenses and excesses in actual over expected earnings on assets—that is, actual compared to the expected claims, expenses and earnings assumed in the original premium calculation. So, since these are refunds to policyowners of excess premiums paid, insurance dividends are not considered to be income for tax purposes, although interest paid on accumulation of those dividends is considered to be taxable income.

Rent

Rent is the payment or series of periodic payments that owners of property receive from others for the possession, occupancy and/or use of that property. It is the form of earnings return received from income-producing real property (such as farm, residential and business real estate) or from income-producing *personal* property (such as rental machinery, equipment, vehicles and the like).

Royalties

Copyrights on the works of authors and composers, and patents on the works of inventors, are assets—and often income-producing assets. The earnings that owners receive on copyrights and patents are called *royalties.* Such royalties usually are payments based on specified amounts or percentages of price per copyrighted item or patented article sold.

A royalty may also be a share of the product or profit reserved for the owner of a valuable right that has been granted to someone for use or exploitation. Examples of recipients of such royalties are grantors of oil and mining leases.

Annuities

Annuities are a special kind of income-producing asset. They combine both periodic returns of earnings on the principal and portions of the principal itself, into equal periodic income payments over specified periods of time such that both interest and principal are exhausted at the exact end of the specified income period.

Temporary annuities (fixed-period or fixed-amount incomes) are most often provided by life insurance companies, though they may be provided by other financial institutions. Life annuities, however, are available only from life insurance companies because only life insurance companies are empowered by law to employ life contingency factors required in life-income contracts.

Gross Return—Capital Growth

Capital growth means increase in the value of the asset itself. There are several ways that such an increase can occur. For one, the earnings can be plowed back into the asset (say, a business) to increase its capital value. Alternatively, labor or material can be added to increase the capital value of the asset. However, these really are reinvestments or additional investments that make the combined old and added values more than the original value alone.

Appreciation

Appreciation is a type of capital growth that increases the value of an asset (in excess of its depreciable cost) due to economic and other conditions, as opposed to factors that increase the value of an asset due to improvements or additions made to it.

Here is an example of appreciation in asset value: 100 shares of XYZ stock are purchased at $30 per share, or a total of $3,000. Two years later, the market price is $40 per share, so the value of those 100 shares is up to $4,000. The $1,000 increase in value ($10 per share) is not an earnings return. It is appreciation in the asset's capital value and, if the stock is sold, represents a capital growth return on the asset.

Investment Costs

Up to this point, our discussion of investment return has been limited to gross return, earnings and capital growth. Now let's consider the *costs* of investment, which can be broken down into three major categories: (1) acquisition costs, (2) holding costs and (3) disposition costs. "What about taxes?" you might ask. Applicable taxes (income, sales, gift, estate and any other taxes involved) fall into one of the three major categories of costs above, and they will be included in the following discussions of those categories.

Acquisition Costs

Acquisition costs are the costs associated with purchasing or otherwise acquiring investment property or other financial resources. In addition to the basic purchase price (usually the cost basis), these costs normally include some of the following.

Sales costs (charges, fees, commissions, etc.) frequently fall in this category. Some investments involve only one such sales cost, while others may involve more than one. Stocks and bonds, for example, involve a sales cost payable by the buyer and seller—the broker-dealer and the sales representatives' commission. Mutual funds may have no sales charge (no load), an upfront sales charge (front load) or a back-end sales charge (a back-end load).

Sometimes these sales costs are obviously charged directly to the investor/buyer, but other times this is not so obvious. For example, frequently the sales charge, fee or commission is simply added onto the net value of whatever is being purchased and included in the price that the investor pays. This is often the case even when technically the seller pays this cost.

Taxes payable by a person when he or she comes into possession of assets, are also acquisition costs that pertain to some investments and other financial resources. In the transfer of stocks on the New York Stock Exchange, for example, there are certain state transfer taxes and SEC fees (which are virtually the same as taxes) payable. Generally, these taxes and fees are paid by the seller. However, it is difficult to say they are not included in the price the seller was willing to accept on the exchange auction—the price the buyer paid—even though the seller technically paid those taxes.

Another example of taxes as acquisition costs are inheritance taxes. As discussed, inheritance taxes are imposed by states on property passed to heirs. Although inherited property is not acquired by purchase, the inheritance tax certainly is an acquisition cost, and one that may be meaningful if the property is held and later disposed of as an investment property.

There are other *miscellaneous* acquisition costs applicable to various investments, such as attorney fees, appraisal fees, finder fees, title search fees or title insurance premiums, loan points, buyer's closing costs, etc.

Holding Costs

While an individual holds investment property or other financial resources, there are certain costs that occur because of and during that holding.

Advisory and/or *management fees,* as well as operating costs, are generally charged to owners of shares in managed funds, or property in trusts, or professionally managed rental property and so on while those assets are held.

Repairs, maintenance and *needed improvements* may arise during the holding of some assets. If so, they may be considered as holding costs—although some of them may be considered as capital improvements for tax purposes. Rental properties are assets that commonly involve this kind of holding cost.

Various forms of *property insurance* may also be needed or required by law, and the *premiums* on such coverages would be holding costs. Any losses (say, by fire, storm, flood, accident or the like) not covered by insurance would also be a holding cost.

Taxes are still another kind of holding cost. These include *income taxes* on interest, dividends, rents, royalties and other earnings returns (received or accrued) on properties held—except for those types of income specifically exempted (such as interest on municipal bonds) and those specifically tax deferred (such as earnings on qualified retirement plans, IRAs and so on) until those earnings are actually received.

And, of course, there are *intangibles taxes, personal property taxes, real estate taxes,* etc., that various state and local taxing jurisdictions assess just for a person's owning and holding those various assets.

Disposition Costs

Disposition costs arise because of, and at the time of, the disposition of investment property and other financial resources. In addition to debts against the property, such costs include the following:

Sales costs (charges, fees, commissions, etc.) that the seller must pay are, of course, disposition costs. In the case of stocks, for example, the seller pays a broker a commission for selling just as the buyer pays a broker a commission for buying. In most instances, even though some of the sales costs may be shifted to the buyer in the price, the seller generally pays the larger part, if not all, of the sales costs in selling real estate and most assets other than stocks.

Taxes are another major disposition cost. Any untaxed earnings returns, including those deferred under qualified retirement or other tax-deferred plans, generally are subject to *income tax* on disposition or liquidation of the assets. Any capital growth returns are generally subject to a *capital gains tax.* Transfer of property to someone else by gift subjects those assets to *gift tax.* Transfer at death subjects those assets to *estate tax* and usually to *inheritance tax.* Any transfers of stocks on an organized exchange are subject to an SEC fee and usually to an exchange *transfer tax,* both generally paid (at least technically) by the seller. Periodic income distributions resulting from the disposition of both the capital and earnings value of an asset are subject to the rules governing the taxation of annuities.

Net Return—Earnings

The *earnings* form of *net return* includes all the gross earnings discussed earlier (interest, dividends, rents, royalties and so on) *less* any of the *costs applicable to earnings* such as advisory and management fees, operating costs, repairs, maintenance and needed improvements other than capital improvements, property insurance premiums, income taxes on earnings, intangibles taxes, personal property taxes and real estate taxes.

Gross earnings minus costs equal the net earnings return on any asset or combinations of assets. Net earnings are generally expressed as a percentage of net periodic earnings return on the net capital value of the asset or assets. They are usually determined on a periodic basis, but can be totaled or averaged over an entire holding period.

Net Return—Capital Growth

The *capital growth* form of *net return* includes the gross value at time of valuation (usually the gross sales price plus any capital distributions since acquisition) *less* any *indebtedness, less* the *cost basis* (usually the basic purchase price plus any subsequent capital investments and capital improvements but less any indebtedness), *less* any of the *costs affecting capital values* at time of acquisition or disposition or while holding.

Those costs affecting capital values include such items as: sales costs; taxes and fees incurred through acquiring, holding or disposing of assets; and other costs incurred with respect to acquisition or disposition, such as closing costs whenever incurred (including legal and appraisal fees, title search fees or title insurance premiums, costs of acquiring, establishing or providing clear title, loan points incurred to obtain financing and so on).

In short, the capital growth form of net return at any given time equals the net capital value less the net capital costs. As with the earning form of net return, the capital growth form can be expressed as a percentage of net periodic return on the net capital value of the asset or assets.

Such forecasts of future capital growth, combined with the previously discussed forecasts of earnings, can be very helpful in determining whether certain assets should be acquired, held or disposed. This depends upon how those forecasts relate to an individual's financial objectives, which will be discussed shortly.

■ EFFECTS OF INFLATION AND DEFLATION

Two important economic influences on much of what has been discussed to this point, especially on measures of net worth and investment return—and on management of financial resources per objectives—are inflation and deflation.

The words *inflation* and *deflation* are commonly used, and most people have at least a general idea of what those words imply. Competent financial analyzers and advisors must have a more complete understanding of the meanings of inflation and deflation.

Inflation

Webster's defines *inflation* as "an increase in the volume of money and credit relative to available goods, resulting in a substantial and continuing rise in the general price level." An *inflationary spiral* is "a continuous rise in prices that is sustained by the tendency of wage increases and cost increases to react on each other." (See Ill. 1.3.)

In his book, *Economics,* Paul Samuelson says that inflation means "a time of generally rising prices for goods and factors of production—rising prices for bread, cars, haircuts, rising wages, rents, etc." Two causes of inflation are labeled *demand-pull* and *cost-push.*

Demand-Pull Inflation

Demand-pull is the conventionally recognized economic situation in which too much spendable money bids for the limited supply of goods and services available at full employment and thus *pulls up* prices and wages. *Webster's* defines it as "an increase or upward trend in spendable money that tends to result in increased competition for available goods and services and a corresponding increase in consumer prices."

Economists are in general agreement that the *demand-pull* cause of inflation can be controlled by application of proper monetary and fiscal policy: holding down unemployment by enough expansion to lead the economic system to the brink of full employment, but not so much expansion that purchasing power goes over the edge and causes price inflation; curbing an inflationary gap by cutting back by just enough to return the system reasonably close to full employment, without going so far as to cause recession or depression unemployment.

Cost-Push Inflation

Cost-push is defined by *Webster's* as "an increase or upward trend in production costs (as wages) that tends to result in increased consumer prices irrespective of the level of demand."

Cost-push inflation is activated by the rise in a firm's cost of doing business. Some of the factors responsible for cost-push inflation are higher labor costs, interest rate increases, higher government taxes and changes in exchange rates. These factors

ILL. 1.3 ■ *Impact of Inflation on Earning Power*

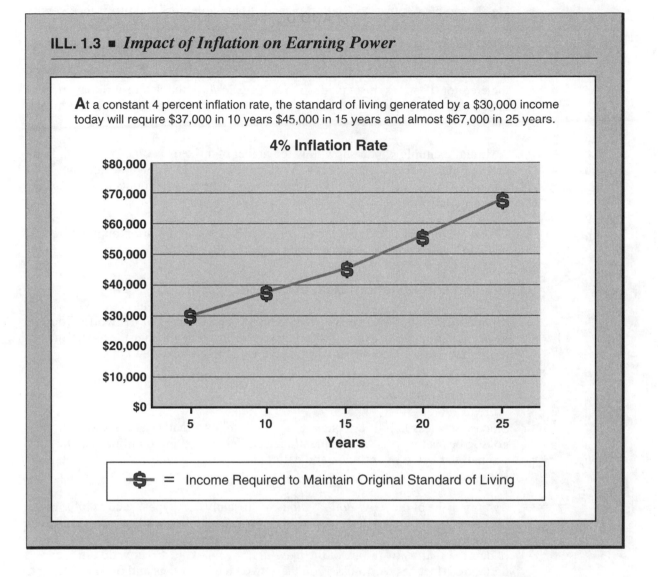

At a constant 4 percent inflation rate, the standard of living generated by a $30,000 income today will require $37,000 in 10 years $45,000 in 15 years and almost $67,000 in 25 years.

4% Inflation Rate

$— = Income Required to Maintain Original Standard of Living

work in concert with each other and can increase production costs, thereby *pushing up* prices—and this *cost-push* up of prices triggers yet another round of inflation.

While cost-push inflation was responsible for the hyperinflation of the late 1970s and early 1980s, in recent times we have seen a lowering of interest rates, a strong dollar, steady labor costs and a lowering of the tax rates for both corporations and individuals. These factors have effectively kept inflation in check; however, the Federal Reserve Bank must remain vigilant to ensure continued relative prosperity.

Deflation

The opposite of inflation, *deflation* is defined by *Webster's* as "a contraction in the volume of available money or credit that results in a decline of the general price level." Samuelson says simply that, "By *deflation* we mean a time when most prices and costs are falling."

He also points out that ". . . *inflation* tends to favor debtors and profit receivers at the expense of creditors and fixed-income receivers. *Deflation* has the opposite effect." The logic of this is obvious. If a person owes $10,000 payable at the end of six years and prices double in that period (*inflation*) the debtor will pay off the debt with *half* the purchasing power—certainly good for the debtor and unfavorable for the creditor. If prices, instead, drop to half (*deflation*), the debtor will pay off the debt with *twice* as much purchasing power—good for the creditor and bad for the debtor.

A similar example would show how the holder of a fixed-income-producing financial resource (a fixed-income bond, pension, etc.) would receive decreasing amounts of purchasing power with inflation or increasing amounts of purchasing power with *deflation.*

We are now ready to discuss the effects of inflation and deflation on measures of net worth and return on investment.

Inflation and Deflation: Measures of Net Worth

Inflation and deflation have substantial effects on measures of net worth. The degree and direction of the effects depend primarily on whether the assets and liabilities are of the fixed-dollar value or the variable-dollar value kind.

Assets and Liabilities

Since assets less liabilities equal net worth, it follows that as assets and liabilities go, so goes net worth. As was mentioned earlier, assets and liabilities can be substantially affected by inflation and deflation, depending on the kind of assets and liabilities.

Assets may be of the *fixed-dollar value* kind (usually debt types, such as bills, notes, bonds, mortgages, etc.) or the *variable-dollar value* kind (usually owner types, such as stocks, fund shares, real estate, etc.). On the other hand, liabilities (being forms of debt) virtually always are of the *fixed-dollar value* kind. So how do inflation and deflation affect net worth based on these two kinds of assets and one kind of liability?

Fixed-dollar value assets and liabilities. When prices rise (inflation), the *purchasing power values* of fixed-dollar value assets and liabilities go down (bad for creditors, good for debtors) while the *dollar values,* of course, remain constant. If prices go down (deflation), the *purchasing power values* of fixed-dollar value assets and liabilities go up (good for creditors, bad for debtors) while the dollar values remain constant. *Net worth,* which is based on such assets and liabilities, obviously reacts to inflation and deflation in the same ways those assets and liabilities do.

Variable-dollar value assets and fixed-dollar value liabilities. When prices rise (inflation), it is commonly believed (although not always proven true) that *purchasing power values* of variable-dollar value assets tend to remain constant, while fixed-dollar value liabilities (virtually all liabilities are), if any, tend to reduce—such that the resulting *net worth* tends to remain constant or rise somewhat in *purchasing power value* as a result of inflation. In terms of *dollar values,* the assets would tend to increase, the liabilities to remain constant and the resulting net worth to rise.

If, on the other hand, prices drop (deflation), the *purchasing power values* of variable-dollar value assets tend to remain constant but fixed-dollar value liabilities, if any, tend to increase—such that the resulting net worth tends to remain constant or drop somewhat in *purchasing power value* as a result of deflation. In terms of *dollar values,* the assets would tend to decrease, the liabilities to remain constant and the net worth to drop.

Current Value

Current value (whether a market value, a replacement value, a book value, an appraisal value, a forced sale or distress sale value or other—and whether in terms of purchasing power, dollars or what have you) is a *value of the moment,* and so is not in itself a reflector of either inflation or deflation.

However, the current value can be higher or lower at one point in time than at another, and the *change* often does reflect inflation or deflation. But a current value at some future point in time is really not a current value. Instead it is a *future value,* or a *present value* that is simply the expression of a *future value* in terms of its discounted value today.

Future and present values. These two values (both previously discussed) are affected by inflation and deflation. Consequently, allowances for expected rates of inflation or deflation should be made wherever possible in the projection or evaluation of a *future value,* or in the discounting of a future value to determine a *present value.*

The procedures are much the same as previously discussed for projecting or discounting except that the expected inflation or deflation rate is used or included in the projecting or discounting calculations.

Determining an inflation or deflation adjusted *future value* is important to facilitate understandable comparisons with other inflation or deflation adjusted future values. Likewise, determining an inflation or deflation adjusted *present value* of, say, a known future value is necessary to permit understanding and comparisons in terms of today's values.

Inflation and Deflation: Return on Investment

Much of what was said concerning the effects of inflation and deflation on assets and liabilities—that is, net worth or net capital value—is also applicable to the earnings and growth returns on such financial resources or investments.

Fixed-Dollar Earnings

While their dollar values remain constant, fixed-dollar earnings (such as interest on debt-type assets, fixed rent, conventional annuities, etc.) tend to decline in purchasing power with inflation or to rise with deflation.

Variable-Dollar Earnings

Variable-dollar earnings (such as earnings on equity-type assets, nonfixed rent, royalties, variable annuities, etc.) tend to remain constant in purchasing power, but to increase in dollar value, with inflation. Such earnings remain constant in purchasing power but decline in dollar value with deflation.

Capital Appreciation

Capital appreciation is an increase in the value of an asset. The effects of inflation and deflation on the value of an asset pertains here. Of course, true appreciation is the increase that would occur if there were no inflation or deflation. Capital growth should be adjusted to eliminate the effects of any inflation or deflation to determine true appreciation or real capital growth.

Costs of Investment

The costs of investment are also affected by inflation or deflation and such effects should be taken into consideration when analyzing or evaluating financial resources. Increases or decreases in asset values tend to increase or decrease sales costs, management fees, operating costs, applicable taxes, property insurance premiums and other costs of acquiring, holding or disposing of the assets. Such increases or decreases clearly affect the increases or decreases in real earnings and appreciation on assets.

In other words, those increases or decreases in investment costs, caused by inflation or deflation, also affect the earnings and capital growth forms of net return on investments and other financial resources.

■ MANAGEMENT OF FINANCIAL RESOURCES PER OBJECTIVES

Sound, professional management of financial resources requires continuous effort to maximize the financial objectives of the individual. This means efforts must be made at time of acquisition, throughout the holding period and upon disposition of each asset. This also means continuous evaluations and comparisons with alternative assets that might do a better job of maximizing objectives.

Some financial objectives are conflicting—for example, maximizing safety of principal and maximizing current yield. Such conflicts may be impossible to resolve fully; in such cases, good financial management requires making trade-offs that most nearly satisfy the objectives in keeping with the individual's priorities.

There will also be uncertainties as to what the future holds—with respect to the individual's own objectives and needs in the future as well as the future economy and the future performance of various financial resources. Here, sound financial management calls for selection of assets that provide the flexibility required to make needed or desired adjustments or changes in the future while satisfying current objectives to the maximum extent possible.

Moreover, careful consideration should be given to the opportunity costs of each selection; that is, what other assets (including all they have to offer) must be passed or given up to own each asset selected.

Suggested Evaluation Procedure

Following is the basic outline of an effective evaluation procedure that may be used in answering the question, "Should this particular financial resource be owned by this particular individual?" It can be used to help answer this question at time of acquisition, while holding or when considering disposition.

Step 1. Clearly establish the financial objectives and priorities of the individual. The vital first step in evaluating a financial resource is determining exactly what the person wants to accomplish with that resource.

Step 2. Carefully and critically examine the particular financial resource being considered, in terms of its ability to satisfy the specific objectives established in Step 1.

Step 3. Compare the ability of this financial resource with that of other available resources to satisfy the specific objectives in Step 1. Give the same consideration indicated in Step 2 to every resource being compared.

Step 4. Evaluate the financial resource as an investment or estate asset to satisfy the specific objectives of this individual only, based on the results of Step 2 and Step 3. (From a practical standpoint, keep in mind that the expected satisfactions should always be in line with acceptable cost and risk, as well as with the particular circumstances and temperament of the individual.)

Common Financial Objectives

Step 1 in the preceding four-step evaluation procedure calls for clearly establishing the individual's financial objectives. Here are eight objectives most commonly voiced:

1. Maximizing safety of principal

2. Maximizing current yield

3. Maximizing after-tax return

4. Maximizing liquidity

5. Maximizing appreciation potential

6. Maximizing present value of future earnings and future sale price

7. Maximizing satisfaction of conflicting objectives

8. Maximizing best selection of alternative resources

Use of the four-step evaluation procedure, combined with an understanding of particular financial resources, should prove most helpful in making the right decisions whenever a question arises as to the propriety of buying, holding or disposing of a particular financial resource.

Moreover, it should provide the best possible means of avoiding or unscrambling an estate that consists of "an unorganized mass of property . . . accumulated over a period of years . . . often without regard to the special needs of the owner, the family or the estate"—as a famous judge once described the typical estate.

The use of this evaluation procedure will permit as high a degree of objectivity as can be expected in weighing the components of a given estate. The investment of a person's money is often charged with emotion and when an opinion is expressed that is contradictory to the estate owner's convictions, it is apt to stir up a hornet's nest. The frequent result is a stalemate that results in the loss of a potential client and an estate still wandering around at loose ends.

However, if a penetrating look at an estate can be made in the cool light of analytical appraisal and if the various estate items can be weighed against the objectives the estate owner has personally stated, then often the choice of acquisition, holding or disposition becomes semiautomatic.

■ SUMMARY

This chapter introduced investment planning, including the concepts of net worth, asset allocation, measures of investment returns, inflation and deflation, and the management of financial resources. Net worth is the value of an owner's total assets less liabilities. Assets include both tangible assets, such as real estate, and intangible assets, such as stocks and bonds. Future, present and market values are asset measurements based on timing while replacement and book value are related to the accounting of an asset. Asset allocation is the partitioning of investable funds within the three major assets categories: stocks, bonds and cash. Studies have determined that this process is responsible for nearly all of a portfolio's long-term investment performance. The return on investment includes interest, dividends and capital gains and encompasses the acquisition, holding and disposition costs of an asset.

All assets are influenced by the effect of inflation and deflation that can subtly alter an asset's true return. Some of the most common financial objectives that a practitioner should evaluate are preserving safety of principal, maximizing yield and return, and clarifying the all too common problem of conflicting objectives. There are numerous types of investment planning software packages that will perform asset allocation, education planning, portfolio management and tax planning functions. Although there are numerous websites where consumers can obtain financial data, the expertise of a trained practitioner brings value to the client and value can never be replaced.

■ CHAPTER 1 QUESTIONS FOR REVIEW

1. Net worth equals which of the following?

    A. Liabilities plus assets

    B. Cash minus intangible assets

    C. Assets minus liabilities

    D. Present value of assets plus future value of liabilities

2. Which of the following terms describes the price at which a buyer and seller, dealing at arm's length, are willing to exchange an asset?

    A. Replacement value

    B. Market value

    C. Book value

    D. Future value

3. Which of the following most accurately describes insurance policy dividends?

    A. Distributed earnings on equity investments

    B. Earnings on loan investments

    C. Distributions of excess premiums

    D. Payments received for use of insurance premiums

4. The costs of investment do NOT include which of the following categories?

    A. Acquisition costs

    B. Holding costs

    C. Variable costs

    D. Disposition costs

5. The first step a person should take in determining whether to buy a particular asset is to establish which of the following?

    A. The costs of investment

    B. The expected return

    C. The asset's anticipated future value

    D. Financial objectives and priorities

6. An asset's book value is determined by

    A. subtracting depreciation and any liabilities

    B. adding depreciation and all liabilities

    C. subtracting fair market value

    D. adding replacement value

7. Simple interest is

    A. interest computed on the original principal only
    B. interest computed on the original principal and accrued interest
    C. interest computed on the original principal minus accrued interest
    D. none of the above

8. The Rule of 72 describes the time period or interest rate required for an asset to

    A. double in value
    B. triple in value
    C. quadruple in value
    D. stay the same value

9. Holding costs for an asset include all of the following EXCEPT

    A. management fees
    B. repairs and maintenance
    C. property insurance and taxes
    D. appreciation

10. Some common financial objectives include all of the following EXCEPT

    A. maximizing after-tax return
    B. maximizing safety of principal
    C. maximizing appreciation potential
    D. minimizing best selection of investment alternatives

2

Individual Retirement Planning

The subject of qualified retirement plans would not be complete without a discussion of qualified *individual* retirement plans. Not only are more people living until retirement, but they are also living much longer during the retirement years. This has created a need for insurance and financial planners to understand the magnitude of the financial requirements facing the retiree and to help the client understand the planning alternatives that are available to help assure financial independence during retirement. In this chapter we will cover these alternatives, focusing on individual retirement accounts (IRAs), simplified employee pensions (SEPs), tax-sheltered annuity or 403(b) plans and plans for the self-employed.

Retirement planning is one of the fastest growing specialty areas in the fields of insurance and financial planning. The general public is far more aware of problems facing soon-to-be retirees than ever before. Even with an employer-sponsored retirement plan and Social Security benefits, an individual and his or her spouse may not have adequate funds to maintain a preretirement standard of living during the retirement years. Employer-sponsored retirement plans will rarely provide 100 percent of the income needed for an adequate retirement.

As this chapter will show, many wage earners and self-employed persons can provide for their own retirement or supplement an employer's plan with an individual plan which offers these five outstanding features:

1. income tax-deductible contributions within the limits established by law;

2. accumulation of interest and dividends free of current tax;

3. 100 percent vested benefits;

4. fund transfers from one financial institution to another when the employee changes jobs; and

5. withdrawals restricted from distribution before the age of 59½ to encourage "forced" saving.

In short, the individual plans in Illustration 2.1 offer most of the advantages of an employer-sponsored plan. Let's begin with a discussion of Keogh plans.

■ ■ ■ ■ ■

■ KEOGH PLANS FOR THE SELF-EMPLOYED

A retirement plan is a sound business investment regardless of the type of organization. Many sole proprietors and partners have recognized this fact and have established such plans for themselves and their employees. These plans are commonly called *Keogh plans* or *HR-10 plans*. Though the rules governing Keogh plans are generally the same as those discussed in the previous chapter for qualified retirement plans, Keogh plans still deserve a brief analysis to identify special legal and practical differences.

Keogh Act Approach

In 1962, Keogh plans were established to provide a way for self-employed individuals to save for retirement. Up to that time, only employees of a business were allowed to participate in a qualified plan, and since proprietors and partners are employer-owners, they did not qualify as employees. What the original Keogh legislation provided was, simply, that self-employed individuals are to be treated for qualified retirement plan purposes as *employees* of their particular enterprises. In the case of sole proprietors, they are deemed to wear two hats: an employer hat and an employee hat. As employers, they are permitted to deduct contributions made to pension and profit-sharing plans established for the benefit of themselves and their employees. And just as with employees, they are not taxed currently on such contributions made in their behalf or on the income earned during the accumulation period. They are taxed on the benefits when received after retirement. The same result is reached in the case of partners. They are considered to be *employees* of partnerships and as such may participate in their plans established by their partnerships.

Who Are the Self-Employed?

Although the answer to the question "Who are the self-employed?" would seem to be self-evident, the law gives a precise definition as to what is meant by the term *self-employed.*

Sole Proprietors

Obviously included in the definition is the sole proprietor—the businessperson who owns an unincorporated business outright. In addition, the individual professional person—the physician, the attorney, the dentist—is self-employed if he or she is the owner of an unincorporated professional practice. It is not enough that the individual simply have an ownership interest in the business to be self-employed. He or she must also be actively involved in its operations and not merely a passive investor.

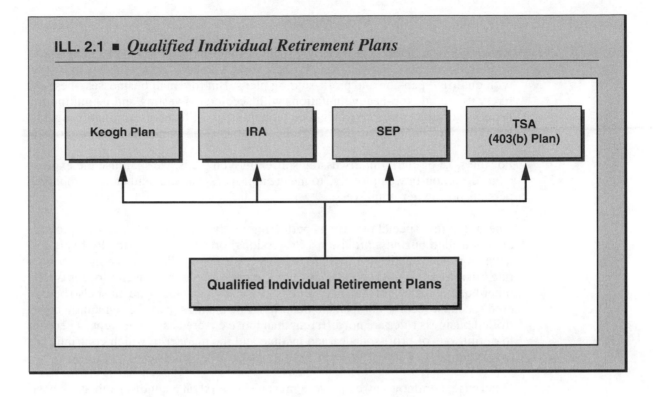

ILL. 2.1 ■ *Qualified Individual Retirement Plans*

Keogh Plan   IRA   SEP   TSA (403(b) Plan)

Qualified Individual Retirement Plans

Partners

Partners likewise are self-employed regardless of their particular partnership interest. For example, if a junior partner in a sizable law partnership has but a 5 percent partnership interest, he or she nevertheless is regarded as self-employed.

A distinction should be drawn between the active general partners and the passive limited partners. Even though limited partners directly recognize income and losses of the partnership, their ownership is limited to passive roles. They acquire an investment in the form of an interest in a partnership but do not actively participate in the partnership. Thus, limited partners are not considered self-employed for Keogh purposes. However, general partners, because they carry on the affairs of a business and are actively involved, are considered self-employed.

Owner-Employees

For purposes of applying special rules, the Keogh Act introduced a special term—*the owner-employee.* It has significance, however, only in the case of partnerships. A sole proprietor owns 100 percent of a business or profession; he or she is in every case both self-employed and an owner-employee. Unless a partner owns *more than 10 percent* of either the capital interest or the profit interest of the partnership, he or she is not an owner-employee. For example, the junior partner in the law partnership mentioned above is self-employed but not an owner-employee since this individual has only a 5 percent interest in the partnership. For purposes of simplicity, the nonowner self-employed will be referred to as a *junior partner.*

Who May Participate in a Keogh?

Keogh plans were once restricted by special rules that discriminated against the self-employed person. Now, Keogh plans are governed in most respects in *parity* with qualified pension and profit-sharing plans. But for small businesses, these are likely to include top-heavy limitations with accelerated vesting and its minimum benefit requirements. *Parity* might be thought of as uniform discrimination against small businesses in the area of fringe benefits—instead of just the self-employed.

For the sake of clarity in discussing self-employed plans, we shall use the expression "common-law employees" to mean employees who are neither self-employed persons nor owner-employees.

One of the few special provisions pertaining to plans covering the self-employed are controlled business provisions. Professional practices are especially likely to have a private practice (self-employed) while also controlling one or more corporate businesses. If a Keogh plan covers an owner-employee, the employees of all other businesses where that individual is also an owner-employee must also be covered (or must receive comparable benefits). For the most part the remaining controlled business rules are not different than those covered earlier, except as pertains to definitions of profits, net earned income and the manner in which contributions are deducted.

Otherwise, common-law employees must be covered on a nondiscriminatory basis without regard to which controlled business they are employed by. This used to create significant problems due to the special restrictions inherent in Keogh plans. However, with the uniform top-heavy plan provisions and general parity in provisions, this is no longer as much a concern.

Spouse's Participation

A question frequently asked is whether a self-employed's spouse may participate in a Keogh plan. The answer is an emphatic "yes" when he or she, in fact, is on the payroll as disclosed on Form W-3. It is not an optional decision—a spouse must be covered if he or she meets the same tests applicable to any other employee. Merely filing a joint return, however, would not constitute an employee relationship. Many spouses are, in effect, donating their labor when they do not draw a salary or wages to avoid additional self-employment tax liability. Often a Keogh plan makes reporting such employment attractive.

Employee Participation

A self-employed proprietor may set up a qualified retirement plan even though he or she either has no employees, or none who is required to be covered. In such a case the employer is the only plan participant.

Even if an owner-employee currently has no employees or no eligible employees, the plan must provide for their eventual inclusion. The eligibility requirements for plans operated by proprietorships and partnerships are no different from corporate plans. However, sometimes it is hard to establish the precise point in time when a self-employed individual actually commenced employment.

Definitions

To sum up, the following five expressions apply to Keogh plans:

1. *Self-employed individual or person* means a person who has an ownership interest in an unincorporated business, trade or profession, which may be either a sole proprietorship or a partnership.

2. *Owner-employee* means a self-employed person who is a sole proprietor or who owns more than 10 percent interest in a partnership.

3. *Junior partner* means a self-employed person who has an ownership interest of 10 percent or less in a partnership.

4. *Common-law employee* means an employee who is not a self-employed person but is employed by a sole proprietorship or a partnership.

5. *Employee* means any one of the persons described in 1, 2, 3 or 4.

Covering Owner-Employees in an Existing Retirement Plan

You may encounter a sole proprietorship or partnership that has already set up a retirement plan for its common-law employees that does not cover the sole proprietor or the partners. For example, a large law partnership may already have a regular qualified plan in operation for its common-law employees.

The question could arise whether or not this existing plan could be amended in such a way as to permit the self-employed to participate. The answer is "yes."

An employer may choose to amend the plan to include all employees. Owner-employees no longer have to consent to plan participation. The normal coverage tests apply to Keogh plans. Thus, if owner-employees opt out of participation, the tests may fail to be met.

A basic principle of any qualified retirement plan is that deductible contributions made to the plan are not taxed to the participants until they actually receive their benefits. This same approach is taken for Keogh plans. The tax on the deductible contributions is deferred until such amounts are distributed under the terms of the plan.

Need for Proper Funding/Administration

Keogh plans are also required to meet the standards of funding, disclosure and administration.

The proper funding and administration of a Keogh plan is perhaps as important as its design. Without a corporate sponsor behind the retirement plan and generally fewer participants and less total dollars, it is crucial that the Keogh plan be properly funded and that plan administrative and investment expenses be kept low. In many unincorporated businesses the accounting records and employment information are not so well organized or available in useful form, adding to the need for personal service work (although availability of personal computers may greatly improve tax planning, even in the family business).

Another distinction can be made. The unincorporated business lacks some of the alternative planning options available to the big corporation. The Keogh plan may have to do the work of a group term life program as well as provide retirement income. In some cases this is the practical cost restraint of operating multiple plans. In others, technical provisions still cause problems. For example, in the case of group life, the cost of benefits for self-employed or shareholder-employees in an S corporation would not be deductible.

Insured Plans

Before insuring a plan, ideally the following conditions should be envisioned:

1. a predictable, ongoing level of contributions, particularly if fixed-premium policies are used;

2. a turnover rate that, when combined with the vesting schedule, does not unnecessarily burden the plan with forfeitures;

3. consistent timing of contributions or a side fund to hold adequate reserves for premiums as they become due; and

4. a comprehensive needs analysis to determine how much life insurance death benefit is needed and how it can best be arranged.

Being small, the sole proprietor is typically not diversified by customer base, by industry, by supplier, by geographic location or even by product line. This can subject earnings to relatively greater fluctuation than a large corporation.

In the past, when fixed-premium retirement income endowment policies were a major funding vehicle for Keogh plans, a special Internal Revenue Code (the code) provision allowed an income averaging procedure so that level premiums could be maintained. This provision has been repealed. Without it the fully insured funding approach is almost impossible. An exception may be found where such large amounts of income are being earned, or small enough contribution/benefit levels are selected, that fluctuations are not material. A properly designed defined benefit pension plan may provide sufficiently stable funding to use this vehicle.

Although perhaps not to the same extent as corporate plans, Keogh plans are finding split-funding more attractive. The owners have become more aggressive in their plan funding, trying to take advantage of shelter for income from interest sensitive products such as universal life, low-premium term life insurance and variable products.

Annuity-Funded Plans

In many respects, the annuity contract (either group or individual) may be the ideal funding vehicle for the Keogh plan. As offered in various forms, the flexibility in selecting features is almost limitless; however, consider these general advantages:

1. *Regular billings or premium notifications.* Since the majority of employers operating under this business form do not have sophisticated employee benefits personnel, the premium reminders can avoid lost deductions. Also, by funding a plan on a monthly or quarterly basis, some dollar-cost averaging may be obtained (variable products) and the pain of large lump-sum contributions near tax time is avoided. Interest may be earned on a larger portion of the funds throughout the year.

2. *A separate fund.* A policy psychologically separates this asset from personal investments. It is immediately identified for its own purpose, avoiding unintentional raiding of policy values during financial emergencies.

3. *Investment options.* With some selective purchasing, the annuity can be nearly risk free (e.g., a fixed, guaranteed rate or one tied to T-bills) or aggressive (e.g., a variable annuity investing in a segregated account of small capitalization common stocks, or "junk" bonds). With discretion, this may allow individual participants to maximize their own needs through the plan.

4. *Diversification of assets to minimize risk and to comply with ERISA.* It is sometimes hard for small plans to adequately diversify. The annuity reserves give Keogh participants access to a broadly mixed portfolio.

5. *Flexible premiums.* The self-employed business owner may increase or decrease funding levels to suit available cash flow, provided minimum funding standards are met. Most policies offer flexible premium payment features.

6. *Investment rollover.* Under a self-directed fund, for example, a Keogh plan might lock in a yield by purchasing bonds (corporate debentures with coupons). However, when the coupons mature, this means reinvesting the money, which entails reinvestment risk. Later, when the bonds mature, the proceeds must be rolled over into new investments. This can be tedious. Competitive yields may not be available. The amounts may be too small to buy minimum units. Partial units may not be available.

   The reserves of an annuity are efficiently reinvested with no effort on the part of the client. An enormous portfolio of different bond maturities and mortgages is held by the insurance company. This makes average yields more stable than might otherwise be available.

7. *Death benefit.* While usually only equal to the sum of the premiums paid into the contract (as a maximum), this offers some assurance against loss.

8. *Named beneficiary.* This is particularly important to the Keogh owner who may need the plan to supplement other business continuation plans. The check can be processed without liquidating specific investments.

9. *Settlement options, including lifetime fixed or variable benefits.* Often this can supplement liquidation proceeds from sale of the business under either a buy-sell agreement or deferred payment contract.

From the practitioner's standpoint, most annuities pay only a moderate rate of commission. If the dollar contribution is also small, the revenue generated may be less than one might make by sticking with life insurance sales. However, by doing total financial planning, this problem may become an opportunity.

The self-employed person is most susceptible to the hazards of disability. By integrating the retirement planning (IRA, SEP, Keogh, etc.) with solid disability protection, additional commissions (and where permitted, fees) are earned. When the client realizes how dependent his or her business is on personal talents and efforts, business continuation is a logical planning step. Only one product "buys a person's human life value" and that is life insurance.

Because Congress chose to expose qualified plan death proceeds to harsh treatment under the federal estate tax and income tax, planning in this area is of utmost importance.

For the reasons given, life insurance and annuity products are quite often seen as product solutions for financial planning for self-employed individuals. This is not to suggest that other vehicles cannot further enhance the Keogh plan or that other planning opportunities will not place demands on available client dollars. The whole package should be assembled so as to maximize returns.

Installation of a Keogh Plan

The steps involved in installing a Keogh plan are similar to those followed when installing a regular qualified plan. Similarly, the process involved is not overly difficult since the proper guidelines are available. The most important concept to remember is that the plan is a bona fide plan established by the employer, even though no separate taxable entity is present, for its employees.

As in the case of a regular qualified plan, many of the steps involved are determined by the funding medium or media used to accumulate the benefits under the plan and the type of plan to be installed. A Keogh plan investing wholly in annuity or insurance contracts, face-amount certificates or government bonds may be established without either a trust or a custodial account. Plans investing solely in mutual fund shares or solely in annuity and retirement income insurance contracts may use a custodial account with a bank or other competent entity in lieu of a trust. Plans desiring greater investment latitude should be administered by a bank or other competent entity as trustee.

Regardless of the method of administration, however, in today's Keogh market, the steps in installing a plan are highly simplified by the use of a prototype or master plan. Insurance companies (and other financial institutions) may sponsor master or prototype plans. Keogh plan prototypes are filed by sponsors on specially designed IRS Request for Determination forms.

Contributions to the Plan

In addition to the creation of a written instrument, a contribution must be made by the self-employed person to bring the plan into being. If the plan is administered by a trustee or custodian, contributions must be made to the trustee or custodian who, in turn, maintains the records and makes the investments called for by the plan and any accompanying agreements. Under a direct investment plan, premiums paid to the insurance company represent the self-employed individual's contribution to an insured Keogh plan.

Income Tax Deduction for the Self-Employed Person

The market for Keogh plans is huge and in many cases, an excellent one for development since many self-employed persons and unincorporated professionals have not had the time or inclination to tackle the complex task of designing, installing and funding their own tax-qualified retirement plans.

As with corporate tax-qualified retirement plans, perhaps the key selling point and motivation for the client to go forward with installation of a new qualified pension plan is the tax incentive provided under federal law. It minimizes after-tax cash flow required to fund the plan for eligible employees each year (or, in the case of profit-sharing plans, in years in which company operations permit a cash contribution).

Earned Income Rule

As we have seen, the definition of earned income and compensation (the term used in the Code to calculate annual plan contributions) is complicated for a self-employed person maintaining a Keogh plan. In these cases, a self-employed's earned income is determined *after* deductions for normal business expenses have been calculated for the Form 1040, including the deduction for the Keogh plan contribution itself. In addition, one-half the amount of self-employment tax due each year must be subtracted from the self-employed individual's earnings in determining net income for the year.

The Top-Heavy Rule

In the case of a self-employed Keogh plan covering one person, the top-heavy rule plays an important role in defining the maximum contribution that can be made to the plan.

A qualified retirement plan is top-heavy if the present value of the cumulative benefits for key employees under the plan exceeds 60 percent of the value for all employees. In addition, only the first $160,000 of an employee's compensation may be considered in the calculation of deductible contributions or benefits under the plan. Though the $160,000 amount is indexed annually for increases in the cost of living, it does limit the self-employed's flexibility in establishing a Keogh plan.

Keogh Plan Loans to Self-Employed Persons

The fiduciary rules and prohibited transaction rules of ERISA deny plan fiduciaries the right to engage in certain types of proscribed conduct. One such type of prohibited activity is the granting of a loan, otherwise available to participants in a Keogh plan that provides for loans under qualifying conditions, to an owner-employee under a Keogh plan.

However, an owner-employee covered under a Keogh plan with loan provisions may apply to the Department of Labor (DOL) for a prohibited transaction exemption (PTE) exempting the owner-employee from the prohibited transaction rules of ERISA. (Note, however, that there is no blanket exemption for loans to owner-employees. The owner-employee must make application to the DOL and show good cause why the PTE should be granted.)

■ INDIVIDUAL RETIREMENT ACCOUNTS (IRAs) AND ANNUITIES

In simplest terms, an IRA is a method by which an eligible individual can divert a portion of his or her earned income for retirement and gain some distinct tax advantages. IRAs are long-term programs and should be established and maintained only on that basis. The provisions of the law that govern IRAs discourage their use for short-term purposes. An individual establishing an IRA should plan to make contributions to it from the time the plan is opened until the time the individual retires.

There are many vehicles available for the investing of IRA assets. The law purposely imposes few restrictions in this regard, leaving the decision in the hands of the individual IRA participant (or plan trustee), who can make the selection based on individual needs and objectives. The common types of IRA accounts include:

- individual fixed-dollar retirement annuities

- individual variable retirement annuities

- a bank time deposit open account

- a bank certificate of deposit

- a savings and loan fixed-term savings deposit

- a savings and loan certificate account

- an insured credit union account

- mutual fund shares

- common trust funds or common investment funds

- self-directed brokerage accounts

Financial products that may *not* serve as IRA accounts are life insurance contracts and collectibles such as stamps, artwork, antiques and precious gems.

Tax Advantages

There are two prime tax advantages to be gained from an IRA:

1. *Most* IRA contributions are tax deductible. This means that they can be made and deducted from gross income, with no taxes due or payable. Thus, these savings are tax deferred until distributed. (Some contributions will not qualify as deductible, as we will discuss later.)

2. *All* IRA earnings (whether they are attributable to deductible contributions or not) accumulate tax free. Unlike a savings account, CD or money-market account, annual earnings do not have to be reported, as long as the IRA is maintained as a retirement savings plan.

Establishing an IRA

There are three rules that must be met for an individual to establish a personal IRA:

1. The individual must have *earned income.*

2. The individual must be under the age of 70½.

3. The amount contributed must not exceed *$2,000 per year,* or 100 percent of compensation, whichever is less.

Earned income includes compensation for personal services, wages, tips, commissions, self-employment earnings, even alimony. It does not include retirement income, deferred compensation or other such passive income. A single individual whose only source of income, for example, is dividends from inherited stock is not eligible to open an IRA. The age limitation was established to insure that these accounts would be used for retirement purposes and not as a means by which to perpetually shelter income and earnings from taxes.

An IRA must be established by a written document with certain standard provisions. Insurance companies and other financial institutions normally have IRS-approved forms.

Deductibility of Contributions

There are two rules that affect the deductibility of IRA contributions:

1. An individual cannot claim an IRA deduction if the individual is an active participant in an employer-sponsored retirement plan *and* has an adjusted gross income above certain levels.

2. An individual cannot claim an IRA deduction in the year he or she attains age 70½.

Thus, while most workers qualify to set up and contribute to an IRA, some will not be able to take a tax deduction for their contributions. Illustration 2.2 shows how these deductibility rules apply. Let's take a closer look at the active participant rule.

Active Participant Rule

In general terms, the *active participant rule* states that if an individual is an active participant in an employer-sponsored retirement plan and has earned income in excess of certain levels, that person *cannot* take an income tax deduction for an IRA contribution. An individual is considered to be an active participant in a retirement plan if he or she "participates in":

ILL. 2.2 ■ *Individual Retirement Account Rules for Deductibility of Annual Contributions*

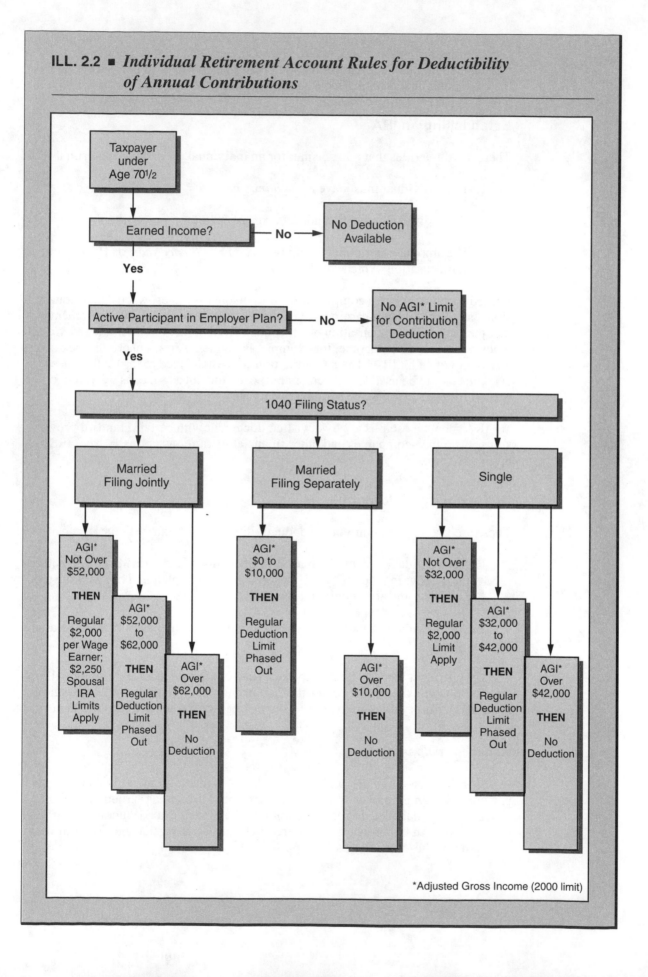

*Adjusted Gross Income (2000 limit)

- a qualified defined benefit plan

- a qualified defined contribution plan

- a qualified profit-sharing plan

- a 401(k) plan

- a government-sponsored retirement plan

- a 403(b) annuity or 403(b) custodial account plan

- a simplified employee pension plan

Only active participants who have adjusted gross income above specified limits will see their deductions affected. These individuals are subject to *phaseout rules,* meaning that as their AGI rises, the deductible amount of their IRA contribution is reduced. At the upper end of these income limits, *no deduction is available.* The following shows these phaseout levels that were indexed beginning in 1998. The phaseout limits for single taxpayers and head of household returns are increased as follows:

1998	$30,000–40,000
1999	31,000–41,000
2000	32,000–42,000
2001	33,000–43,000
2002	34,000–44,000
2003	40,000–50,000
2004	45,000–55,000
After 2005	50,000–60,000

The phaseout limits for married taxpayers returns are increased as follows:

1998	$50,000–60,000
1999	51,000–61,000
2000	52,000–62,000
2001	53,000–63,000
2002	54,000–64,000
2003	60,000–70,000
2004	65,000–75,000
2005	70,000–80,000
2006	75,000–85,000
After 2007	80,000–100,000

For taxpayers who are married and filing separately, the phaseout begins with AGI of $10,000 and above.

Active participants whose deductions are phased out or eliminated can still make contributions up to the $2,000 limit and have the earnings on those contributions grow tax deferred until they are distributed.

Individuals not covered by an employer-sponsored retirement plan may deduct their full IRA contribution (limited only by the $2,000 or 100 percent of income requirement), no matter what their earned income or AGI levels are.

Spousal IRAs

The nonworking spouse of an eligible worker may establish a special spousal IRA, provided that the other spouse has earned income. As of 1998, the nonworking spouse may invest up to $2,000 in the spousal IRA. Nonworking spouses who are married to active participants are not subject to the maximum deductible phaseout range of $52,000 to $62,000 that is applicable to married active participants in 2000. For example, Ed is a participant in his company's 401(k) plan, his wife Zoe is not employed, and their combined AGI is $125,000. Because their AGI is below $150,000, Zoe may make a deductible IRA contribution.

Rollover IRAs

Individuals can transfer assets from an IRA or a qualified employer plan to another IRA, provided certain conditions are met. The new IRA account is called a *rollover IRA,* and its purpose is to provide flexibility of transfer and investment for retirement savings. Rollover IRAs can be more than one IRA, and any amount of a qualifying distribution to the taxpayer can be transferred to a rollover IRA without being taxed if the transfer is direct from the plan (or old IRA) to the new IRA, or completed within 60 days of the distribution.

Individuals establishing rollover IRAs can be active participants in an employer's retirement plan. It is best to limit the rollover of a single sum to one rollover account, since single-sum distributions are eligible for a one-time, five-year forward averaging election if received after age 59½.

Qualified retirement plans must give participants the right to have eligible distributions transferred directly to an IRA (or other qualified plan) in a direct rollover. Generally, all qualified plan distributions are eligible for rollover except an annuity payable for the life of the participant (or his or her spouse) or for at least 10 years. Also, nontaxable parts of any plan distribution (including nondeductible contributions) cannot be rolled over. In addition, IRS rules specify certain miscellaneous kinds of distributions, including the P.S. 58 cost of current life insurance protection, and the minimum distributions required after the participant reaches age 70½, as ineligible for rollover.

With the tax laws simplified in this area, and direct transfers encouraged to avoid withholding from the distribution, plan participants are increasingly likely to make direct rollovers not only upon retirement, but also when changing jobs and receiving plan distributions in mid-career. Insurance and financial planners can assist such prospects or customers by making IRA rollover vehicles available. These career events are also an opportune time to review the client's overall insurance and financial needs.

IRA Distributions

Income is taxable when distributed from the IRA (unless rolled over to another IRA as just discussed). To restrict IRA tax benefits to retirement savings, IRA distributions are also restricted in much the same manner as qualified retirement plan distributions by the 10 percent early withdrawal tax (for distributions before age 59½), the 50 percent penalty tax (for failing to distribute adequate amounts after age 70½) and the 15 percent excise tax (for excess retirement distributions and accumulations). Clients rely on their retirement financial planners to guide them to an IRA distribution schedule that eliminates (or minimizes) these taxes while providing the desired retirement income stream.

▪ THE ROTH IRA

The Roth IRA is a new kind of IRA that offers tax-free income in retirement as opposed to a traditional IRA's tax-deferred income. Contributions to a Roth IRA are not tax deductible; however, if the account has been in existence for at least five years **and** the withdrawal is made after the account owner has attained age 59½, the earnings in the account will be totally tax-free income. In addition, tax-free withdrawals can be made on account of death, disability or a qualified first time home mortgage. If earnings are withdrawn from an account that does not meet these restrictions, they will be subject to income tax that may also include a 10 percent penalty. For an investor to qualify for a Roth IRA or convert their traditional IRA to a Roth IRA, the investor must have earned income that does not exceed certain limits. (See Ill. 2.3.)

There are two scenarios where a Roth IRA makes the most sense. First, if an investor cannot deduct their contribution to a traditional IRA, they should definitely contribute to a Roth IRA. The second scenario arises when an investor is older than age 70½, is taking mandatory distributions that they do not need and the account is set up so that the entire balance must be paid out upon the investor's death. By converting the traditional IRA to a Roth IRA, the investor gets a second chance to take advantage of the estate planning benefits offered by the Roth that can provide tax free income to the investor's heirs for many years to come. (See Ill. 2.4.)

There are many factors to consider when contemplating either an investment to a Roth IRA or a conversion from a traditional IRA, such as present and future tax brackets, the balance of the traditional IRA, conversion taxes and the present age of the investor. The practitioner should undertake a thorough analysis of the investor's situation before making any recommendations.

▪ THE SIMPLIFIED EMPLOYEE PENSION PLAN (SEPs)

A *simplified employee pension plan* has its roots in two parts of legislative pension programs: the individual retirement account and the Keogh plan for self-employed individuals.

The SEP was introduced to help employers establish a retirement plan for their employees without the burdensome administrative costs and governmental paperwork that most qualified plans endure. With the SEP, Congress created one of the most innovative and effective retirement programs ever designed.

ILL. 2.3 ■ *Roth IRA—Planning Considerations*

Beginning January 1, 1998, a new individual retirement account/annuity (IRA) named for Senator William J. Roth, allows taxpayers to choose between traditional IRAs and the new Roth IRAs. The following chart lists the major attributes followed by some questions about converting a traditional IRA to a Roth IRA.

	TRADITIONAL IRA	ROTH IRA	
		Contributory	Conversion
GENERAL ELIGIBILITY	Individuals who are under age 70½ with earned income.	Income limits exist. The phaseouts are $95,000 to $110,000 AGI for single filers and $150,000 to $160,000 AGI for joint filers. There is no age limit.	Individuals with AGI of less than $100,000 (excluding the conversion amount) and, if married, must file jointly.
CONTRIBUTIONS	The lesser of $2,000 ($4,000 if filing jointly) or 100 percent of earned income. Individuals can roll over funds held in other retirement plans such as 401(k), 403(b), tax-free to a traditional IRA.	The lesser of $2,000 ($4,000 if filing jointly or 100% of earned income)	Rollovers from other Roth IRA or traditional IRA only.
TAX IMPLICATIONS			
• **Deductibility Limits Per AGI**	Individuals may deduct all or part of their contribution, subject to limitations.	Contributions are not deductible.	Contributions are not deductible.
• **Distributions**	Total amount in IRA is taxable in year distributed, except for any prior nondeductible contributions. A 10 percent federal penalty tax may also apply if owner is less than age 59½ and no other exception applies. Required minimum distributions must begin at age 70½.	Tax free for qualifying distributions, where annuity values remain in the Roth IRA for 5 years and the individual: • is 59½ or older; or • dies; or • becomes disabled; *or* • uses amounts distributed (up to $10,000 during lifetime) to purchase first home. Nonqualifying distributions in excess of Roth IRA contributions are taxed as ordinary income and may be subject to a 10 percent federal penalty tax. No required minimum distributions.	Tax prorated over a 4-year period (1998–2001) *only* if converted in 1998. After 1998, amounts converted or rolled over are taxable as ordinary income in year of conversion (except for nondeductible contributions. The 10 percent penalty tax does not apply to conversions or rollovers to a Roth IRA. The penalty may apply to nonqualifying distributions of converted or rolled over amounts (and if the nonqualifying distribution involves 1998 conversions or rollovers, the federal penalty tax may be increased to 20 percent). No required minimum distributions.
• **Distributions After Death of IRA or Roth IRA holder**	Fully income taxable to beneficiaries.	Income tax free to beneficiaries unless holder dies within the 5-year holding period which may cause some income tax to be paid.	Income tax free to beneficiaries unless holder dies within the 5-year holding period which may cause some income tax to be paid.

ILL. 2.4 ■ *Planning for an Inherited Roth IRA*

Numerous articles have been written about the benefits made available to eligible taxpayers by a Roth individual retirement account (IRA) but few have highlighted some of the exciting estate planning aspects concerning this arrangement.

Remember that eligible individuals can make nondeductible contributions to the Roth IRA and as long as the annuity has remained in force for at least five years and the Roth IRA owner is over age 59½, distributions can be taken from the annuity income tax free. In effect, if an individual is willing to fund his or her annuity with after-tax dollars now, then the proceeds of the annuity will be distributed tax free in his or her retirement years. This is generally good news for most clients but what happens when the Roth IRA owner dies and a spouse or another third party beneficiary inherits the annuity?

As with traditional IRAs, Roth IRA assets are included in the deceased owner's gross estate. If left to a spouse, no estate taxes would apply due to the unlimited marital deduction. If left to a nonspousal beneficiary, estate taxes might apply depending upon the total value of the deceased's taxable estate. While estate taxation is the same for both Roth IRAs and traditional IRAs, there are several distinct income tax advantages for Roth beneficiaries.

When a traditional IRA is inherited by a beneficiary, either spousal or nonspousal, the issue of whether the decedent died before or after the required beginning date (April 1 following attainment of age 70½) is a major factor in determining the income taxation of the inherited IRA. Generally, if the IRA holder dies after age 70½, distributions to the beneficiary must continue at least as rapidly as they were paid to the original IRA owner.

Upon the death of a Roth IRA owner the surviving spouse, if the sole beneficiary, may elect to treat the Roth IRA as his or her own. Unlike a traditional IRA, there are no minimum distributions required at the spouse's attainment of age 70½. So in this regard, the spouse would not be required to make any distributions during his or her lifetime and the annuity could continue to grow income tax free.

The surviving spouse could then designate another beneficiary, such as a son or daughter, who would receive the distributions from the Roth IRA after his or her death. This could allow for many more years of tax-free growth of the annuity. The surviving spouse could always access the annuity income tax free for income should the need arise, assuming the Roth IRA had been established for at least five years before the original owner's death.

If the surviving spouse is *not* the sole beneficiary, then another set of rules apply and the annuity would have to be distributed in either of two ways:

1. the entire Roth IRA must be received prior to December 31 of the fifth year following the year of the owner's death; or

2. the entire Roth IRA must be received over the beneficiary's lifetime, beginning one year after the owner's death.

Unlike the traditional IRA, the Roth IRA owner's age at death has no effect on how distributions must be taken, but the annuity must be in existence at least five years to offer income-tax free distributions. There may be income taxes due on the distributions if the Roth IRA is held for less than a five-year period.

The Roth IRA owner may have chosen which rule to apply when the annuity is established or the choice may have been left to the beneficiary. In the latter case, an election must be made by December 31 of the year following the year of the Roth IRA owner's death. A nonspousal beneficiary is not permitted to make regular or rollover contributions to the inherited Roth IRA, nor can it be combined with any other of the beneficiary's Roth IRA. Even so, there can be favorable planning opportunities for the Roth IRA owner and the beneficiary in this scenario.

ILL. 2.4 ■ *Planning for an Inherited Roth IRA (continued)*

When either a spouse or nonspouse beneficiary inherits a Roth IRA, the beneficiary inherits both the Roth IRA assets *and* the holding period of the original Roth IRA owner. For example, Robert is a 65-year-old widower and has accumulated $600,000 in a Roth IRA. He has sufficient assets outside the annuity and does not foresee the need to use any of it to maintain his standard of living. Robert has designated his son James, age 40, as the beneficiary of his Roth IRA.

If Robert were to die at age 80, and assuming an 8 percent rate of return on the annuity for 15 years, it would be worth a little over $1,900,000. James, age 55, would then be required to either take the annuity by the end of a five-year period or over his lifetime. James's life expectancy at age 55 is 28.6 years; so, if he elected payments over his lifetime, his first annual distribution would be approximately $66,000 ($1,900,000/28.6).

In the following year, assuming the annuity continues to grow at 8 percent, then James's second distribution would be $71,000 ($1,900,000–66,000)/27.6). As you can see in this example, James is receiving a yearly increase in his distribution and both the original inherited amount and all subsequent appreciation, is income tax free!

The Roth IRA is also a powerful tool for planning for grandparents. For example, Bill, a 70-year-old grandfather, wishes to establish an irrevocable trust for the sole benefit of his 3-year-old granddaughter, Tiffany. Bill plans to fund the trust with the proceeds of his Roth IRA after his death. If Bill lives until age 85, and assuming the trust is properly structured, after Bill's death, the trustee can elect to receive the distributions from the Roth IRA in accordance with Tiffany's life expectancy, which at that time will be 63.9 years.

If we assume the Roth IRA is worth $800,000 at the time of Bill's death, then the first distribution to Tiffany would be approximately $12,500 ($800,000/63.9). Once again these distributions from the Roth IRA would continue to Tiffany for her *entire* lifetime and are entirely *income tax free.*

In these examples, the beneficiaries could conceivably inherit a permanently income tax-free asset that could provide then with income on a tax-free basis for the remainder of their natural lives.

Basically, a SEP is an IRA established and maintained solely by the employee, but to which his or her employer can contribute. Eligibility, contribution limits, vesting and many other features associated with a tax-advantaged qualified plan are all present in a simplified employee pension plan, with some major additional benefits. A SEP has the administrative simplicity of an IRA, but also has a higher contribution limit; employees may also contribute to the plan and take advantage of lower income tax rates because of that deferral. Best of all, hard-earned company funds do not have to be spent on administrative or technical assistance. The money could be used to enhance the simplified employee pension plan.

Advantages of a SEP

Simplified employee pension plans carry three prime advantages: they have tax advantages for both the employer and the employee, they are extremely simple to establish and operate and they allow plan participants the ability to select the contribution and investment options that most precisely meet their budgets and retirement objectives.

Tax Advantages for the Employer

For an employer having just begun to see daylight with his or her business and seeking to further the gains, a SEP has some extremely attractive tax advantages.

First, all contributions made to the plan by the employer are tax deductible as an ordinary and necessary business expense. For the individual business owner, this can be an important factor in having to pay a tax rate of 15 percent as opposed to 28 percent, or even 28 percent as compared to 31, 36 or 39 percent. If the employer is a fledgling corporation, the tax difference can range from 15 to 40 percent of corporate taxable income.

For the employer's contribution to be deductible, it must meet two basic requirements:

1. The contribution must be an ordinary and necessary business expense.

2. The compensation on which the deductible contribution is based must be for services actually performed by the employee.

Tax Advantages for the Employee

A SEP operates in the same fashion as a 401(k) plan: all employee-participant contributions to the plan are treated as a deferral of taxes and a reduction of taxable income. In addition, all earnings accumulate tax free to the participant and taxes do not have to be paid until the funds are withdrawn.

Nontax Advantages for the Employer

There are several nontax advantages when an employer establishes a simplified employee pension plan. These include:

- *Having a specialized retirement plan.* Employers who want their employees to have a retirement plan identical in scope and coverage to the pension plans found in the larger corporations can establish a SEP that meets all those expectations. With a SEP, the employer can answer his or her employees' concerns over their future retirement security.

- *The ability to attract and retain employees.* An employer operating in today's labor market must be able to provide prospective and current employees with a retirement program similar to, if not better than, the plans being offered by his or her competitors.

- *Increasing productivity and reducing turnover.* Costs of production in today's business arena are a vital factor in determining whether or not a business will be a success or a failure. If an employer can satisfy the legitimate concerns over the future, individual and company productivity will increase since employees will stay. Training and recruiting costs are reduced, which also leads to a more favorable profit and loss statement at year-end.

Participation Requirements

Employers who have established a SEP and make annual contributions to the plan must include all employees who:

- are age 21 or older;

- have worked for the employer *three* out of the last *five* years (there is no stated minimum of hours of service such as 1,000 hours per year, just the three-out-of-five rule, though the employer can select a shorter waiting period than the rule stated); and

- received at least $400 of compensation that year.

An employee who meets all three of these requirements must be included in the SEP plan. However, an employer may select requirements that are less stringent than those cited.

Employees who do not meet the minimum eligibility rules may be excluded from the SEP. In addition, the law also allows the exclusion of union employees and non-resident aliens who have no United States income.

Contributions to a SEP

A SEP is really very similar to a profit-sharing plan in that the employer does *not* have to make a contribution to the plan each year.

Employer contributions to individual employees, when made, are limited to the *lesser* of:

- 15 percent of an employee's annual compensation; or

- $25,500 (for 2000, subject to annual adjustment for inflation).

Employee Contributions

The limit on an employee's contribution to a company's SEP is $10,500 (in 2000 and indexed for future years).

SEP Nondiscrimination Rules

Though the rules on SEPs are the most liberal in the IRS Code, an employer is bound by the strict nondiscrimination rule that he or she cannot make contributions for one class or group of employees and not for others.

The 1.25 ADP Rule

SEPs must meet the 1.25 ADP test. Employee contributions to a SEP by highly compensated employees cannot exceed by 1.25 times the average annual contributions of the nonhighly compensated employees. "ADP" refers to *actual deferral percentage,* or the percentage of income that an employee elects to defer (contribute) to the plan. For example, assume that the average annual deferral of the non-highly compensated employees in a firm was 8 percent of their compensation. Eight percent multiplied by 1.25 equals 10 percent. This means that the average annual deferral for the highly compensated employees cannot exceed 10 percent of compensation.

Excess Contribution Rule

Any amount contributed on behalf of an employee in excess of the 15 percent/$25,500 limitation is treated as an *excess contribution,* subject to a 6 percent penalty tax. This tax is nondeductible on an individual tax return and must be paid by the *employee,* not the employer.

If excess contributions have been made to a SEP, the employee has three options for correcting the excess:

1. He or she can withdraw the excess on or before April 15 of the following year and pay ordinary income tax rates on the amount withdrawn.

2. The excess can be withdrawn after April 15 of the following year (this will not avoid the penalty, though).

3. The excess can be carried over to the next tax year and be worked off through no contributions being made until the excess is cleared.

The $160,000 Rule

Paralleling the excess contribution rule is the *$160,000 rule,* which states that only the first $160,000 of compensation may be taken into account in calculating SEP contributions (subject to future indexing). This is to prevent discrimination in favor of highly compensated employees.

To show how the $160,000 rule works, assume that Executive A earns $240,000 a year and Employee B earns $20,000 a year. If the company's SEP calls for a 10 percent contribution, Executive A would have a contribution of $24,000 (the maximum), and Employee B would have a contribution of $2,000.

With the $160,000 rule in effect, Executive A could only use the first $160,000 of pay on which to base his or her contribution. This means that Executive A cannot achieve a $24,000 contribution (nor can anyone else); the maximum contribution given the 15 percent limit is now $24,000 (15 percent of $160,000). And for Executive A to get his or her $24,000, the overall contribution rate will have to be 15 percent of compensation. Consequently, Employee B's contribution would be $3,000 (15 percent of $20,000).

Excess Employee Contributions

Excess employee contributions, or the amounts contributed above the $10,000 (indexed) annual limit, can place the SEP plan in conflict with the 1.25 rule. Should excess employee contributions affect this rule, any excess deferrals contributed by highly compensated employees will be subject to a nondeductible 10 percent penalty tax, to be imposed on the *employer*.

■ TAX-SHELTERED ANNUITIES (§403(b) PLANS)

In addition to the previously discussed qualified retirement plans available to corporations and to self-employed individuals, a market exists in which employees of public schools and certain tax-exempt organizations also have favorable income tax treatment working for them in saving for retirement. This is the tax-sheltered annuity (TSA), sometimes referred to as the tax-favored or tax-deferred annuity or the 403(b) plan.

Many practitioners have neglected this market, perhaps because the list of potential clients is less obvious than for other types of plans. The two prime groups of individuals eligible for this coverage are teachers and medical personnel. In many instances this market is viewed strictly as a group market: the group variable annuity is commonly used for medium-sized to large-sized enrollments.

Many institutions whose employees are eligible for this program have restricted competition by granting exclusive sales/enrollment permission to one or a few practitioners. The choice can become political since administrators are often appointed officials or committee members who don't report directly to anyone. However, an overly restrictive policy can make all the institution's TSA accounts into a "pension plan" regulated by the Department of Labor, which the institution may want to avoid.

Despite complicating factors in this market, there are many practitioners who find it to their liking. These reasons include:

1. There are limited numbers of other practitioners working in this market.

2. Being a salary reduction plan in most instances, the sale is made to the employee. It requires no employer outlay, little or no administrative support and simple payroll and premium remittal procedures.

3. Institutions whose employees are eligible also include small churches, private schools and nonprofit organizations, often totally overlooked.

4. The employers whose employees are eligible provide services rather than products. These service industries have grown at a relatively fast pace.

5. A high percentage of those employees are spouses of a two-income family. These individuals, therefore, have a high marginal propensity to save. Also their spouse (family) becomes a referred lead for an IRA, life insurance and financial planning.

Qualified Employer

To be eligible for a TSA, an employee must work for an employer that is tax exempt under Code §501(c)(3) or for a public school system. Such employers are referred to as *qualified employers*.

Organizations covered by 501(c)(3) are not only tax exempt, but are entitled to receive tax-deductible charitable contributions from others. They comprise non-profit corporations, funds and foundations organized and operated exclusively for religious, charitable, scientific, literary or educational purposes, for the prevention of cruelty to children or animals or to foster national or international amateur sports competition (as long as they do not furnish athletic supplies or equipment). The income of such an organization is specifically exempt from federal income taxation. Parochial school systems and most private schools and colleges are included in the types of organizations covered by 501(c)(3).

A school or college operated directly by a civil government or agency also qualifies for the special treatment of a TSA plan, even though the employer cannot come under 501(c)(3). Normally, an organization operated by a state, county or city will not qualify for such plans. However, a public school system is specifically included as a qualified employer under 403(b). Also, for annuity purposes, a charitable cor-poration owned by a governmental unit, such as a hospital, may file separately as a 501(c)(3) organization. In the event a publicly owned school is operated by a sepa-rate educational instrumentality, it may qualify both as a 501(c)(3) organization and a public school.

There are some types of tax-exempt organizations that are exempt under sections other than 501(c)(3), and accordingly are not qualified employers for TSAs. The nonqualified employers include trade associations, civic leagues and labor unions. To obtain a tax-exempt status under 501(c)(3), an organization must have filed a request for such status with the district director of Internal Revenue. A direct inquiry should be made to determine whether a particular organization has obtained an exemption or not.

Eligible Employees

A TSA may be purchased only for common-law employees (part-time or full-time) of qualified organizations. A self-employed individual, or an independent contrac-tor who performs services for such an organization is not eligible. Although not conclusive, payment of Social Security taxes by the organization is strong evidence that an individual is an employee of the organization. Borderline cases will arise, however, as to whether an individual is an employee or an independent contractor. In such an event, the so-called *common-law rules* are applied.

Common-Law Rules

Under the common-law rules, the key is control. Individuals are considered to be employees if the organization for whom they render services has the right to direct and control them in the way they work, both as to the final results and as to details of when, where and how the work is accomplished.

The following questions highlight some of the elements of control:

- Is the individual required to comply with instructions regarding the perfor-mance of assigned duties?

- Must the individual devote his or her full time to the business of the employer?

- Does the individual receive reimbursement for any business and travel expenses?

- Has the individual made a significant investment in facilities in performing the service?

- Is the individual subject to summary dismissal?

- Does the individual receive training in company procedures?

An affirmative answer to these questions should be weighed and compared with those which point to an independent contractor status.

Employees of §501(c)(3) Organizations

TSAs may be made available for some or all employees of a 501(c)(3) organization, including those performing services as social workers, members of the clergy, teachers, professors, clerks, secretaries and others.

Physicians working for a qualifying hospital also are eligible for tax-deferred annuities. However, the relationship between physicians and a hospital often is not one of employer and employee. To aid in determining the relationship between a hospital and a physician, the IRS has offered the following guides which are based on the common-law test:

> *Physicians may be employees if they agreed that they would not assume outside duties to the detriment of their primary services to the hospital, would not furnish services to other hospitals without the employer's consent, would comply with all rules and regulations of the hospital, and, if their percentage remuneration did not equal a guaranteed amount per year, would receive an adjustment. Moreover, each case must be determined on its own facts and no clear-cut rule can be laid down in advance that will apply to all cases.*

Employees of Public Schools

A person is an employee of a public school if he or she performs services as an employee directly or indirectly for such institution. For example, the principal, teachers, clerical employees and custodial employees of a public school are eligible employees.

Employees who do not work at a school but are involved in the operation or direction of an educational program of a public school system are performing services indirectly. The elected or appointed official of a public school also is an eligible employee if he or she is trained or experienced in the field of education.

The Advantages of a Tax-Sheltered Annuity Plan

In general, the tax advantages under a TSA plan permit an employee to exclude from his or her gross income employer contributions made toward the purchase of an annuity contract, up to a specified limit. The tax on these contributions is deferred until retirement when the employee's income probably will be reduced.

Elective Contributions under TSAs

The amount of the contribution that an employee may exclude cannot exceed the employee's exclusion allowance for the tax year. The exclusion allowance formula is the following: (20 percent × employee's includable compensation) × years of service – amounts previously excludable.

In addition, there are limits on the maximum amount that an employee can elect to defer for any taxable year. An employee covered by at least one TSA can defer up to $10,500 each year (in 2000 and subject to future indexing). But, for an employee with at least 15 years' service with an educational organization, hospital, home health service agency, health and welfare service agency, church or convention or association of churches, the $10,500 limit is increased each tax year by the *smallest* of the following:

- $3,000;

- $15,000, reduced by increases to the $10,500 limit allowed in earlier years; or

- $5,000 *times* the number of years of service *minus* the total elective deferrals made under the plan for earlier years.

Flexible Features

In establishing a TSA plan, a qualified employer has two choices: (1) it may agree to make premium contributions to the employee-owned annuity that are in addition to the employee's regular current compensation or (2) it may authorize any employee who so chooses to have a certain percentage of his or her salary reduced and the amount of the reduction channeled into an annuity.

In any event, the employer applies for the annuity and makes premium payments directly to the insurance company. The employees own the annuities and name their own beneficiaries for the death benefits under the plan.

There Must Be an Agreement

To satisfy the requirements for a TSA, an employer must enter into an agreement with the employee. The agreement must cite whether contributions are to be made from a salary reduction or in addition to current income. And the amount of the exclusion allowance is based on the employee's includable compensation for the taxable year.

Although an employee is free to terminate the agreement at any time, he or she must not be allowed to enter into more than one agreement during a taxable year. For purposes of this requirement, an agreement that gears contributions to a percentage of salary that ultimately requires a change in contributions because of an increase or decrease in compensation, is not considered a new agreement. Also, a change in the insurer does not constitute a new agreement.

Approved Tax-Sheltered Annuities

The tax-exempt contributions made to a TSA plan must be applied toward the immediate purchase of an annuity contract. Included in the Internal Revenue Service's definition of *annuity contract,* is the commercial annuity offered by most life insurance companies. In addition, the Employee Retirement Income Security Act of 1974 (ERISA) expanded the definition of annuity contracts to include mutual funds purchased through a custodial account. An approved annuity contract may be issued by an employer who establishes a separately funded retirement reserve subject to the supervision of the state insurance department. Contributions to a separate fund maintained by a state teachers' retirement system may constitute contributions to a TSA.

Nonforfeitable Rights and Nontransferable

The employer pays the premiums on the contract, but the employee has nonforfeitable rights to the policy purchased on his or her behalf. Thus an employee is entitled to the full rights in the policy at the time contributions are made. There may be no contingencies that will cause the employee to lose his or her rights.

The policy also must be nontransferable when issued. This means that the employee cannot sell, assign, discount or pledge as collateral for a loan his or her interest in the contract, except to the insurance company.

Salary Reductions

Frequently a tax-exempt organization cannot make contributions in addition to present salary. Here the salary reduction approach can be used effectively. A new employment agreement can be executed that reduces an employee's current salary. The employer can then purchase an annuity for the employee and pay the premiums with the difference between past and future salary.

Although a legally binding salary reduction agreement is authorized, an employee may make only one such agreement with his or her employer during any one taxable year. It is also essential that the employment contract calling for the salary reduction be *prospective* in its effect—it applies to future earnings only, and is not retrospective to any income already received.

Nondiscrimination

TSA programs must meet IRS nondiscrimination rules that depend on which of the flexible features the employer chose. If the employer is making premium contributions in addition to the employee's regular current compensation, the plan, like a qualified corporate retirement plan, must meet one of the *percentage test, ratio test* or *average benefit test,* and also the *50/40 test,* for employee coverage, discussed in Chapter 10. And if the employer makes matching contributions in addition to employee salary reduction contributions, the plan must meet the special nondiscrimination test for matching contributions also discussed Chapter 10. The contributions under the plan must also be nondiscriminatory in amount. For this purpose, the IRS has issued guidance allowing employer contributions for highly compensated employees to range from 100 to 180 percent of the contributions for nonhighly compensated employees, depending on the percentage of the employer's lower-paid workers who are covered by the plan and the percentage of plan participants who are lower-paid workers.

If, however, the employer only authorizes employees to make salary reduction elections, all that is required is that each nonexcludable employee be allowed to contribute at least $200 per year if he or she so elects. Excludible employees are those who work fewer than 20 hours per week, students who are not subject to Social Security taxes, nonresident aliens or participants in certain other types of plans.

Tax-Free Exchanges or Transfers

In general, an individual can apply for a similar but better yielding contract with the same or another insurer, have proceeds directed from the first to the second and avoid a current taxable distribution provided the proper procedure is adhered to.

Additional Advantages

In addition to the tax advantages, the tax-favored annuity plan also offers these advantages to the employee of a qualified employer. You should stress these advantages when you first open up a TSA case.

The annuity plan is flexible. Its maturity date can coincide with the employee's retirement date. If an employee should decide to elect an early retirement under the retirement plan, he or she also can elect an early income under the annuity plan. By the same token, the plan can coincide with the employee's Social Security retirement benefits. If the employee elects an early retirement date under Social Security, he or she may do the same with the annuity.

The annuity plan relieves the employee of investment responsibility. The insurance company does the investing and diversification is achieved by spreading the premium deposits among various investments. These investments also reflect the maximum in yields consistent with safety.

The Plan Benefits All Concerned

From the employees' standpoint, the plan presents a unique opportunity to supplement their regular retirement program with tax-sheltered dollars.

From the employer's standpoint, the annuity plan can be an attractive and sound business investment. On one hand, there is no cost to the employer unless it agrees to make annuity payments for an employee that are in addition to current salary. On the other hand, it can help attract and retain employees of high caliber. Retirement benefits are virtually a required form of compensation among employees who are intent upon a career with an employer.

Installation of a TSA Program

If a practitioner is going to install a TSA program, he or she must:

1. obtain the permission and support of the employer; and

2. consult with each employee on the advantages of:

- the TSA concept;

- the annuity product or products offered; and

- dealing through and with the practitioner.

Introducing the Plan to the Employer

Qualified employers include schools, charitable organizations, hospitals, clinics, churches and other not-for-profit organizations. Whom do you approach? This can be a difficult matter. For the most part, you will be encountering the sale by first establishing a need by the individual employee. This, then, is the first place to ask. Some employees will know who handles such business matters at his or her place of employment. For a pastor this may be the board of elders or the church secretary. For a teacher this may be a business office either in the building or located within the district, township or state.

Once a person is located in a sufficient position of power, an agreement is usually obtained that authorizes this person to sign agreements on behalf of the employer. This eliminates the need for board members or officers to be involved in the daily affairs of the program and protects the practitioner because the signature authorization also states that the organization is truly one of the type whose employees qualify for a TSA. A TSA program may already be in operation, in which case this preliminary groundwork may already have been accomplished.

As the role of government and nonprofit services expands, more and more individuals are eligible for 403(b) plans. The practitioner has a lot to gain by being aware of those eligible for this benefit. Although many larger school districts generally already have programs, many will allow another insurer to enter the system if the product offers a combination of unique or outstanding features. Small private schools, churches and even hospitals offer, perhaps, less competitive environments.

■ SUMMARY

Retirement planning has become a trillion-dollar market. As more and more individuals become aware of the limitations surrounding Social Security, there is an increasing demand for competent advice from the qualified practitioner. Individual retirement plans include Keogh plans, IRAs, Roth IRAs, SEPs and TSAs. Keogh plans offer small business owners the ability to provide retirement benefit plans to their employees in much the same manner as large employers. Contributions to a Keogh plan are tax deductible to the business and tax deferred to the employee until retirement. IRAs are investment accounts that can be opened by any individual with earned income. Although the initial contribution may not be tax deductible, the invested assets are tax deferred until retirement. A SEP is a retirement plan with high contribution limits and tax deductibility. The advantages to the plan are the minimal recordkeeping requirements specifically designed for the self-employed individual with few employees. TSAs are available to employees of public schools and not-for-profit organizations. Investment to a TSA are tax deductible and tax deferred and sometimes have higher contribution limits than 401(k) plans.

There are several software programs designed for the practitioner to be used in conjunction with the retirement planning market from design and implementation to portfolio management. Retirement planning is already a a very large market and is becoming larger each year. The practitioner who excels at understanding its varied components will benefit both the client and himself or herself.

■ CHAPTER 2 QUESTIONS FOR REVIEW

1. A Keogh plan is designed to provide qualified retirement benefits for which group?

   A. Key corporate employees

   B. Highly compensated corporate employees

   C. Rank-and-file corporate employees not covered by a qualified plan

   D. Self-employed individuals

2. Which of the following best defines *earned income?*

   A. Earned income is gross income less expenses less capital expenditures.

   B. Earned income is gross income plus expenses less self-employment tax.

   C. Earned income is determined after deductions for normal business expenses.

   D. Earned income is determined after deductions for back taxes owed.

3. Sam Hunter, a corporate employee, is single, earns $36,000 a year and is covered under his employer's profit-sharing plan. How much may Sam *contribute* to an IRA annually?

   A. $0

   B. $1,000

   C. $2,000

   D. $9,000

4. Julie White earns $28,000 a year and participates in her employer's simplified employee pension. What is the maximum that the *employer* may contribute on Julie's behalf for the year?

   A. $1,000

   B. $2,000

   C. $4,200

   D. $7,000

5. Which of the following is the maximum annual employee deferral to a TSA plan?

   A. 25 percent of salary or $30,000, whichever is less

   B. $2,000

   C. $9,500

   D. 20 percent of compensation less the previous year's contributions to the plan

6. The deduction for a couple, both being participants in their companies' plan, with a $100,000 AGI making the full $4,000 IRA investment is

   A. $0
   B. $1,000
   C. $2,000
   D. $4,000

7. Eligible TSA employees include all of the following EXCEPT

   A. public school employees
   B. church employees
   C. nonprofit employees
   D. self-employed individuals

8. The most stringent eligibility requirements for a SEP plan are

   A. age 21 or older
   B. worked for the employer a minimum of three of the last five years
   C. received at least $400 in compensation for the year
   D. all of the above

9. All of the following financial products are allowable IRA investments EXCEPT

   A. life insurance
   B. mutual funds
   C. certificate of deposit
   D. variable annuity

10. An owner-employee is a self-employed person who owns more than how much interest in a partnership?

    A. 5 percent
    B. 10 percent
    C. 20 percent
    D. 50 percent

3

Federal Income Taxation of Life Insurance and Annuities

An understanding of the federal income tax treatment of life insurance and annuities is necessary if the financial services professional is to be effective in the fields of business insurance, retirement plans, estate planning and investment planning. We begin this chapter by examining the unique tax advantages of life insurance and continue with a discussion of the tax treatment of insurance death proceeds, policy loans and annuity payments.

Remember the old saying about the certainty of death and taxes? There is probably no arguing that the person who attempts to avoid them completely isn't going to succeed. Yet when it comes to taxes, there are opportunities for planning and control. For example, we can reduce our taxes by utilizing the tax advantages of life insurance.

Life insurance enjoys certain tax advantages that are not found elsewhere. By knowing what these advantages are and when they apply, you will increase your value to your prospects and clients and strengthen your sales presentations.

Over the past several years there have been several changes to the code and many investments no longer receive favorable tax treatment. However, tax-deferred buildup of life insurance cash values has been preserved, making cash value life insurance an extremely attractive financial alternative.

Emphasizing favorable tax treatment is not the only way to sell life insurance, nor are tax advantages the only reason to buy it. To be totally effective in the fields of business insurance and estate planning, however, you must have a working knowledge of this important subject. The knowledge you gain here will serve as a valuable foundation for your future consultative endeavors.

This discussion will concentrate on the *federal* income taxation of life insurance and annuity contracts. Please consult your specific state for the applicable state income tax laws.

■ ■ ■ ■ ■

■ THE TWO MAIN TAX ADVANTAGES

The two main tax advantages of life insurance are the following:

1. The internal cash buildup within the contract is tax deferred.

2. Death proceeds are generally received income tax free.

The main tax advantages of annuities are the tax-deferred internal cash buildup within the contract.

Currently, no other form of financial product, other than tax-qualified or tax-advantaged retirement plans, permits the taxpayer to postpone, sometimes forever, income tax on the return of premium invested. Some forms of investment such as tax-exempt mutual funds are exempt from income tax; however, they do not have the unique ability to create a sizable, liquid estate, with little or no risk of loss of investment in the manner that life insurance does.

Today, competing forms of investments are at an even greater disadvantage compared to life insurance products. For example, individual retirement accounts (IRAs) now are subject to stringent rules for taxpayers covered by an employer's tax-qualified or tax-advantaged retirement plan. Many of your prospects and clients who once were able to make the maximum annual deductible contribution to an IRA may be limited in the amount of a tax-deductible contribution that can be made, and in cases, many persons are now ineligible for an IRA deduction. Tax-qualified employer-sponsored retirement plans are now subject to even more stringent rules and limitations on benefits for employees. Tax-sheltered investments, the most common form of which is the limited partnership, have also lost their major attraction to many investors—the ability to offset taxable income from other sources with paper losses for income tax purposes.

The advantages of life insurance and annuity products are very competitive when compared with other forms of financial instruments. In simplistic terms, life insurance protects against dying too soon, while annuities protect against living too long.

■ WHAT IS LIFE INSURANCE?

The life insurance industry has changed markedly in the last several years. Universal life, variable life, variable universal life and other investment-oriented products have altered traditional notions of what life insurance is or is not. The popularity of these emerging products prompted Congress to enact a comprehensive definition of life insurance for federal income tax purposes. To qualify for favorable tax treatment, a policy issued after 1984 must meet the definition of life insurance under applicable state law *and* it must meet one of two tests to qualify for favorable federal income tax treatment: (1) the cash value accumulation test or (2) the guideline premium/cash value corridor test.

If a policy fails to meet one of the two alternative tests, it will be separated into its pure insurance and savings portions. Income earned on the savings portion will be

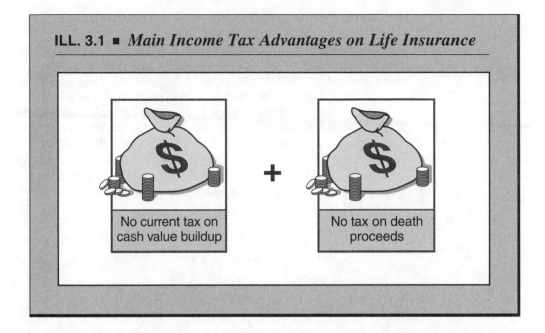

ILL. 3.1 ■ *Main Income Tax Advantages on Life Insurance*

No current tax on cash value buildup

+

No tax on death proceeds

taxable to the policyowner each year, much like a savings account or mutual fund. Moreover, the policyowner will be taxed on policy income from all *previous* policy years. Only the pure insurance portion of a disqualified policy will be eligible for the income tax exemption for death proceeds. If income earned on the savings portion is taxable, income is calculated without reduction for any policyholder dividends paid during the current year.

Cash Value Accumulation Test

Under this test, the cash surrender value of a life insurance policy cannot exceed, at any time over the term of the policy, the net single premium that would be required at such time to fund the future benefits of the policy.

The cash surrender value of the contract is the policy's cash value without regard to surrender charges, policy loans or reasonable termination benefits. The net single premium is determined by using:

- a 4 percent annual interest rate or the interest rates guaranteed in the contract, whichever is greater;

- the mortality charges specified or, if not specified, the charges used in computing statutory reserves for the contract; or

- any other charges specified in the contract.

The cash value accumulation test is usually the first item that the life insurance illustration software will test. If the policy does not pass this first test, then the software will check the guideline premium.

Guideline Premium/Cash Value Corridor Test

This is really two tests combined into one overall test, *both* halves of which must be satisfied. The *guideline premium* half is met if the aggregate premiums paid to date under the contract do not, at any time, exceed the greater of the *guideline single premium* or the sum of the *guideline level premiums*. The *guideline single premium* is that one-time premium that would fund the future benefits of the contract. The *guideline level premium* is that level annual amount that would fund the future benefits of the policy over a period lasting at least until the insured's 95th birthday and not later than age 100. A policy will satisfy the cash value corridor half of the test if the death benefit available under the policy is at all times no less than the applicable percentage (based on the insured's age) of the cash surrender value in the following table:

Insured's Age	Applicable Percentage	Insured's Age	Applicable Percentage
40 or less	250	61	128
41	243	62	126
42	236	63	124
43	229	64	122
44	222	65	120
45	215	66	119
46	209	67	118
47	203	68	117
48	197	69	116
49	191	70	115
50	185	71	113
51	178	72	111
52	171	73	109
53	164	74	107
54	157	75–90	105
55	150	91	104
56	146	92	103
57	142	93	102
58	138	94	101
59	134	95 or more	100
60	130		

For purposes of the above table, the insured's age is determined as of the beginning of the contract year, not his/her birthday.

Amount Includable in Taxable Income

If a life insurance contract fails to meet one of the two alternative tests, the policyholder may be subject to current income taxation on a portion of gain on the savings element. The amount of income, if any, on the savings portion of a life insurance policy that must be included in taxable income each year of the policy's term is computed as follows:

$$
\begin{array}{rl}
 & \text{Increase in net surrender value} \\
+ & \text{Cost of pure life insurance provided} \\
+ & \text{Dividends received} \\
- & \underline{\text{Premiums paid}} \\
= & \text{TAXABLE INCOME}
\end{array}
$$

In arriving at this computation, the cost of pure life insurance protection is the lesser of:

1. the cost of individual life insurance on the insured; or

2. the mortality charge, if any, set forth in the policy.

Because the consequence of a disqualification could be disastrous for the policy-holder, most insurance companies monitor policies each year in order to avoid this situation. Unforeseen disqualification may also result in underpayment of estimated tax by the policyowner.

▪ FEDERAL INCOME TAXATION OF LIFE INSURANCE PROCEEDS AND ANNUITIES

A discussion of the income tax treatment of life insurance and endowment proceeds must be divided into two general classifications:

1. proceeds payable as a result of the insured's death; and

2. proceeds paid at maturity or surrender of the policy (including annuity benefits).

First, let's examine the taxation of life insurance proceeds resulting from the insured's death.

Income Taxation of Death Proceeds in General

As a general rule, life insurance death proceeds are received income tax free by the beneficiary. However, in some circumstances, the proceeds may not be fully exempt from federal income taxation. Even when the general rule applies, the exact tax treatment of proceeds paid to a beneficiary upon the death of the insured depends on whether the proceeds are received in one lump sum or under one of the settlement options.

To start our discussion, we will consider contracts that are not exempt and how their death proceeds are treated for income tax purposes. Then we will examine the tax treatment of contracts that qualify for exclusion of death proceeds, beginning with those payable in a lump sum and moving through those distributed under the various available settlement options.

Contracts with Death Proceeds Not Excluded from Income Tax

Generally, death proceeds are excludable from the beneficiary's gross income. Only in limited situations are the death proceeds of traditional life insurance contracts treated as taxable income for federal income tax purposes. An example of this would be death proceeds received under a contract that had been transferred for valuable consideration, such as with a sale of the policy from one shareholder to another.

Not all transfers for valuable consideration, though, result in taxation of the proceeds. The transfer-for-value rule does *not* apply to a transfer:

1. to the insured, a partner of the insured, a partnership in which the insured is a partner or a corporation in which the insured is a shareholder or officer; or

2. where the recipient's tax basis in the policy is determined, to some extent, by the basis of the party who transferred it.

For example, in a tax-free corporate reorganization, the basis in a policy owned by the former company would be the same in the hands of the reorganized company. (In the first exception, note the absence of a transfer to a shareholder in a corporation in which the insured is a shareholder. The transfer-for-value rule would apply to such a transfer.)

When death proceeds are not excluded from gross income, the amount by which those death proceeds exceed the net investment in the contract (generally, premiums paid) is subject to federal income taxation. Since the death benefit usually is many times the net investment in a life insurance contract, a tremendous amount of appreciation is subject to ordinary income tax treatment when the death proceeds are not excluded from gross income.

Federal Income Tax Treatment of Excluded Death Proceeds

The vast majority of life insurance policies provide death proceeds that are excluded from gross income of the beneficiary for federal income tax purposes. Proceeds of all fixed-premium policies (with the exceptions indicated above) and of flexible premium policies that meet the tests or exceptions prescribed by law are excluded.

The federal income tax treatment of excluded life insurance death proceeds depends upon whether the proceeds are received in a lump sum or under one of the settlement options. The following is a discussion of the traditional treatment of death proceeds distributed in each of the typical ways.

Proceeds Paid as Lump Sums

If the beneficiary, at the insured's death, receives the proceeds in a lump sum, *the entire amount of the proceeds is received income tax free.* In addition to the policy's face amount, this tax-free sum includes any proceeds paid under a double indemnity provision, paid-up additions, one-year term insurance purchased by dividends, accumulated dividends and any accumulated interest.

ILL. 3.2 ■ *Federal Income Taxation of Life Insurance Death Proceeds*

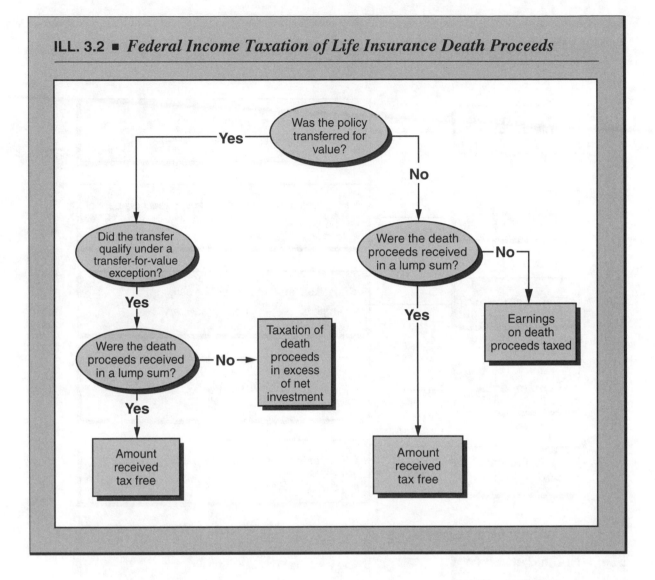

For example, assume that the insured under a $100,000 whole life policy dies as a result of an accident. B, the beneficiary, receives in a lump sum the $100,000 face amount of the policy, $100,000 as a result of a double indemnity provision in the policy and $2,500 in dividends and interest that the insured had allowed to accumulate. The entire $202,500 received by B as a result of the insured's death is received income tax free. Illustration 3.2 displays the federal income taxation of life insurance proceeds.

Proceeds Paid Under Settlement Options

Sometimes it will be more advantageous for the beneficiary to receive the proceeds under one of the settlement options, rather than in a lump sum. While you already may be familiar with the various settlement options, we will review them here before discussing the tax treatment applicable to each. (See Ill. 3.3.)

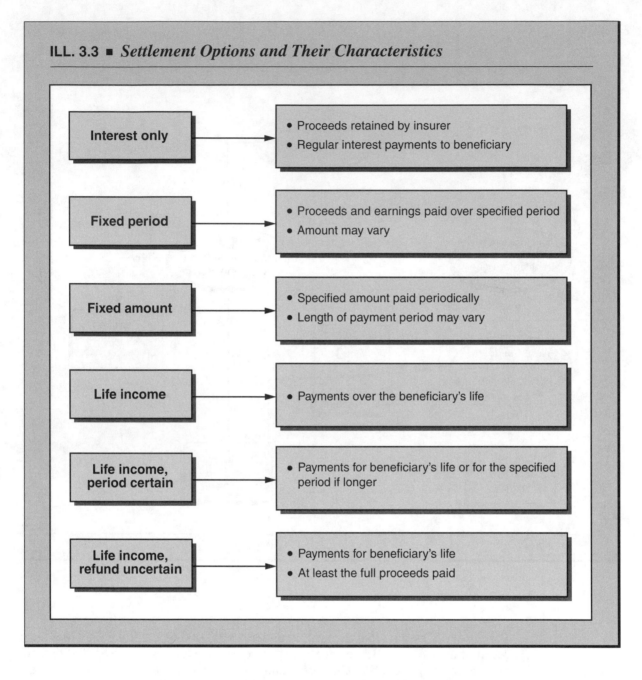

ILL. 3.3 ■ *Settlement Options and Their Characteristics*

Interest only
- Proceeds retained by insurer
- Regular interest payments to beneficiary

Fixed period
- Proceeds and earnings paid over specified period
- Amount may vary

Fixed amount
- Specified amount paid periodically
- Length of payment period may vary

Life income
- Payments over the beneficiary's life

Life income, period certain
- Payments for beneficiary's life or for the specified period if longer

Life income, refund uncertain
- Payments for beneficiary's life
- At least the full proceeds paid

The Interest-Only Option. Under the interest-only option, proceeds are retained by the insurance company and interest is paid to the beneficiary on a regular basis.

It is a flexible option. In addition to the interest, a beneficiary may be given an unrestricted privilege to withdraw any amount of the proceeds at any time. Alternatively, the withdrawal privilege may be limited to a certain maximum amount per year. A beneficiary may also be given the opportunity to switch to some other option in the future. Where the beneficiary is given these privileges, there are income tax ramifications that deserve careful consideration.

Fixed-Period Option. The fixed-period option spreads the payment of the proceeds, plus earned interest, over a stated time. Each payment is part *principal* (the original amount of the proceeds) and part interest. Under the fixed-period option the insurance company is told how long payments are to continue. Once set, the period will not vary. If proceeds are more or less than originally counted on, the amount of each installment will be proportionately increased or reduced. Any excess interest cannot extend the period, so it is customarily paid annually.

Fixed-Amount Option. The fixed-amount option is similar to the fixed-period option. Under the fixed-amount option the company is told how much each payment is to be. Once fixed, that amount cannot vary. As a result, any variation in the available proceeds will extend or shorten the period of payments. The regular installment payment stays the same. Any excess interest will increase the period rather than the amount of any installment.

The Life-Income Option. Like the fixed-period and fixed-amount options, the life-income option maximizes income by distributing both principal and interest in each payment. In addition, it guarantees that those payments will continue over the lifetime of the beneficiary, no matter how long that may be.

A number of variations of the life-income option are offered. The two most common are *life income, period-certain* and *life income, refund-certain.* To avoid confusion, it should be emphasized that the "certain" feature has no bearing on the settlement for the primary beneficiary. The beneficiary will receive an income for life in any event. Instead, the certainty refers to safeguarding the interest of the contingent beneficiaries.

For example, life income, 20-year certain, first guarantees that payments will continue to the primary beneficiary for the rest of his or her life. In addition, contingent beneficiaries are protected by the assurance that payments will continue for a minimum of 20 years following the insured's death, even though the primary beneficiary might die within the 20-year period.

Refund-certain is another frequently encountered variation. It provides that income will be paid to the primary beneficiary for life, but if he or she dies before receiving an amount equal to the full proceeds, the installments will continue to be paid to contingent beneficiaries until a stated balance has been paid.

We are now ready to examine the tax treatment of death proceeds under each of these options.

Taxation of Settlement Option Payments

In general, when life insurance proceeds are paid under settlement options, only the *interest element* of each payment is taxable. Where death proceeds are involved, the interest element of the payment is the amount that exceeds the total that would have been payable had the beneficiary received the proceeds in a lump sum at the time of the insured's death.

In other words, the amount payable in a lump sum does not lose its tax-free character simply because the beneficiary elects to receive the death proceeds in installments. When death proceeds are paid under a settlement option, a portion of each payment is tax-free insurance proceeds and a portion is taxable interest.

Let's examine the specific rules under the various life-income options.

Interest-Only Payments

Under the interest-only option, the interest income is *taxable in full to the beneficiary who receives it.* And it is taxable without regard to whether the insured or the beneficiary elected the option.

The interest income is taxable to the beneficiary even though he or she may not have the privilege of withdrawing the principal. Even if the beneficiary has the insurance company accumulate the interest income for *later* benefit, it is still taxable *currently* unless he or she is *not entitled* to the accumulated interest until a certain date. In other words, at the time the beneficiary is *permitted* to withdraw the accumulated interest, it becomes taxable. This is because of the *constructive receipt rule,* discussed later in this chapter.

Fixed-Period Payments

It is simple to determine the taxable portion of each installment under a fixed-period option. The amount payable in a lump sum under the policy is divided by the number of payments to be made. That portion represents principal and is not subject to tax. The balance of the payment is interest and is taxable. Any excess interest received, of course, would be taxable. *Excess interest* refers to any interest in excess of the assumed rate set by state law and regulation for the type of contract involved.

Here is an example of the income tax treatment of death proceeds under a fixed-period option:

Assume that $100,000 of life insurance is payable to a surviving spouse under a fixed-period option for 20 years at a guaranteed interest rate of 5 percent. This will provide a monthly income of $650, or an annual income of $7,800 (excluding any excess interest) for 20 years. Dividing the $100,000 face amount by the 20-year period produces a tax-free payment of principal of $5,000 per year. Subtracting this $5,000 from the annual payment of $7,800 leaves annual reportable income of $2,800.

Annual Payments ($650 × 12 months)	$7,800.00
Annual Tax-Free Payments ($100,000 ÷ 20 years)	−5,000.00
Annual Taxable Portion	$2,800.00

Fixed-Amount Payments

When death proceeds are paid under the fixed-amount option, the number of guaranteed payments required to exhaust the proceeds must be determined before the taxable element can be found. You can find the number of guaranteed payments by referring to the fixed-amount option table in your rate book. Then, the procedure is similar to that for the fixed-period option.

For example, assume that a surviving spouse is to receive $25,000 of life insurance proceeds in the amount of $200 a month until the proceeds are exhausted. The guaranteed interest rate is 5 percent. The rate book table shows that it will take 14 years, six months, to exhaust the $25,000 of initial proceeds. The initial amount is then divided by the number of monthly payments to arrive at the excluded portion of each payment. Dividing $25,000 by 174 (the number of guaranteed monthly payments) produces a figure of $143.68, which is the nontaxable portion of each payment. The balance of each payment, $56.32, is taxable interest income. Over a one-year period, the spouse would receive reportable income of $675.84 ($56.32 × 12 months).

Monthly Payments (14½ years × 12)	174	
Monthly Tax-Free Payments ($25,000 ÷ 174 months)	$143.68	
Monthly Taxable Portion ($200.00 – $143.68)		$ 56.32
		× 12
Annual Taxable Portion		$675.84

Excess Interest—In a fixed-amount option, excess interest is applied to increase the *number* of payments rather than the *amount* of each payment. Thus any installments that extend beyond the guaranteed period (such as the 14-year-and-six-month period in the preceding example) would not include any principal, but would consist entirely of excess interest. These additional payments would be fully taxable to the beneficiary.

Life-Income Payments

In determining the taxable portion of payments under a life-income option (either life only or life with guaranteed payments), it is necessary to know the life expectancy of the primary beneficiary at the time of the insured's death. This figure is then divided into the amount that would be received in a lump sum to find the tax-exempt portion of each payment. In other words, the beneficiary's life expectancy plays the same role under a life-income option as the number of fixed payments do under an installment option.

Sex-Neutral Tables to Allocate Interest and Proceeds—The law requires companies to use sex-neutral mortality tables to determine what portion of each payment is interest. This rule will not prevent companies from making payments to beneficiaries based on their own tables. It applies only to determine what portion of each payment is an excludable death benefit and what portion is attributable to interest.

Life-Only Option

If the beneficiary is to receive the proceeds under a life-income option without a refund or period-certain feature, the initial proceeds are simply divided by the beneficiary's life expectancy at the insured's death. The result is the annual tax-free payment of principal; the balance of each annual payment is taxable income to the beneficiary.

To illustrate, assume that $25,000 of proceeds are left to a surviving spouse, age 54, under a life-only option. Also assume payments will total $142.50 monthly or

$1,710 annually. Further assume that at age 54 the spouse's life expectancy is 29.6 years. Dividing $25,000 by 29.6 produces for the spouse an annual tax-free return of proceeds of $844.60. Subtracting this figure from the spouse's total annual payments of $1,710 results in taxable annual interest income of $865.40 to the beneficiary.

Annual Payments ($142.50 × 12 months)	$1,710.00
Annual Tax-Free Payments ($25,000 ÷ 29.6 life expectancy)	– 844.60
Annual Taxable Portion	$ 865.40

If the beneficiary exceeds his or her life expectancy (and the investment in the contract has been recovered), the tax-free portion of the income flow stops and the entire payment becomes taxable. (For payments that began before 1987, the tax-free portion remains as long as the beneficiary lives, even though he or she lives longer than expected.)

Life Income with Guaranteed Payments

When a period-certain or refund feature is part of the life-income option, an additional step is necessary. It involves a downward adjustment in the amount that is divided by the primary beneficiary's life expectancy. This adjustment is based on the actuarial chance that guaranteed payments may extend beyond the primary beneficiary's death.

The amount of the adjustment is stated in percentage or decimal form and is obtained from the life insurance company that issued the policy. Once it is applied to the death proceeds payable under the policy, the reduced figure is divided by the primary beneficiary's life expectancy. This creates a smaller tax-free portion of the life income payments, reflecting the fact that payments will continue if the beneficiary dies before the end of the guaranteed period. Following are examples under both the period-certain and refund-certain options.

Life Income, Period-Certain—A surviving spouse, age 63, is to receive $20,000 of proceeds under a life income, 10-year certain option paying $120 a month. The spouse's life expectancy at the insured's death is 21.7 years. The actuarial value of the period-certain feature is 8 percent based on government annuity tables. This 8 percent figure means that, actuarially, the contingent beneficiaries have an 8 percent interest in the proceeds at the insured's death since the spouse, in spite of a 21.7 year life expectancy, might die during the 10-year guaranteed period. Thus the $20,000 original proceeds must be adjusted downward 8 percent, or $1,600, resulting in adjusted proceeds of $18,400.

Dividing the adjusted proceeds of $18,400 by the primary beneficiary's 21.7-year life expectancy results in $847.93 of annual tax-free principal. Subtracting this figure from the total annual payment of $1,440 leaves the spouse with annual reportable income of $592.07 as long as he or she lives.

Adjustment for Refund Feature ($20,000 × 8%)	$1,600.00	
Adjusted Face Amount ($20,000 – $1,600)	$18,400.00	
Annual Payments ($120 × 12 months)		$1,440.00
Annual Tax-Free Payments ($18,400 ÷ 21.7 years)		– 847.93
Annual Taxable Portion		$ 592.07

If the spouse dies during the period certain, the secondary beneficiaries will receive the entire amount tax free until the end of the guaranteed period.

Life Income, Refund-Certain—The procedure for arriving at the taxable portion of payments under a life income, refund-certain option is the same as that for the period-certain option, except that the number of guaranteed payments must be found. This is done by dividing the original proceeds by the annual payments. The result, rounded off to the nearest year, is the number of guaranteed payments.

For example, assume the above beneficiary receives the $20,000 proceeds under an installment refund option instead of the 10-year certain option. His or her monthly income will be $112, and annual payments, $1,344. Dividing $20,000 by $1,344 shows that it will take 15 years (rounded off) to return the guaranteed principal. Thus, in effect, the refund option becomes a 15-year period-certain option.

Assuming the actuarial value of the refund feature to be 13 percent, the original proceeds are adjusted downward $2,600 ($20,000 × 13%). Dividing the adjusted proceeds of $17,400 by the surviving spouse's 21.7-year life expectancy produces a tax-free principal payment of $801.84 each year for life. The balance of each annual payment, $542.16, is lifetime taxable income to the spouse.

Annual Payments ($112 × 12 months)		$1,344.00
Total Annual Guaranteed Payments (20,000 ÷ $1,344)	15	
Adjusted for Refund Feature ($20,000 × 13%)	$ 2,600	
Adjusted Face Amount ($20,000 – $2,600)	$17,400	
Annual Tax-Free Payments ($17,400 ÷ 21.7 years)		– 801.84
Annual Taxable Portion		$ 542.16

If the beneficiary dies before receiving the guaranteed amount, the refund to the secondary beneficiary is tax free.

Points to Emphasize

Despite the fact that the interest element of installment and life income options is subject to income tax, *excluded* life insurance death proceeds still receive preferential income tax treatment when compared to other types of investments. Bear in mind that the *principal* is distributed to beneficiaries free of federal income tax. Principal is the policy's death proceeds, a sum that an insured seldom accumulates during his or her lifetime. Yet this appreciation of death proceeds over premiums paid—often tremendous—is an income tax-free gain to the beneficiary.

The preferential tax treatment of excluded life insurance death proceeds will not, in itself, sell life insurance. But the tax advantages can be important supporting factors in your presentation. Emphasize the significance of the preferential taxation; bring to the client's attention the difference between this and the tax treatment of other kinds of investments.

Income Taxation of Living Proceeds

When an insured surrenders a life insurance policy for its cash surrender value (or when an endowment policy matures), there are income tax consequences. As we will see, in some cases the tax treatment is the same as the tax treatment of death proceeds, and in other instances the treatment differs somewhat.

First, we are going to examine the taxation when the benefits are paid in a lump sum or left on the interest-only option. Then we will examine the treatment when the benefits are received in installments. There we will see that living life insurance benefits paid in installments are taxed in the same way as annuity benefits.

Lump-Sum Payments

When the proceeds of a surrendered life policy (or a surrendered or matured endowment or retirement income contract) are paid to the insured in a lump sum, any excess of such proceeds over the *cost* of the policy is taxed as ordinary income in the year received. Obviously then, before any taxable gain can be determined, it is necessary to find the cost of the contract.

A participating policy refers to insurance contracts sold mainly by Mutual Insurance Companies. This allows each policyholder to "participate" in the surplus earnings of the company from which dividends are paid.

If the policy is nonparticipating, the cost is generally the sum of premiums paid, less any policy loans outstanding. If the policy is participating, dividends must be considered in determining the cost. Dividends paid in cash, or applied against the gross premium or policy loan, are subtracted from total gross premiums to arrive at the net cost of the contract. Thus, if at surrender or maturity, total gross premiums are $7,000, and $1,000 in dividends has been paid in cash or applied against premiums or loans, the net cost of the contract is $6,000.

There are a few more points to keep in mind. If dividends are used to buy paid-up additions or left to accumulate at interest, the net cost at surrender or maturity is generally the sum of the gross premiums, less any outstanding policy loans. Furthermore, the amount of the premium that pays for the waiver of premium and accidental death benefits is excluded from the gross premium in determining the net cost. Finally, policy loan interest does not enter into the computation of cost.

In all these situations, the gain is taxed as ordinary income in the year the proceeds are received by the insured. The following example illustrates how the gain is computed.

Assume that a $100,000 nonparticipating contract is surrendered and that the insured receives the cash surrender value, $57,000, in a lump sum. The total gross premium payable under the contract is $42,000, $500 of which is attributable to a waiver of premium clause in the contract. In addition, there was a $5,000 loan against the policy. Thus, the gain under the contract would be computed as follows:

Total Proceeds Received		$57,000
Gross Premiums Payable	$42,000	
Waiver of Premium Cost	– 500	
Policy Loan	– 5,000	
Cost of Policy		–36,500
Taxable Gain		$20,500

Constructive Receipt

The general rule is that gain on a policy is taxable in the year the proceeds are received. There is, however, one exception—the *constructive receipt* rule. Constructive receipt means that upon surrender or maturity of a policy, any gain is taxable income to the insured if he or she has full right to the proceeds, even though that right is not immediately exercised. Income is constructively received in the taxable year during which it is credited to a taxpayer's account or set apart so that he or she may draw upon it at any time.

For example, if the insured leaves proceeds with the insurance company but retains the right to withdraw the funds at any time, he or she has constructively received the proceeds in the year of maturity or surrender. As a result, if the insured realizes a gain on the policy, the gain is taxed as ordinary income in the same manner as a lump-sum payment—even though the insured does not actually receive the proceeds at that time. However, income is not constructively received if the taxpayer's control of its receipt is subject to substantial limitations or restrictions.

There is one key exception to this constructive receipt rule. If within 60 days after the proceeds become available (and before the insured receives any cash payment), the insured elects to receive the proceeds under an installment or life-income option, then the proceeds are *not* considered to be constructively received. For this reason, the insured will not be taxed on gain at the time of maturity or surrender if such an election is made.

Interest-Only Option

When the proceeds of an endowment contract or a matured or surrendered life insurance policy are left with the insurance company under the interest-only option, the interest is taxable to the recipient when received. The constructive receipt rule can result in an additional taxable gain in the year the option is exercised.

Living Proceeds Paid in Installments and Annuities

The same rules that govern the income taxation of amounts received under annuity contracts also govern living benefits of life insurance and endowment contracts that are received in installments. Both are taxed under what is known as the *annuity rule*. Under the annuity rule, a fixed portion of each payment is excludable from gross income as a return of capital, and the balance is treated as taxable income. This remains so until the annuitant has recovered the cost in the contract.

To determine the amount excludable from gross income, an *exclusion ratio* must be computed. This ratio is simply the total dollar investment in the contract divided by the total expected return. For example, if the total cost of an endowment contract is $15,000 and the total expected return is $20,000, the exclusion ratio is $15,000/$20,000, or 75 percent. So if $2,000 is the amount received from the contract in a given year, $1,500 ($2,000 × 75%) is the amount excludable from gross income. The remaining $500 would be taxable. The cost factor in the contract is computed just as in the case of a lump-sum payment.

In the examples below, under each of the installment options, we use a shortcut method of computing the excludable portion of each payment. The result will vary by no more than a few cents from the result that would have been derived had the entire computation of the exclusion ratio been used. Therefore, you may want to use this shortcut method when illustrating the tax results under various options. However, be aware that the technically correct method involves the use of the exclusion ratio.

Fixed-Period Option

The excluded portion of each year's payments under the fixed-period option can be found by dividing the dollars accumulated in the contract by the number of years in the fixed period.

Assume that the insured's $20,000 ordinary life contract has a cash value of $10,700. The insured's investment in the contract is $9,000. The insured has elected to receive the cash value over a period of 15 years. With a guaranteed interest rate of 5 percent, this option will provide annual payments of $1,001.52 (excluding any excess interest). Dividing the insured's dollar accumulation of $9,000 by 15 (the number of years the payments will be received) gives an annual tax-free return of principal of $600. Thus $401.52, plus any excess interest, will be taxable each year.

Annual Payments	$1,001.52
Annual Tax-Free Payments ($9,000 ÷ 15 years)	− 600.00
Annual Taxable Portion	$ 401.52

Fixed-Amount Option

To determine the tax-free portion of each payment under the fixed-amount option, we divide the total investment in the contract by the number of guaranteed payments. For example, assume that the insured's $20,000 20-pay life policy has a cash value of $12,310 at age 65. However, dividend accumulations (including untaxed interest) have boosted total surrender values to $15,000. The insured has paid gross premiums of $12,900. This is the investment in the contract because the insured did not withdraw dividends. The insured has elected to have this $15,000 paid at the rate of $200 a month until the proceeds are exhausted. The guaranteed interest rate is 5 percent. The applicable fixed-amount table shows that it will take seven years and four months to exhaust this $15,000. The insured's investment is then divided by the number of monthly payments to arrive at the excluded portion of each payment. Dividing $12,900 by 88 (the number of monthly payments) produces a figure of $146.59. The balance of each payment, $53.41 ($200 – $146.59), is taxable income. On an annual basis, the insured would have reportable income of $640.92 ($53.41 × 12 months).

Number of Monthly Payments	88	
Monthly Tax-Free Payments ($12,900 ÷ 88 months)	$146.59	
Monthly Taxable Portion ($200 – $146.59)		$ 53.41
		× 12
Annual Taxable Portion		$ 640.92

Remember that payments received in excess of the guaranteed period—payments as a result of excess interest—are fully taxable.

Life-Income Payments

To find the taxable portion of payments under a life-income option, we need to know the life expectancy of the insured at the time the payments begin. This figure is then divided into the cost of the policy. The quotient is the tax-exempt portion of each payment.

Under all of the life-income options, a portion is tax exempt only until the investment in the contract is recovered. However, if the payments started before 1987, the exclusion ratio applies to all payments during the annuitant's life.

Life-Only Option

If the insured elects to receive the surrender or maturity proceeds under a life-only option, the cost of the contract is divided by normal life expectancy at the time payments begin. The result is the annual tax-free return of principal; the balance of each payment is taxable gain.

For example, assume that an insured, at age 65, elects to take the proceeds from a $100,000 maturing annuity under the life-only option. This will pay $794 monthly, or $9,528 annually. The insured has invested $50,000 in the contract. At age 65, the insured has a life expectancy of 20 years. Dividing the net accumulation of $50,000 by 20, results in annual tax-free return of $2,500. Subtracting this figure from the total annual payments of $9,528 produces $7,028 of taxable income to the annuitant. Excess interest increases the amount of taxable income.

Annual Payments ($794 × 12 months)	$ 9,528
Annual Tax-Free Payments ($50,000 ÷ 20 life expectancy)	– 2,500
Annual Taxable Portion	$ 7,028

Life-Income with Guaranteed Payments

When a period-certain or refund-certain feature is part of the life-income option, the insured's investment must be adjusted downward before it is divided by the insured's life expectancy to determine the tax-exempt portion of each payment. The annuitant's taxable portion is increased through the downward adjustment; dividing life expectancy into a decreased dollar accumulation produces a lower tax-exempt return of principal.

The adjustment is based on the actuarial probability that the secondary beneficiary may receive a part of the guaranteed payments. The amount of the adjustment is determined from the actuarial value of the period certain or refund feature. This value is stated in percentage form, and is found in Table III of the Commissioner's Annuity Tables. The percentage figure from the table is multiplied by the insured's investment, or the total amount of guaranteed payments, whichever is less. The result is subtracted from the investment to arrive at the adjusted investment figure. From there on, the procedure is the same as under the life-only option. You are already familiar with the procedure from the examples in the settlement option section.

Surrenders of or Cash Withdrawals from Deferred Annuity Contracts

In addition to any regular income tax liability, a penalty tax equal to 10 percent of the amount included in gross income applies in the case of early withdrawals from an annuity. The penalty applies to withdrawals before the owner reaches the age of 59½, dies or becomes disabled. An early withdrawal will not be penalized, however, if it is part of a series of substantially equal periodic payments made over the life of the owner or the lives of both the owner and a beneficiary.

■ LIFE INSURANCE POLICY LOANS

Normally, loans from life insurance policies are tax free, as are withdrawals and partial surrenders up to the total amount of premiums paid. However, certain withdrawals during the policy's first 15 years are partially taxable.

If a policy change within the first 15 years reduces benefits and results in a cash distribution to the policyholder, the portion of the distribution that does not exceed the *recapture ceiling* will be treated as income to the extent that cash value before the distribution exceeded the investment in the contract. Whether a loan on a life insurance policy will be treated as a partially taxable distribution depends on whether the loan reduces benefits under the contract. A loan probably will not be considered to reduce the benefit. Although a loan that has not been repaid when the insured dies is deducted from the death proceeds, the death benefit is not reduced; part of it merely is used to repay the loan. However, a loan might reduce benefits in other ways; for example, dividends or the amount of income credited to the policy might be reduced because of the loan.

As noted above, only the portion of a distribution that does not exceed the recapture ceiling will be subject to these rules. Calculation of the recapture ceiling depends on whether the withdrawal occurred during the first five years or the 6th through 15th years. For a withdrawal during the first five years, the recapture ceiling is the amount required to be paid out of the policy to meet the cash value accumulation test or the guideline premium/cash value corridor test, whichever is applicable. For a withdrawal during the 6th through 15th years, the recapture ceiling is the amount by which the cash value immediately before the distribution exceeds the maximum permissible cash value corridor test, regardless of whether that test is otherwise applicable to the policy.

The tax treatment of a policy loan will also depend on whether the policy is a modified endowment contract. This is any policy, entered into on or after June 21, 1988, that meets the definition of life insurance but fails the seven-pay test. A policy is deemed a modified endowment contract if the accumulated amounts paid under the contract during the first seven years exceed the sum of net level premiums that would have been paid (on or before such time) if the contract provided for paid-up future benefits after seven level annual premiums. This means that any distributions from a modified endowment contract, such as assignments, dividends received in cash or left to accumulate at interest, surrenders of paid-up additions as well as policy loans and automatic premium loans, are taxed last-in-first-out (LIFO) to the extent of the gain in the policy. The taxable portion of a distribution from a modified endowment contract is subject to a 10 percent penalty tax. This penalty tax is waived if the policyowner has attained age 59½, is permanently disabled or elects a life income settlement option.

■ SUMMARY

A thorough understanding of the federal income tax treatment of life insurance and annuities is of major importance to the practitioner. Life insurance and annuities enjoy special dispensation with regard to income taxation. The two major tax advantages of life insurance are the tax-deferred internal cash buildup within the policy and the income tax-free death benefit. The major tax benefit to annuities is the tax-deferred internal cash buildup within the policy. For a policy to be considered life insurance, it must pass either the cash value accumulation test or the guideline premium/cash value corridor test. The death benefit of a policy that has been transferred for value may not be completely income tax free. There are several settlement options that the beneficiary may choose such as interest only, fixed period and life income with a period certain. Unlike a life insurance policy, an annuity will usually have a cost basis that is taken into consideration when calculating the income tax on the settlement payment. This is called the exclusion ratio, which exempts that portion of the annuity payment from income tax.

Advantages of life insurance policies are the loans that may be taken from the policy. In most cases, these loans do not need to be paid back are merely subtracted from the death benefit upon policy maturity. Life insurance and annuity taxation are intricate fields of study and our discussion has been basic. There are many software programs with detailed analysis on this subject as well as websites. The practitioner would be well advised to continue to learn more about this ever-changing field of tax law.

■ CHAPTER 3 QUESTIONS FOR REVIEW

1. Which of the following is NOT a tax advantage of life insurance?

   A. Cash value grows tax free until distribution.

   B. Death proceeds are generally tax free.

   C. Premiums are deductible.

   D. Policy loans are generally tax free.

2. What is the result if a contract fails to qualify as life insurance under one of the tests set out by the Internal Revenue Code?

   A. The death proceeds are fully taxable.

   B. The gain on the savings element is taxable.

   C. The pure insurance element is taxable.

   D. The premiums are deductible.

3. The transfer-for-value rule

   A. states that death proceeds are usually taxable.

   B. provides that a transfer of a policy for valuable consideration makes the death benefit nontaxable.

   C. is used to determine the exclusion ratio of annuity payments.

   D. carves out an exception to the usual treatment of death proceeds.

4. When life insurance death proceeds are paid out in a settlement option, what portion of a payment is subject to taxation?

   A. The entire amount

   B. The portion representing interest on the death proceeds

   C. The portion representing payment of the death proceeds

   D. None

5. Constructive receipt is

   A. an exception to the transfer-for-value rule

   B. a rule that taxes gain on a policy's surrender to the policyowner if he or she has a right to the proceeds, even if the right is not exercised

   C. a method of recovering the tax-free element of life income payments if the beneficiary lives beyond his or her life expectancy

   D. a method of avoiding taxation of life insurance cash values under the corporate AMT

6. Under the corridor test, a 38-year-old male policyowner's cash value may not be more than what percent of the death benefit?

   A. 25

   B. 40

   C. 50

   D. 100

7. A participating policy is usually sold by

   A. a mutual insurance company

   B. a stock insurance company

   C. a dividend insurance company

   D. someone other than an insurance company

8. The tax treatment of a policy loan that is considered to be a modified endowment policy is

   A. taxed as LIFO (last-in, first-out) to the extent of policy gain

   B. taxed as FIFO (first-in, first-out) to the extent of policy gain

   C. is not taxable

   D. none of the above

9. The law requiring companies to use sex-natural mortality tables is used to determine

   A. the portion of each payment that is excludable death benefit from taxable interest

   B. prevents insurance companies from making payments to beneficiaries based on their own tables

   C. both of the above

   D. none of the above

10. Certain withdrawals from life insurance policies during the first how many years can be partially taxable?

    A. 5

    B. 10

    C. 15

    D. 20

Section Two

Business Entities

4 Proprietorships

P roprietorships constitute nearly three-fourths of the nation's businesses and offer a vast market for the financial advisor. The independence and simplicity of this form of business entity make it very attractive to many businesspeople. At the same time, there are special problems that arise at the death of the proprietor—regardless of whether the business is liquidated, retained or sold. In this chapter, we will see the role that life insurance can play in resolving these difficulties.

The sole proprietorship is the simplest way to own and operate a business. That's probably why sole proprietorships are far more popular—and prevalent—than partnerships or corporations. There's something comfortable and yet exciting about being your own boss without going through the complexities of setting up partnership agreements or doing what it takes to create an entirely new entity with a corporation.

Even the sole proprietor, however, does not escape the many complexities of operating a business, such as complying with the rules and regulations of the different taxing authorities and, in the case of professionals, meeting licensing, bonding and continuing education requirements.

According to recent government census figures there are about 15 million proprietorships, not including farms. They account for nearly 74 percent of all businesses nationally. Obviously, sole proprietorships play a big role in the nation's economy, and they offer a vast market for life insurance sales.

Why? Because proprietorships are supporting still more millions of family members. The income generated by the business while a proprietor is there to run it may be lost at his or her death. Unless effective plans are made by the proprietor during life, the chief source of income for the family may be lost through death.

In this chapter, we'll discuss the methods of correcting this potential problem. But first, let's develop an understanding of the proprietorship form of doing business to give you an appreciation of the kind of problems created when a business owner dies.

■ ■ ■ ■ ■

■ PROPRIETORSHIPS IN GENERAL

A sole proprietorship is an unincorporated business enterprise owned entirely by one person. Customarily, the owner—the proprietor—manages the business. He or she may do this either alone or with the assistance of any number of employees.

The creation of a proprietorship involves relatively few legal requirements as compared with a partnership or corporation. A certificate, known as a DBA (doing business as), must be filed with the proper authorities if a proprietor wishes to operate the business under a name other than his or her own. This distinguishes it from the partnership, which is created by a legally binding agreement between the partners, or from the corporation, which is created by certain legal steps leading to a corporate charter granted by the appropriate governmental unit, such as a state.

Assets and Liabilities of the Proprietorship

Since a sole proprietorship is owned by one individual and there is no legal entity apart from the proprietor, the assets of a sole proprietorship are the personal assets of the proprietor. If the proprietor dies, the business assets become a part of his or her estate. Thus, when an individual creates a sole proprietorship, no new property rights are formed. This is another important difference between the proprietorship and the other forms of business organization. Furthermore, there is no distinction between personal debts and business liabilities created by a proprietor. In either case, the proprietor is fully liable for all financial obligations, and this liability is unlimited and borne by the individual alone.

Advantages and Disadvantages of a Proprietorship

The principal advantage of the proprietorship method of doing business is, of course, its relative simplicity. The business may be started without any formal organizational procedure. Once established, its operation is flexible. The owner can make immediate decisions unhampered by approval of other owners or a board of directors. The proprietor can enter new fields and abandon old ones with freedom of choice. Finally, unlike partners and stockholders, the proprietor is entitled to all the profits.

However, simplicity of structure is also the sole proprietorship's chief disadvantage because the same proprietor who is entitled to all the profits must also bear all the losses. The disadvantage that most concerns us in this discussion, though, is that the *proprietorship* ends with the death of the proprietor. This is because it is not a separate legal entity. Unless effective plans have been made by the proprietor for continuation of the business, it will cease upon his or her death. Furthermore, a once profitable source of income may be lost to the surviving family.

In this chapter, we deal primarily with different methods of disposing of a sole proprietorship at the proprietor's death. Generally, there are three methods of orderly disposition available:

1. orderly liquidation (conversion of business assets into cash);

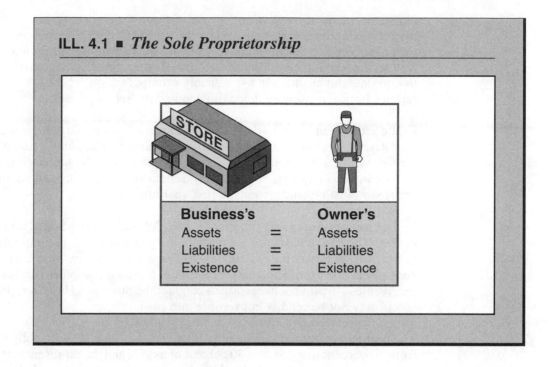

ILL. 4.1 ■ *The Sole Proprietorship*

Business's		Owner's
Assets	=	Assets
Liabilities	=	Liabilities
Existence	=	Existence

2. retention of the business in the family; or

3. sale of the proprietorship to an employee or outsider.

We will see that life insurance is crucial to carrying out any one of these three alternatives. First, however, let's turn to the adverse consequences thrust upon the estate and family of a sole proprietor who fails to take proper steps prior to death.

■ WHAT HAPPENS WHEN A PROPRIETOR DIES?

If the proprietor did not have a will, or if his or her will contains no express provision regarding the disposition of the business, the legal representative (the executor, personal representative or administrator) of the proprietor's estate is legally bound to discontinue the business immediately, except to the extent necessary to complete unfinished business and wind up its affairs. The legal representative must take possession of all assets, convert them to cash and pay all administrative expenses, taxes and personal and business obligations of the decedent—only then distributing any remaining estate assets to surviving heirs.

Forced Liquidation

In converting business assets to cash (liquidating the business), the legal representative will frequently try to sell the proprietorship as a going concern. Attempts will be made to find a buyer for the business as a whole rather than liquidate it piecemeal. The value of a successfully operating business as a going concern is considerably greater than the value of its tangible net assets.

However, in the absence of any special plans to the contrary created during the proprietor's life, the representative is under a primary duty to terminate and liquidate the proprietorship promptly. In very few instances will the representative be able to find an immediate buyer. In the majority of cases, the representative will be forced to liquidate the business in a reasonably prompt fashion. There is a tremendous difference between a *forced* liquidation and an *orderly* liquidation.

Estate settlement costs—administration expenses, taxes and debts—must be paid in a relatively short period of time. Subject to certain extensions, federal estate taxes are due within nine months after the estate owner's death. Otherwise, penalties, or at least interest charges, are imposed. Generally, other debts and administration expenses must be paid within the first year after death.

In the case of typical sole proprietors, most of their money is tied up in their businesses. They have worked hard through the years to build up their enterprises and in the process have often put any excess earnings into their businesses. Most business assets consist of inventory, real estate, fixtures, equipment and accounts receivable—the things necessary to conduct the business. However, these business assets may not be readily convertible into cash.

The problem of forced liquidation arises because typical estate obligations range from 10 percent to more than 30 percent of assets, and the representative usually has no alternative but to quickly liquidate business assets to raise cash. Forced sale usually brings only a fraction of what the business was worth during the proprietor's lifetime.

The business may have been counted on to remain in the family and while certain tax breaks help to reduce the estate tax on family farms and businesses, the need for liquidity remains. If the cash needed to satisfy taxes and other estate liabilities cannot be obtained from other sources, forced liquidation of business assets may be necessary.

A proprietor should be aware that the forced liquidation of proprietorship assets may result in the following:

- Accounts receivable may be impossible to collect in full.

- The sale of inventories will usually bring only a fraction of their worth.

- Equipment may be sold or repossessed by creditors, often at a great sacrifice.

- Goodwill, an intangible asset that often accounts for a significant percentage of the value of the proprietorship, evaporates completely—its value is totally lost at the death of the entrepreneur.

Stoppage of Income

The forced liquidation of the business also means that all income from the business stops. If income from the business was the family's primary source of income, the family will be in desperate straits unless the survivors can call upon other sources of income.

Continuation Attempts

To avoid the severe financial effects of forced liquidation and the resulting termination of family income, the representative may attempt to continue the business. This course of action, however, is fraught with risk.

A legal representative who continues to operate a deceased proprietor's business without authority becomes personally liable for all business debts. In addition, he or she is personally responsible to the beneficiaries of the estate for losses. On the other hand, the representative cannot share in profits, which belong to the estate. Thus, for the legal representative, unauthorized continuation is "Heads you win, tails I lose."

In some instances, the legal representative may obtain the consent of all the heirs to continue the business. However, the heirs, by their own consent, may forfeit the right to hold the representative liable. Even with the heirs' consent, the representative remains liable to current estate creditors to the extent of estate assets. The representative may also be personally liable to any new creditors of the business. As you can see, such a plan is generally undesirable for all concerned.

In some states the legal representative may be authorized by court order or statute to continue the business for a limited time for the purpose of selling it as a going concern. While more advantageous than unauthorized continuation, or continuation by consent of the heirs, formal authority is seldom the ideal solution to the problems involved when a proprietor dies. As a going concern, the business usually reflects the ability, industry and personality of its owner. It is unrealistic to expect the legal representative to match the proprietor's skills and efforts in this regard.

Three Alternatives

It's easy to see that it is not a good idea to wait until a proprietor dies to determine the fate of the business. A far better idea is for the proprietor—while alive—to plan for the most efficient disposition of the business. This is almost certain to result in a better plan than one scraped together by legal representatives, the courts or the statutes.

In formulating plans, the proprietor should consider first the needs of the surviving family. Generally, with that thought in mind, there are three alternatives to be considered:

1. If there's no family member capable of taking the business over—and no prospective outside buyer—the best option may be an *orderly liquidation* of all business assets.

2. If there is a family member trained to take over the business, the proper legal and financial moves are necessary to assure its *orderly retention*.

3. If there is an employee or other individual who wishes to purchase the business, plans must be made to initiate and complete a *sale*.

Any of these alternatives—orderly liquidation, retention or sale—may be appropriate, depending on the situation and the needs and wishes of the proprietor. However, each alternative requires proper planning prior to the proprietor's death. Let's review each alternative in more detail.

■ ORDERLY LIQUIDATION OF THE BUSINESS

In the majority of cases, the typical proprietor will have neither a family member nor an employee who is capable of, interested in or willing to operate the business after the proprietor dies. The only alternative, therefore, is to make sure that the representative can liquidate the business in an orderly manner.

Orderly liquidation (as opposed to *forced* liquidation) requires (1) a properly drawn will and (2) adequate insurance on the proprietor's life.

A Properly Prepared Will

The proprietor's will should give the representative authority to continue the business until it can be disposed of in the most advantageous way possible. The will provisions should, generally speaking, free the representative from personal liability during this period.

With this freedom from liability, the representative can attempt first to sell the business as a going concern. The representative must proceed promptly, however, for claims of estate creditors must be satisfied. A sale of the entire business will usually bring a larger price than a piecemeal sale of the assets because some value may be realized for the goodwill of the business, its credit standing and other intangibles. However, the price received for the business as a whole still will be substantially less than what the business was worth to the proprietor and his or her family while the proprietor was alive.

In the event the representative cannot sell the business as a going concern, generally he or she has the authority—without personal liability—to continue the business until the assets can be liquidated piecemeal by the most profitable means, provided estate creditors are paid or consent to the continuation. This prevents a hurry-up, *forced* liquidation. But even with ample time to search for buyers, the representative will discover that the sale of the business assets on a piecemeal basis will bring substantially less than their true value. Moreover, the value for goodwill and credit standing will be lost. Thus even an *orderly* liquidation generally results in a startling shrinkage in the value of business assets.

Adequate provision in the will prevents an immediate liquidation but even an orderly sale of the business, either as a whole or piecemeal, cannot forestall substantial shrinkage. Such shrinkage can cause serious harm to the deceased proprietor's family unless a second arrangement, working in conjunction with a properly drawn will, comes into play. This arrangement is insurance on the life of the proprietor.

Adequate Life Insurance

Insurance on the life of a sole proprietor will accomplish three important objectives where the representative is authorized to liquidate the business in an orderly fashion.

1. *Life insurance will pay estate settlement costs.* Adequate liquidity will be made available to meet business debts as well as all other costs.

2. *Life insurance will make possible an orderly sale or liquidation.* Even though the representative is authorized to continue the business, this will be impossible if cash is not available to pay estate liabilities. The proceeds from a life insurance policy will provide the funds needed to enable the representative to continue the business until the best price for the business can be obtained.

3. *Life insurance will offset the diminishing value of the business.* Shrinkage will result even with an orderly liquidation. Dollars are needed to replace this shrinkage for the purpose of providing income to the proprietor's family. Life insurance provides these dollars.

Now let's apply these uses of sole proprietor business life insurance to a practical example.

Case Study: Liquidation of the Sole Proprietorship

Mr. Miller, age 47, is the sole owner of a small but prosperous retail business. Through the years, he has poured most of his earnings back into the business. Having no one in his family to take over the business at his death, he has provided in his will for its orderly liquidation. He feels that given sufficient time, his representative will be able to dispose of the assets for about 50 percent of their present worth. Miller rents his place of business and has no business real estate. Here is a picture of the value of the business assets before his death and after death (assuming an orderly liquidation of the company).

	During Lifetime	*After Death*
Cash Value of Merchandise	$100,000	$50,000
Fixtures and Furniture	28,000	14,000
Accounts Receivable	12,000	6,000
	$140,000	$70,000

Miller has business debts of $17,000 and personal debts of $4,000. He also has a $120,000 mortgage on a $200,000 home. He has $100,000 of life insurance, which has attractive income options and favorable interest rates. (The insurance was purchased to provide income for his family's benefit.) He has other personal property and savings worth $20,000.

If Miller were to die today, his estate, assuming his representative could liquidate the business assets for $70,000, would look like this:

Assets		*Liabilities*	
Home	$200,000	Estimated Funeral and	$ 29,000
Personal Property and Savings	20,000	Administration Expenses	
Life Insurance (payable to wife)	100,000	Mortgage on Home	120,000
Business Assets	70,000	Business Debts	17,000
	$390,000	Personal Debts	4,000
			$170,000

Miller needs $170,000 in estate liquidity to take care of the costs of settling his estate, clearing up his debts and paying off his mortgage. Furthermore, Miller wants his current life insurance to be used for family income. He doesn't want his other property liquidated to come up with the $170,000. He also recognizes that more money may be needed to provide for his family's total needs. What should he do?

Miller solves both his estate and his family problems by purchasing $250,000 of additional life insurance protection. The proprietor cannot deduct the premiums paid on this insurance for income tax purposes but *the proceeds will be received income tax free.* First, he earmarks $170,000 of the proceeds to pay funeral and administration expenses, the mortgage and his debts. Until these proceeds are actually used for their intended purpose, they will also serve as a reserve enabling Miller's representative to continue the business until its assets can be liquidated for the best price.

The predeath value of his business is $140,000. Miller wants to leave a dollar equivalent to his family. Therefore, he next earmarks $70,000 of insurance proceeds for his family's benefit to offset the shrinkage value of his business assets after his death; this can be paid to them in the form of income or in a lump sum as investable capital to provide income.

The $70,000 that the business assets should bring under an orderly liquidation can be used by Mrs. Miller in a number of ways. She can channel the money in an annuity to provide additional guaranteed lifetime income; she might use the funds to provide a higher education for her children; she might use part as an emergency fund, part as an income fund and part for education.

In any event, the remaining life insurance proceeds coupled with the $70,000 realized on the sale of the business assets, enables Miller to transfer a dollar value to the family equal to the physical value of the proprietorship during his life.

Now let's explore how life insurance can help the proprietor who desires to have the business retained for the family's benefit after death.

■ ORDERLY RETENTION OF THE BUSINESS

Occasionally a sole proprietor will have a spouse or an adult child capable and desirous of carrying on the business. Under such circumstances, every effort should be made to assure successful continuation of the business. The most effective way to accomplish this is through an outright bequest of the business to an heir under the proprietor's will. To ensure that the desired transfer will take place, however, the proprietor must also provide for adequate estate liquidity and adequate income for other family members. Let's consider each problem and look at how, once again, life insurance is the perfect solution.

Provision for Adequate Estate Liquidity

The representative must have adequate cash to pay funeral and administration expenses, personal and business debts and death taxes. This is particularly important with respect to debts. Always remember that directions in the will for the continuation of the business will not be allowed to interfere with the right of existing creditors and tax collectors to receive their money when the proprietor dies. If the estate lacks sufficient cash or nonbusiness assets that can be liquidated to raise cash, the representative will be forced to liquidate business assets. This, of course, can severely impair, or completely destroy, the value of a business to the heir.

Insurance on the proprietor's life—payable to the estate—is the simplest method of providing adequate liquidity to assure a prompt and safe transfer of the business to the intended heir under the proprietor's will.

Provision for Other Family Members

An estate that is short on cash for liquidity needs often will provide little in the way of needed income for the proprietor's surviving spouse. The proprietor's interest has been left under the terms of a will to the child or other designated relative. In many situations, there will be little left to provide a life income for the spouse or to equalize inheritances among the children who aren't active in the business.

What the proprietor will have to do is to create a new source of income separate from the proprietorship interest. Again, the logical choice is life insurance. Life insurance will provide a cash sum when needed—at death—and through the annuity principle a monthly income can be assured for the proprietor's spouse for life. Alternatively, the spouse can take the cash in a lump sum and invest it to provide investment income.

Life insurance can also be used to equalize inheritances between the child or relative who inherits the business and the other relatives. In fact, an heir not associated with the business might prefer a gift of a smaller sum in cash to a larger inheritance tied up in a business enterprise in which he or she has no interest.

Now let's see how the bequest of a proprietorship to an adult child works.

Case Study: Retaining the Sole Proprietorship

Mrs. Martin, age 52, owns an advertising agency. She has built up a business and clientele over the past 25 years that has brought her family a comfortable living. Martin's daughter, Mary, age 28, has worked for her mother the past six years and has become experienced in the business. Martin wants to leave the business to her daughter. By the same token, she wants her husband, Bob, a university professor, and their son, Jim, age 25, to be treated equitably.

Martin rents her office, but has about $15,000 tied up in equipment, furniture and fixtures. Her accounts receivable average about $55,000 and her business debts about $1,500. If Martin were to die today, her estate picture would look like this:

Assets		*Liabilities*	
Home (owned jointly with husband)	$200,000	Funeral and Administration Expenses	$ 20,000
Personal Property and Savings	20,000	Mortgage on Home	124,000
Life Insurance (payable to husband)	60,000	Business Debts	3,000
Business Equipment	15,000	Personal Debts	3,000
Accounts Receivable	55,000		$150,000
	$350,000		

Martin, in her will, directs that her business assets—the business equipment ($15,000) and the accounts receivable ($55,000)—be transferred to her daughter. Giving Mary the accounts will impress upon customers that the business will continue to operate as a going concern. If the representative were directed to collect the accounts for the estate's benefit, customers might assume from the action that the business was being liquidated.

Martin's home, which is owned jointly with her husband, and her life insurance will automatically pass to Bob. In addition, the $20,000 of personal property and savings will pass to Bob by means of her will.

Martin needs at least $150,000 of estate liquidity to achieve her various objectives. This amount would enable her to leave the family's home unencumbered by a mortgage. It will also assure that her funeral and administration expenses are paid promptly and that her personal debts are cleared. Finally, this cash will clear her business debt, enabling her daughter to take over a going business unhampered by debt.

Martin also wants to treat her son on an equitable basis with her daughter. Thus, she needs an additional $70,000 to leave Jim at her death. To resolve this issue and to guarantee a successful transfer of the business to her daughter, Martin purchases $220,000 of additional permanent insurance to supplement the current $60,000 insurance on her life.

She designates her estate the beneficiary of $150,000 of the proceeds to provide her representative with the needed estate liquidity and names Jim beneficiary of $70,000. Life insurance makes it possible for Martin to perpetuate her business and, at the same time, carry out her wishes and obligations to all family members.

We are now ready to examine a plan that can solve the financial problems inherent in the sale of a proprietorship to an employee or other buyer.

■ SALE OF THE BUSINESS

In many proprietorships, the owner has no one in the family capable of running the business, but does have an employee ready and willing to step in and take his or her

ILL. 4.2 ■ *Liquidation or Retention—Life Insurance Is the Solution*

As you have learned, a proprietorship and its owner are legally inseparable. As a result, the death of a proprietor usually means the end of the business. It is the obligation of every proprietor to make sure that the sale or liquidation of his or her business is an orderly one. Life insurance can help accomplish either a sale or an orderly liquidation. The advantages life insurance can provide to a proprietor, both during life and after death are summarized here.

During the Proprietor's Life, Life Insurance. . .

1. *Provides collateral.* The proprietor's personal credit will be enhanced by the presence of life insurance. The policy's cash value is ideal collateral for a business loan.

2. *Creates an automatic reserve fund.* The ever-increasing cash value provides a readily available source of cash at a modest rate of interest as needed for business emergencies or opportunities.

3. *Builds a retirement fund.* When the proprietor is ready to retire, accumulated cash values can be used to provide a guaranteed life income or investment income.

When the Proprietor Dies, Life Insurance. . .

1. *Provides estate liquidity.* The representative will not be forced to sell business assets to raise the necessary cash to pay personal and business debts, death taxes and all administration expenses.

2. *Permits an orderly liquidation.* If the proprietor directs in his or her will that the business should be sold as a going concern or on a piecemeal basis at death, life insurance provides the representative with the necessary cash to continue the business until the business, or its assets, can be sold under the most favorable circumstances.

3. *Permits an orderly retention.* The proprietor who bequeaths the business to an heir can use life insurance both to leave a business free of debt and to treat other family members on an equitable basis.

The flexibility offered by the life insurance contract is ideally suited for overcoming the problems inherent in the sole proprietorship form of business.

place. Such employees may include: (1) the valuable employee who is familiar with every facet of the operation, (2) an outstanding salesperson who is responsible for obtaining a substantial amount of the firm's business or (3) the indispensable "insider" who runs the administrative operation while the owner concentrates on sales.

In each of these instances, the employee's talents are recognized by customers, creditors and suppliers. The employee brings a degree of goodwill to the business distinct from that attributable to the owner. The sale of the business to the employee at the proprietor's death is a "natural," because the sale will preserve the business's going-concern value based on the goodwill built up by the talents of both the employee and the proprietor.

Primary Obstacle

The major obstacle to such a sale is a lack of funds on the part of the employee to buy the business. The employee is usually younger than the owner. Although the employee may earn a good income, the responsibility of raising a family, combined with the high cost of living and the inroads of taxation, make the accumulation of the necessary funds difficult if not impossible. Thus, eager as he or she might be to buy the business, the typical employee may not be able to accumulate the purchase price. Even if the employee is able to borrow the needed funds, he or she would be saddled for years with a crushing—perhaps prohibitive—debt.

When a proprietor is fortunate enough to have a capable employee ready and willing to buy the business at death, he or she should make every effort to facilitate the employee's purchase of the business. This will assure the owner's family that the sale of the business will be for its true worth, rather than for liquidation value.

A Two-Step Plan

A two-step plan can bring about an orderly sale of the business to an employee:

1. An attorney drafts a *buy-sell agreement* that binds the estate and the proprietor respectively to sell the business upon the proprietor's death or retirement. The agreement would bind the employee to buy the business at a mutually agreed upon price.

2. The employee acquires *insurance* on the employer's life in accordance with the terms of the buy-sell agreement. The employee is the owner, premium payor and beneficiary of the policy. The employee cannot deduct premiums paid for income tax purposes, but (in all but exceptional cases) *receives the proceeds income tax free upon the proprietor's death.*

The following example illustrates how the insured buy-sell plan works to the mutual benefit of the proprietor and the employee.

Case Study: Selling the Sole Proprietorship

Mr. Maxwell, age 50, owns a well-established office equipment business. Ten years ago he hired Ruth Jordan, then age 25, as a salesperson for his firm. Because of Jordan's ability to make contacts in the business world, she has enjoyed a financially successful career. In her 10 years with the Maxwell Co., she has also brought some lucrative accounts to the firm.

Maxwell has no one in the family to whom he can leave the business. However, he wants to avoid a liquidation of the business at his death because of the attendant loss to his family, and because he knows that the business can be continued successfully after his death. Both Maxwell and Jordan realize that she is the logical purchaser of the business. She knows and enjoys the operation, has developed accounts of her own and is identified as an integral part of Maxwell Co. by customers and creditors alike.

At age 35, Jordan is in no position to buy the business if Maxwell were to die; however, she can afford to maintain insurance on Maxwell's life equal to the amount of the purchase price. Therefore, Maxwell's life agent raises the possibility of an insured buy-sell agreement with Maxwell and Jordan. They both enthusiastically agree to the plan.

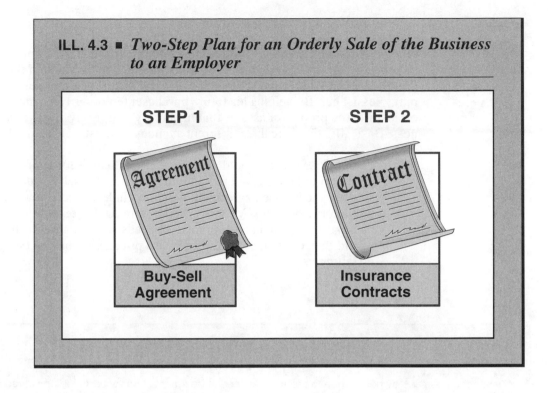

ILL. 4.3 ■ *Two-Step Plan for an Orderly Sale of the Business to an Employer*

STEP 1

Buy-Sell
Agreement

STEP 2

Insurance
Contracts

Determining the Purchase Price

After an "arm's-length" discussion, they arrive at a purchase price of $100,000 for the business. Of this amount, $60,000 is attributable to the net assets of the business and $40,000 recognizes the goodwill created by Maxwell, which will remain in the company after his death, thus inuring to the benefit of Jordan.

A buy-sell agreement incorporating the purchase price, a definite commitment by Jordan to buy the insurance on Maxwell's life in an amount equal to the purchase price and other provisions is prepared by their attorneys. The agreement also allows for a periodic review of the purchase price, with the latest purchase price incorporated into the agreement to prevail.

Jordan buys $100,000 of variable universal life insurance (VUL) on Maxwell's life for approximately $2,000 annually. With the payment of the first premium, Jordan immediately creates the full purchase price for the business. At the same time, she automatically creates an accumulation vehicle for a substantial down payment on the purchase price when Maxwell retires in 15 years. At Maxwell's age 65, the policy's approximate cash value will be $36,000, assuming a 10 percent gross rate of return. This will provide Jordan with 36 percent of the full purchase price. The balance will be paid off in installments according to the terms of the buy-sell agreement.

If the Employee Needs Temporary Help

One potential obstacle to an insured buy-sell agreement is the employee's inability to pay the insurance premiums. If Jordan were unable to maintain the full $2,000 premium for several years, it would be a sound business investment on Maxwell's part to assist her. By helping his future purchaser temporarily finance the insurance on his life, the proprietor assures that his family will receive full value for his business. Basically, there are three different avenues of assistance available to Maxwell.

1. Personal Loan—He could make a personal loan to Jordan for a part of each premium until she could pay the full premium herself. Under these circumstances, the buy-sell agreement would include a special loan schedule that would provide that if Maxwell died before Jordan repaid the loan, it would be repaid first from the insurance proceeds. The balance of the proceeds would then cover most of the purchase price, with the rest being paid off in installments.

ILL. 4.4 ■ *Sale to an Employee—Life Insurance Is the Solution*

When the business owner wishes to sell the business at death or retirement and the employee wants to buy the business in either event, the insured buy-sell agreement offers remarkable advantages to all parties concerned and tremendous sales points for you.

For the Estate and Heirs

1. *The estate receives the full (or substantially all of the) purchase price at once.* The shrinkage in value due to liquidation of the assets and the loss of goodwill are thus eliminated.

2. *The estate is settled promptly and efficiently.* The representative has cash at his or her disposal immediately from the sale of the business to pay the costs of funeral and administration expenses, estate liabilities and death taxes.

3. *The family is relieved of business worries.* In exchange for the going-concern value of the business, the estate receives cash, which may be invested in suitable, worry-free investments to provide income for the spouse and children.

For the Employee

1. *A future business career is assured.* The employee's current career is stabilized and come what may, he or she ultimately will own the business. Without the insured buy-sell agreement, the business—and thus the employee's present career—would be in jeopardy.

2. *The business is stabilized.* Customers, suppliers and creditors, aware that plans have been laid for the orderly continuation of the business, will be favorably disposed toward long-term business dealings with the firm.

For the Proprietor

1. *A buyer for the business at retirement is established.* Through permanent life insurance and the terms spelled out in the buy-sell agreement, the proprietor can look forward to realizing a full return during retirement years for hard and devoted effort during his or her active years.

2. *The services of the employee will be retained.* Rather than leaving to start a competitive business, the employee will be eager to stay and do a bigger and better job for the present employer.

2. Executive Bonus Plans—Maxwell could increase Jordan's salary by an amount sufficient to cover the premium. These plans are discussed in greater detail in Chapter 9.

3. Split-Dollar Plan—The employee pays a small economic benefit based on the policy's face amount and the employer pays the remainder. Split-dollar arrangements are discussed in greater detail in Chapter 9.

Illustration 4.4 summarizes the advantages of an insured buy-sell agreement.

■ THE PROPRIETOR NEEDS YOUR SERVICES

This completes our examination of the sole proprietor as a prospect for life insurance. Regardless of the proprietor's choice as to the disposition of the business at death—liquidation, retention or sale—sales opportunities exist.

The important point to bear in mind in dealing with the sole proprietor is that the *proprietor* must decide whether the business should be liquidated, retained in the family or sold at his or her death. It is not your job to dictate the choice. Rather you should search out the proprietor's personal objectives for the business at his or her death, point out the obstacles that stand in the way of accomplishing these objectives and then demonstrate how life insurance will help overcome these obstacles and transform desires into reality.

Every successful proprietorship has a need for life insurance. Once the proprietor is ready to make a decision with respect to the disposition of the business in the event of death, he or she will be receptive to your ideas. Sole proprietors need your services and your products. Introduce both of them to the proprietor and you will be well rewarded.

■ SUMMARY

In this chapter we have learned that proprietorships account for nearly 74 percent of all businesses nationwide. There are very few legal requirements to establish a proprietorship and there is no legal distinction between the business and the proprietor. Upon the death of the proprietor, forced liquidation and stoppage of income are the two primary concerns for the heirs. Orderly liquidation, family retention or sale of the business are the three methods used to dispose of the proprietorship. A properly planned will and adequate life insurance are a necessity to the orderly liquidation of the business, while estate liquidity and the provisions for family members play an important role in the business being retained by the family. A primary obstacle to the sale of the business is the lack of funds. A properly drafted and insured buy-sell agreement helps overcome this obstacle and offers many advantages to both the buyer and seller of the business.

■ CHAPTER 4 QUESTIONS FOR REVIEW

1. Which of the following statements about sole proprietorships is correct?

   A. The business assets are owned personally by the proprietor.

   B. The owner is not personally responsible for business debts.

   C. The business is a separate legal entity from the owner.

   D. The business form is relatively complex to establish.

2. When a sole proprietor dies without a will that covers the disposition of the business, then the business

   A. passes intact to the heirs under intestate laws

   B. must be discontinued by the legal representative, other than to wind up affairs

   C. is unaffected since it has a legal existence separate from the owner

   D. automatically passes to the coowners

3. If the owner wants his or her business to be retained in the family, all of the following elements are necessary EXCEPT

   A. a family member willing and able to continue the business

   B. a properly drawn will

   C. adequate provision for other family members

   D. orderly liquidation of the assets

4. If a legal representative tries to continue the business without authorization, then the representative is

   A. personally liable for business losses

   B. entitled to keep business profits

   C. legally required to personally buy the business

   D. legally required to incorporate the business

5. The principal advantage of the proprietorship method of doing business is

   A. its relative simplicity

   B. the need for only two directors on its board

   C. the proprietorship is entitled to 50 percent of all profits

   D. the business is started with a formal organizational procedure

6. When a proprietor dies, life insurance

   A. provides collateral

   B. builds a retirement fund

   C. permits an orderly retention of the business

   D. creates an automatic reserve fund

7. Under a buy-sell agreement, all of the following could be used to help an employee purchase insurance on the life of the business EXCEPT

    A. a personal loan

    B. executive bonus plan

    C. split-dollar plan

    D. a 401(k) plan

8. All of the following are alternative plans to transfer the business at the proprietor's death EXCEPT

    A. orderly liquidation

    B. orderly retention

    C. the sale of the business

    D. transfer business to the estate

9. If a business is worth $500,000, the amount of life insurance on the owner, owned by the key employee, should be

    A. $100,000

    B. $250,000

    C. $500,000

    D. $750,000

10. A forced liquidation of a proprietorship usually has the following results EXCEPT

    A. accounts receivables may be impossible to collect

    B. inventories may be worth only a fraction of their real worth

    C. the goodwill of the business is usually lost

    D. the proprietor or the heirs are usually happy with the outcome

5 Partnerships

Partnerships face many of the same difficulties at the death of a partner as a proprietorship faces at the owner's death. Matters are more complex, of course, because two—or more—individuals are involved in the business. The interests of the decedent's family—including, quite often, their need for cash to pay expenses and to continue income—may run counter to the interests of the surviving partners. In this chapter, we will examine the alternatives available to a partnership in these circumstances and the problems faced by both the surviving partners and the heirs of the deceased partner. Also, we will take a detailed look at the concept of the insured buy-sell agreement.

Doing business by virtue of a *partnership* makes good business sense. It enables one person with a particular set of talents to combine with another person with different—but compatible—talents to create an effective business organization. It often results in what people refer to as *synergism,* the phenomenon in which the total effect of combining different skills or assets is greater than the sum of what they can accomplish separately.

■ ■ ■ ■ ■

■ WHAT IS A PARTNERSHIP?

A partnership is a voluntary association of two or more people to carry on a business for profit. (In the interest of clarity, most of our remarks suggest two partners, but the discussion is equally applicable to three or more.) The contract signifying its existence may be written or oral, although in most cases a written contract is preferred.

A partnership is a highly personal relationship in which profits and losses are usually divided among the partners according to their ownership interests in the business. By the same token, the partners are liable for the full amount of partnership indebtedness to the extent not only of their assets in the firm, but their entire personal assets as well. This is a significant characteristic that sets partnerships apart from corporations, which we'll study in Chapter 6.

Our purpose here is to acquaint you with the unique characteristics—and problems—of the partnership. This will help you to assist your partnership prospects in planning the future disposition of their business interests.

■ TYPES OF PARTNERSHIPS

Partnerships generally take one of two different forms:

1. general partnerships

2. limited partnerships

While the vast majority of partnerships are *general,* you need to understand the distinction between these two forms of partnerships in the event you encounter a *limited partnership.*

General Partnerships

In a *general partnership,* each partner contributes capital to the business, either in the form of money or services, and each partner shares in the control and management of the business. Each act of a partner within the scope of partnership activity is an act attributable to the other partner or partners. Further, each partner shares in the profits of the business in whatever proportion is determined under the partnership agreement.

Liability for partnership debts is not limited to a partner's proportionate interest in the business. Each general partner is liable for the full amount of partnership indebtedness to the extent not only of personal assets invested in the business but also to the extent of his or her *entire personal assets.* Partnership assets are applied first to partnership indebtedness. However, if the partnership becomes insolvent, the partners' personal assets are also available to creditors of the partnership for the payment of such indebtedness.

Limited Partnerships

A *limited partnership* is composed of both general partners and limited partners. Limited partners contribute capital to the business, but have no control over the management of the business. If they do, they become general partners as a matter of law. Unless they overstep their sphere and act for the firm, the limited partners' liability for partnership indebtedness extends only to the amount of their capital contribution. Their personal assets are *not* available to creditors of the business. This is the chief distinction between a general and a limited partner.

State laws usually require a limited partnership to record its existence with designated state officers so that the nature of the partnership can become a matter of public record. This makes creditors of the partnership aware of the limited liability of some partners.

Although our discussion in this chapter emphasizes the general partnership, most of the discussion also applies to the general partners in a limited partnership.

■ INCOME TAXATION OF PARTNERS

To assist in fully understanding the partnership concept, it is necessary to take a brief look at how the federal income tax is applied to partners.

The partnership itself is not subject to federal income tax. It is, however, required to file a partnership return, Form 1065, for the taxable year of the partnership. In this return, the gross income of the business is shown, including a separate schedule for each partner (K-1), and business deductions are allowed in computing the net income of the partnership. The *distributive share* of partnership gains and losses to each partner is also reported by the partnership, both to the IRS and to each respective partner.

The partners themselves are required to include in their individual returns the distributive share of the partnership net profits or losses to which they are entitled under the partnership agreement for the taxable year of the partnership. It is immaterial—so far as the tax liability of the partners is concerned—whether or not the profits are actually distributed to them in cash or property. The individuals are required to report the distributive share of profits to which they are entitled, *whether actually distributed to them or not.*

Beginning in 1998, the reporting requirement for large partnerships (over 100 partners) changed. Some of the more pertinent rules are:

- Individual partners are no longer allowed to treat a partnership item differently than the partnership itself.

- The number of items previously required for K-1 reporting has been reduced.

- K-1 schedules must be provided to all partners no later than March 15 after the end of the year.

Additionally, the tax year of a partnership closes with respect to a partner whose entire interest in the partnership terminates, whether by death or liquidation.

For instance, assume A and B are equal partners in the AB Company. In one calendar year the AB Company has a profit of $30,000, but only $20,000 of this is actually distributed, and the balance is reinvested in the firm. Nevertheless, both A and B will have to report $15,000 of partnership income on their respective individual income tax returns. Each partner receives an increase to his or her basis in the partnership interest to reflect any partnership income allocated but not yet received.

■ WHAT HAPPENS WHEN A PARTNER DIES?

Our first step in discussing the problems created by the death of a partner is to examine its legal effect. In this way we can determine how the problems arise and what their practical effect will be.

The law of partnerships as applied when one member of the firm dies is well settled. However, its consequences are all too frequently overlooked by the persons most affected by that law, namely, the partners themselves. This lack of appreciation of crucial problems may lead the partner unwittingly to ignore factors that someday may vitally affect his or her business future. The partner, enjoying the profits of a successful partnership, feels safe and secure from everything except the daily hazards that menace any business. There's a feeling that the partnership organization, through its combination of the judgment and ability of several individuals, gives a degree of protection and lends the business an assurance of continued success the sole proprietorship does not enjoy.

An understanding of the serious problems faced by the surviving partners should alter the complacency of the business owners. Of equal importance are the problems faced by the heirs of the deceased partner. It is, of course, impossible to determine who will and will not be the survivor. Your role in presenting a plan should be to approach each business owner as though he or she could be either the survivor or the decedent. As a survivor, the individual will be faced with serious problems. If on the other hand the individual is the first to die, his or her heirs will be faced with equally serious problems. When the complacency of the business owners is sufficiently disturbed, the life insurance solution in all its simplicity can be effectively presented.

A Partner's Death Dissolves the Partnership

The death of a partner automatically, by operation of law, dissolves the partnership. This means that the partnership is continued *only* for the purpose of winding up the firm's affairs.

The reason for this rule of law is clear. The partnership relation is a voluntary, contractual business relationship in which each partner can act for the others and can subject them to unlimited liability. Because of the nature of this business association, the right to choose one's own partners has always been a basic principle of partnership law. No one can choose a partner for another, nor can he or she unilaterally elect to be the partner of another. This has led to the rule that the disassociation of any partner from a firm dissolves the partnership and gives each associate a new choice of partners.

The Effect of Dissolution

In the absence of any agreement entered into by the partners *before* the partnership is dissolved, the dissolution of the partnership brings an end to the authority of the surviving partner to act for the partnership except to wind up the firm's business. The surviving partner becomes owner of the partnership assets, but only for the purpose of winding up the business. The survivor becomes what is known as a *liquidating trustee.*

As liquidating trustee the surviving partner must, with reasonable dispatch:

- complete all partnership transactions started before the death of the partner but not as yet completed;

- collect the accounts receivable;

- pay the partnership debts;

- convert the remaining assets into cash; and

- in the case of more than one surviving partner, pay to all the surviving partners, and to the representative of the deceased partner, the net amounts owed to each in relation to his or her partnership interest.

If, after all the above transactions, there is a deficit, then each partner (including the estate of the deceased partner) must contribute a proportionate share to make up the deficit. If any are unable, then the others must make up this share. Remember—each *general* partner is liable for the full amount of partnership indebtedness, and this liability extends not only to assets invested in the business, but also to the individual's personal assets.

■ THE PROBLEMS OF THE SURVIVING PARTNER

If suitable arrangements have not been made *before* the death of a partner, the surviving partner faces a choice of two disconcerting alternatives. The partner must either (1) cease business and completely liquidate the affairs of the firm or (2) reach an agreement with other parties and set up a new firm. In other words, the surviving partner has the choice of *liquidation* or *reorganization*. Often this choice is not even in the surviving partner's hands. It may be in the hands of the heirs of the deceased partner.

Liquidate or Reorganize

For years advisors have been telling partners that their firms will be dissolved by death, that the law destroys the business. Too often the partners have refused to become greatly alarmed.

Regardless, the surviving partner's choice between liquidation and reorganization is honest and unexaggerated; this is the fundamental problem that every partner not a party to a *suitable prior agreement* must face when a partner dies. With that death, the business as it exists is ended—and its liquidation becomes the order of the day unless in some manner it can be reorganized and started again with a new partnership group. The survivor cannot continue with the old business, and the creation of a new business will take both a certain amount of time as well as the consent and agreement of various parties.

The surviving partner is faced with an almost insurmountable problem—up against a stone wall through which there are only two gates—one of liquidation and the other, reorganization. The survivor *must* pass through one of them. Surely this story is enough to shake the complacency of almost any business partner. If the choice had to be made tonight, it is not likely that the partner would sleep very well. It would present a real business and personal crisis.

Heirs Really Control Decision

As bleak as this picture may be, it is not the whole story. In the final analysis, the choice will not be the surviving partner's to make. In all likelihood, that choice would be some form of reorganization so that he or she might continue the business. However, the only choice that any partner can demand is the liquidation of partnership affairs. Likewise, that is the only choice that can be demanded by the estate and heirs.

Neither the surviving partner nor the heirs can reorganize the business without the consent of the other. For example, if the surviving partner wishes to continue the business in partnership with the heirs of the deceased partner's interest, the heirs must agree to a reorganization as an alternative to receiving the value of the deceased partner's interest in cash. Likewise, if the heirs wish to form a partnership with the survivor, they cannot do so if the surviving partner prefers to liquidate.

Your job is to make partnership prospects realize that the choice a surviving partner faces with the death of a partner is one between liquidation and reorganization. You should also make them aware that the survivor will not make this choice alone. The estate or the heirs of the deceased partner, thinking of their own interests, will do the choosing, though it may mean the loss of the business, of a lifetime of investment and work, of a protection that was to have sheltered the individual in old age.

Whether the choice is liquidation or reorganization, there are many problems, unless prior plans have been made. Let's look at these problems and then consider the appropriate solution.

■ PROBLEMS IN LIQUIDATING THE PARTNERSHIP

In the previous chapter we saw, in connection with sole proprietorships, just what the sudden and forced liquidation of a going business concern may mean in the way of losses. Most of that discussion applies with equal force to the situation at a partner's death if liquidation of the firm becomes necessary.

For example, we saw that liquidation of the business means the collection of accounts receivable, the payment of outstanding obligations and the forced sale of assets. There's little doubt that liquidation of a business can be accomplished only after serious losses and shrinkage in value.

Every business owner knows these things. The only problem is to make the prospect realize that this is the situation to be faced tomorrow if the partner dies.

Surviving Partners Liquidate Their Own Jobs

Perhaps more critical, however, than the losses in business value that must accompany any attempt to liquidate the enterprise is the surviving partner's loss of his or her business future. The surviving partner settles the business and is out of a job at the same time. Assuming that the business has been relatively successful—and has been the main source of the survivor's income—this becomes a major consideration.

The survivor may find it difficult to begin a business career over again. If it isn't possible to start again from scratch, he or she will probably end up working as an employee, rather than as an employer. If the surviving partner is older, termination of the business may mean permanent unemployment. If the heirs choose to liquidate, there is no choice.

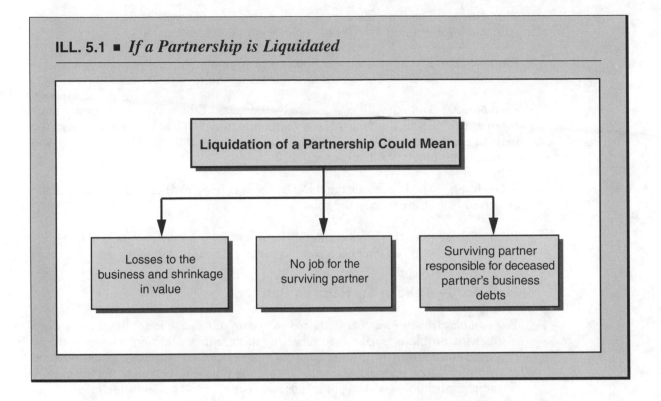

ILL. 5.1 ■ *If a Partnership is Liquidated*

Liquidation of a Partnership Could Mean

- Losses to the business and shrinkage in value
- No job for the surviving partner
- Surviving partner responsible for deceased partner's business debts

Surviving Partners Pay Firm Debts If Estate Is Insolvent

Another point to be considered is that surviving partners are liable for their shares of any deficiency of assets against firm liabilities, if liquidation should result in a deficit. Remember that the assets are being sold at auction prices on a forced sale basis. There is a risk under these circumstances that the business will not realize enough to pay all the outstanding debts. Surviving partners are liable for their share of any deficit that may result. Worse, they may be liable for the entire deficit if the deceased partner's estate should prove insolvent or unable to meet its share of the liabilities.

■ PROBLEMS IN REORGANIZING THE PARTNERSHIP

After the partnership is dissolved, the surviving partner becomes a liquidating trustee. Because liquidation is usually such a drastic course of action, and because it may spell the end of the individual's independent business career, the surviving partner, as liquidating trustee, will sometimes search for ways the partnership can be reorganized. Regardless of which method is chosen, however, there are bound to be legal, financial and psychological obstacles unless there has been proper advance planning.

If the heirs should find reorganization to their advantage, and if it is legally possible to enter into some plan for salvaging the partnership business through its reorganization with new partners, then that reorganization must take one of the following forms:

Plan No. 1. The immediate creation of a new firm that will include the heirs, or someone representing them, as new partners in the business.

Plan No. 2. The immediate creation of a new partnership that will include someone who has purchased or agreed to purchase the heirs' interest as partner.

Plan No. 3. The immediate purchase by the heirs of the surviving partner's interest in the business. Although this is a reorganization plan from the viewpoint of the heirs, it is really a liquidation plan from the viewpoint of the surviving partner who is selling out his or her interest.

Plan No. 4. The immediate purchase by the surviving partner of the interest of the deceased from the estate or the heirs.

Each of these plans involves certain difficulties and presents unique problems. Therefore we will consider each plan separately. (See Ill. 5.2.)

Plan No. 1—Take in the Heirs as Partners

You can choose your partner, but not your partner's heirs. That phrase aptly dramatizes the problem faced by the surviving partner in accepting the heirs of the deceased partner into the business. Individuals select their partners because of some contribution those partners can make toward the ultimate success of the business—financial assistance, good business judgment, unique sales talents, technical training and experience or whatever it may be. A partner's heirs may be selected as associates only because the choice is between taking them in or liquidating the business.

The Heirs as Active Partners

Business ability, unfortunately, does not always run in a family. The present partner may be well qualified, but it is possible that other family members know little about business affairs. After the partner dies, the survivor is either forced to deal with the heirs or accept the alternative of liquidating the business.

Perhaps the heirs decide that one of them should come into the business as an active partner. For instance, a surviving spouse may feel that he or she can protect family interests better by taking an active part in the management of the business. As a consequence, the surviving partner avoids liquidation only by taking in an associate who may be inexperienced in business matters and unqualified for the duties he or she assumes. Few people contemplate with favor being in business with their partner's family. It may be an exhausting and nerve-wracking task for everyone concerned.

It is impossible to tell how much of the business and its responsibilities these new and untried partners will understand. They may prove to be most uncongenial associates. Lacking knowledge of the business and its affairs, often misunderstanding its condition, the new associates may prove to be a constant source of exasperating and needless questions. The new partners may be unwilling to place full confidence in the surviving partner. They may be tempted to question the surviving partner's motives in many business actions, or hesitate in giving their consent to a particular action. They may even criticize what the surviving partner has done. In such circumstances, the new partners can be a most annoying and serious handicap.

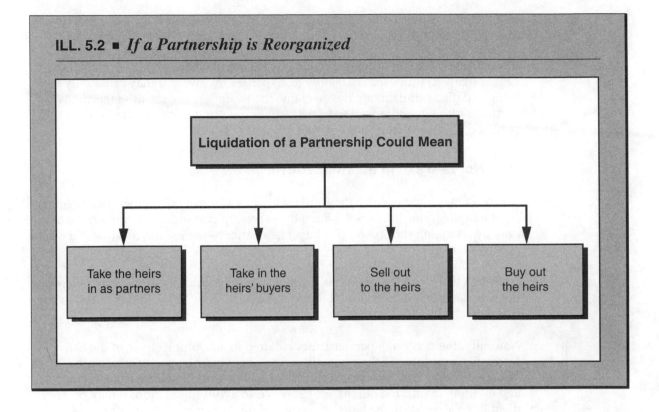

ILL. 5.2 ■ *If a Partnership is Reorganized*

Liquidation of a Partnership Could Mean

| Take the heirs in as partners | Take in the heirs' buyers | Sell out to the heirs | Buy out the heirs |

The Heirs as Inactive Partners

Perhaps the heirs will accept partnership status in the business to preserve it as a business entity and permit its continued operation as a going concern though they prefer not to take an active part in the business. If this is the case, the surviving partner must do all the work, assume all the responsibilities and operate the business without the advice and counsel of the former partner. To make matters worse, the surviving partner may have to divide the profits with others whose only contribution to the business is an interest they inherited! In essence, the surviving partner is supporting two families instead of one.

In addition, these inactive partners may have peculiar notions concerning the income the business can be expected to pay them. For instance, much of the deceased partner's income from the business may have been salary for services performed in carrying on the business. The heirs, however, may expect the business to pay them just as much after the partner's death as it did before. This may be true even though the heirs contribute nothing to the active conduct of the business and the surviving partners must hire additional employees to replace the decedent.

It is also possible that the interests of the surviving partner—whose business future rests on the firm's continued growth—and the interests of the heirs are directly opposed. The business partner usually thinks in terms of expanding the business, investing capital in the business and using profits to increase capacity and operations. On the other hand, the representative of the estate and the heirs may think almost exclusively in terms of their need and desire for current income. One thinks in terms of business construction and sound business practice, the other in terms of current livelihood.

These facts all add up to one conclusion: Any plan that brings the heirs into the business is likely to prove unsatisfactory to all parties involved. It may cause only bickering and discord. Bringing the heirs into the business may result in the surviving partner's ultimate retirement from the business and its collapse in the hands of inexperienced and incapable management.

Plan No. 2—Take in the Heirs' Buyer

The heirs may conclude that they will realize more from a sale of their business than from a liquidation. If this is the case, the surviving partner may avoid liquidation only by accepting the prospective buyer as a partner—unless the *survivor* is the prospective buyer.

Although the surviving partner is the logical purchaser of the decedent's interest, the heirs are not obligated to sell to this individual. They are at liberty to sell to anyone they choose.

Naturally, the surviving partner is not required to accept the buyer of the heirs' interest as a partner. The partner can insist upon winding up the partnership affairs as prescribed by law, paying the firm's debts, converting whatever is left into cash and dividing it with the purchaser. However, to avoid liquidation, it may be expedient to go along with the heirs' plan and accept the buyer of their interest as a new partner.

It is always unpleasant to be forced to accept a stranger into the close relationship of a partnership. It is unpleasant, and often disastrous, to be forced to take in an untried stranger not of the surviving partner's choosing. Most partners will agree that this second reorganization alternative is generally to be avoided.

Although the buyer of the heirs' interest may not be acceptable or may be personally objectionable to the surviving partner, the survivor may have to accept this person as a partner. The only alternative, remember, is *to liquidate the business.*

Plan No. 3—Sell Out to the Heirs

Occasionally, the ultimate solution to the problems presented by termination of the present partnership is the sale of the surviving partner's interest to the heirs or to someone who has acquired their interests.

This solution is adopted most often when the interest of the partners in the business were not equal, and the deceased partner owned a majority interest. Under such circumstances, the surviving partner, with a minority interest, may be asked to sell out and leave the business to the heirs. The only alternative again is liquidation of the business. Often, the lion's share of the proceeds of any such liquidation will go to the others, leaving only a small share to the surviving partner.

This solution might be used more often if it weren't for the fact that, in most cases, a sale to the heirs is out of the question. Under normal circumstances, the heirs are in no position to buy the interest. Usually, the spouse and the other heirs need funds for their own subsistence, and the estate needs funds to meet immediate estate liabilities and debts. Seldom will either the estate or the heirs possess the cash required to buy out even a minority interest of a surviving partner.

Assuming that the heirs are able to finance such a purchase, the surviving partner is not likely to favor such a solution. While this may be an acceptable reorganization plan from the standpoint of the heirs, it is a liquidation plan from the standpoint of the surviving partner. At best, the alternative of selling out to the heirs is a last resort from the surviving partner's point of view. At worst, it is the end of the survivor's business career.

Plan No. 4—Buy Out the Heirs

In an effort to avoid the twin menaces of forced liquidation and the introduction of new and unwanted partners into the business, the surviving partner may try to purchase the interest of the decedent from the estate. There are many stumbling blocks to such a purchase.

First, there is the problem of obtaining the cash needed to make that purchase, at a time when the affairs of the business are in confusion and its future is surrounded with uncertainty. Second, it can be difficult to come to terms with the heirs, who may be inclined to demand a high price for their interest. Third, there is the problem of dealing with the deceased's representative who is frequently unfamiliar with the business and its real worth.

Securing the Money

First of all, the necessity for making this purchase comes at a most inopportune time. Credit lines can be expected to suffer with the termination of the partnership at the death of a partner. The partnership no longer exists and can no longer secure a loan as such. In many partnerships, the firm's credit is largely tied to the personal credit of the partners. Where such is the case, the survivor's sources of credit assistance dry up almost completely.

Even where the surviving partner's personal resources are substantial and personal credit is available, he or she will find that credit materially impaired with the death of the partner, because the future of the business is shrouded in uncertainty. Firm creditors, fearing a forced liquidation of business assets and the resulting impairment of collateral, may demand immediate payment of their claims by the surviving partner. If met out of business assets, the claims will involve a heavy drain upon the resources of the firm. If not satisfied, claims will constitute a cloud upon the personal assets of the surviving partner, since he or she is personally liable for payment of these debts if firm assets prove to be insufficient.

Ask partnership prospects whether they could obtain the money to buy out their partners' interests under these conditions, the conditions they will face when their partners die.

Meeting the Heirs' Terms

Suppose that the survivor can raise the cash. The second problem is whether the survivor and the heirs or the estate can reach an agreement on the price for the deceased partner's interest. For example, unless arrangements have previously been made for sale of the deceased's interest at an agreed price, how does the surviving partner know that the estate and the heirs will not hold out for an impossible price?

While the surviving partner is the logical purchaser, he or she is not necessarily the only purchaser, as we have seen. Since the survivor is the logical purchaser, and control of the business would mean more to him or her than anyone else, the heirs may expect to be paid a premium for their interests. Knowing what control of the business would mean to the survivor, the heirs may expect to be paid more than the true value of the deceased partner's interest.

It may be impossible for the survivor to pay the full purchase price in cash. Yet, the heirs may insist on a cash payment for their interest. Even when the heirs are willing to sell at a reasonable price, they may be unwilling to take the survivor's promissory note for part or all of the purchase price. This is especially true if an installment sale results in substantial postponement of their receipt of the purchase price. The heirs may prefer to take less—through liquidation of the business—in order to get it quickly.

Financing the Purchase

Even the surviving partner who comes to terms with the heirs for purchasing the decedent's business interest through a series of notes may be faced with an installment obligation that is difficult or impossible to carry to completion. While the surviving partner can expect to receive profits on the newly acquired interest in the business in addition to profits arising from the original interest, the net income after taxes may be insufficient to pay the notes as they become due.

Buyout Usually Best

In most cases, the most desirable solution to the problem of partnership liquidation is the survivor's purchase of the deceased's interest. Very often, however, this solution is unavailable, for the survivor must meet two definite conditions:

1. Cash must be available to the survivor to pay for that interest.

2. The heirs must be willing or obligated to sell at a reasonable price.

Failure to meet either of these prerequisites means the collapse of the survivor's plans for purchasing the business and the adoption of one of the alternative measures we have discussed previously.

■ PROBLEMS FACED BY THE DECEASED PARTNER'S ESTATE

We have considered the problems that a partner's death creates largely from the viewpoint of the surviving partner—or partners—of the firm. Generally, it is good sales psychology to approach the presentation of partnership problems with the assumption that the prospect is going to be the surviving partner. It is often easier for prospects to consider the death of a partner than to picture themselves deceased.

The fact remains that partners who expect to survive may themselves be the first to die. There is no guarantee that they will survive . . . no guarantee that their families will not someday be wondering what to do with their interests in a firm. The problems that death brings are not confined to the surviving partners. They exist with equal force and perplexity for the surviving spouse and the estate of the deceased.

Loss of Income

Probably the most serious problem faced by the family of the deceased partner results from automatic termination of the decedent's salary or draw. Typically, a man or woman in a partnership enterprise will not be a tremendously wealthy individual. There are exceptions, of course, but in many instances, substantially all of the capital of a deceased partner will be tied up in the business. A large part of personal income is usually derived from the business. What happens under these circumstances when a partner dies?

The family income from the business immediately stops. Any salary received usually ends at once. Withdrawals made for family living expenses likewise terminate with the partner's death and the winding up of the firm's affairs. The income that had been the mainstay of the family's existence suddenly disappears. In the hour of their greatest need, with funeral expenses and perhaps expenses of the deceased's last illness added to ongoing living expenses, the family finds itself subject not only to the shock and grief of the death, but to a sudden family financial crisis as well.

This may be difficult for the surviving spouse to understand. Often, the spouse views the decedent's income simply as a return from an interest in the business. The realization that part of it was salary for services rendered and only part a distribution of business profits, may come as a distinct shock. It may be difficult to understand why the business that paid the deceased so much now pays the surviving family so little.

Firm Assets Not Available

It may be possible for the surviving spouse to draw upon the resources of the estate and upon potential equity in the business for support allowances during the period of estate settlement.

That is not so ready a solution as may at first appear, if it is available at all. The representative may advance funds to the spouse during the time the estate is being probated and its affairs settled—*if the estate has any funds from which to make such advances!* But, if the bulk of the dead partner's estate and capital resources is tied up in the business, what then? If the principal asset of the estate is the deceased's equity in the partnership, the surviving spouse may find it very difficult to obtain the funds with which to meet family obligations and maintain the home, until the partnership itself has been settled. The hands of the representative are tied by law. Generally, no advances can be made to the spouse against the estate's equity in the business, until the partnership affairs have been settled and the value of the dead partner's share in the partnership has been determined.

The process of settling the partnership affairs requires considerable time. The surviving partner may be in no hurry to liquidate the business. He or she may actually prefer to delay liquidation as long as possible, in order to have more time to work out future plans.

In the absence of other substantial estate assets, the family's problem of surviving the period of business and estate settlement may be acute.

Estate Shrinkage

Assuming the common situation in which the deceased partner's estate consists primarily of an interest in the firm, the *liquidation* of the business—with its serious shrinkage in the value of business assets—may result in an equivalent shrinkage in the value of the estate. Thus it must be kept in mind that liquidation of the partnership is also liquidation of the estate of the deceased partner to the extent of his or her interest in the firm. Every dollar lost in that process means a proportionate loss to the deceased partner's family.

The problem of the *diminishing value* of the business—the difference between the present value of the business as a going concern and its value for liquidation purposes after the partner dies—is as crucial in the partnership context as it is in the sole proprietorship. The deceased partner's family will not receive 100 cents on the dollar for their interest in the business if liquidation occurs. The business interest that constitutes a large part of the estate will reach them at only a fraction of its true worth as a going business.

Reorganization Attempts

One of the various plans of reorganization previously noted may be adopted by the parties as an attempted solution to their mutual problems. Each of these plans involves problems and difficulties for the surviving spouse and the estate that are just as disturbing as the problems faced by the surviving partner. There are two sides to the story of reorganization following a partner's death. Now we'll look at this issue from the heirs' point of view.

Plan No. 1—The Heirs Become Partners

The first reorganization plan involves the entrance of the heirs into the business as active or inactive partners, succeeding to the deceased partner's interest. Such a procedure may prove to be as unattractive to the spouse and the heirs as to the surviving partner.

Suppose the spouse or other heirs enter the business and take an *active* part in its management. Perhaps the deceased did not discuss business problems at home. The spouse may have little business experience as well as a misunderstanding of the status of the firm and the decedent's relations with the other partners. With little business background and little information concerning the affairs of the firm, the surviving spouse may have a difficult time trying to understand the business transactions that take place.

Inexperience and lack of understanding may lead to a distrust of the motives and actions of the surviving partner, and also to friction and dispute in the management of the business. This situation will be aggravated by the fact, as was pointed out earlier, that the interests of the spouse, and those of the surviving partner, often may be diametrically opposed.

With internal dissension, it may be difficult to make substantial progress with the business, and diminishing profits may tend to intensify the conflict of the varying interests. The spouse's situation is not enviable under these circumstances, especially when it is remembered that she or he has been suddenly tossed into the midst of a business that may be entirely new and unfamiliar.

As *inactive* partners, the problems of the heirs remain serious. They are forced to look to the surviving partner(s) for income, without having a direct voice in management affairs. In many instances, the loss of the deceased's salary will come as a shock to the surviving spouse, who thought the deceased's salary and share of the profits both constituted "income from the business."

Further, any plan under which the heirs enter into the business with the surviving partner subjects them to liability for firm debts. If the business falters, the heirs are subject, at least, to loss of their capital invested in the business. The situation is not a desirable one from any standpoint.

Plan No. 2—The Heirs Sell to an Outsider

This second plan, frequently unacceptable from the viewpoint of the surviving partner, will prove little better for the family either.

First of all, it may be difficult if not impossible to find anyone willing to buy the deceased partner's interest. Remember that partnership lines of credit have likely collapsed temporarily and the business may be in a stalemate pending settlement of the firm's and the estate's affairs. A prospective purchaser might well be cautious in attempting to acquire a business enterprise and trying to revitalize it under such circumstances.

Anyone considering the purchase of the interest of the heirs would have to have answers to many serious questions before taking that step.

Even assuming the heirs *do* find a prospective purchaser for their interest, there is no guarantee that the surviving partner will accept this person into the business. It may prove to be someone the survivor finds unsatisfactory, in which event the survivor may proceed with liquidation regardless of the wishes of the heirs. As we have seen, the survivor is not required to accept anyone the heirs select as a new associate.

Plan No. 3—The Heirs Buy Out the Survivor

The third reorganization plan involves the purchase of the surviving partner's interest by the heirs. The plan is rarely available to the heirs, who are usually far more concerned about where they can sell their interest to get some much needed cash than they are about how they can buy the interest of the survivor.

Again, even if the estate of the decedent is in a position to buy out the surviving partner, there is no guarantee that the surviving partner will be willing to sell. There is also no guarantee that the surviving partner will be willing to sell at a price the heirs can afford to pay.

Plan No. 4—The Heirs Sell to the Survivor

The fourth alternative reorganization plan involves the sale of the heirs' interest to the surviving partner. As previously noted, this is by far the most desirable procedure from the standpoint of all parties. The heirs obtain the cash from the business and the surviving partner continues the business. However, we have already noted the stumbling blocks that may arise to defeat such a solution.

Primarily, the surviving partner must have *cash resources* sufficient to make the purchase. Otherwise, the surviving spouse and the heirs may find themselves selling out for a small down payment and long-term notes in lieu of the interest they already own outright in the firm. In addition, the heirs have to rely upon the surviving partner to make a success of the venture to pay off these obligations. We have seen that the problem of securing cash is a difficult one, even to meet installment terms as they come due.

Secondly, there is the question of *terms,* which remain even though the surviving partner may have the funds available to make an outright purchase. The same problems of reaching a fair price between the parties arise under this plan.

■ THE SOLUTION: A BUY-SELL AGREEMENT

It is clear that the plan under which the surviving partner acquires the deceased partner's interest and continues the business, while the estate receives in cash the fair market value of that interest, is usually the best solution to the problems that arise when a partner dies. Such a plan, however, should be *definite, certain and binding* on all the parties, so that the rights of each will be fixed. The plan must be adequately secured and financed so that the surviving partner will be certain to have the funds with which to carry out the agreement.

What plan achieves all these objectives? *The answer is the business insurance buy-sell agreement funded with life insurance covering the partners.* Let's look next at how such an agreement works. (For purposes of our discussion, we'll generally assume partnerships of more than two partners.)

Executing a Buy-Sell Agreement

The first step in the business insurance plan is the execution of a binding *buy-sell agreement* between the partners. Under such an agreement, the interest of any partner who dies will be sold to and purchased by the surviving partners, at a price agreed upon between the parties and stipulated in the agreement.

There is no uncertainty in this plan. The deceased partner has agreed to sell at death; the surviving partners are assured that they will have the right to buy. The survivors have agreed to buy; the deceased's family is certain that it will be able to dispose of the decedent's interest. The price is fixed and agreed upon; the survivors are assured that they will not have to pay too much and the family is assured it will not receive too little.

There is no "option" involved. There are no arrangements for putting the heirs into the business, a move that not only may be subject to legal questions (as in the case of a professional partnership such as doctors, attorneys or CPAs, where the members are subject to strict licensing requirements) but also seldom accomplishes the desires of the surviving partners.

At the death of a partner, the surviving partners receive the interest of the deceased partner and the estate receives the agreed upon purchase price in cash.

Financing the Agreement

The second step in the business insurance plan is the establishment of a fund that will provide the surviving partners with sufficient cash to carry out their purchase obligations upon the death of any partner.

A partnership buy-sell agreement is only as strong as the financial arrangements that support it. The agreement gives the surviving partner or partners the right and power to buy the interest of the deceased—and it must be a valid and binding agreement in every way. However, when the time comes, if the surviving partners do not have the cash to pay for the deceased's interest, the plan collapses.

The power to buy is meaningless, unless the required cash is available. The surviving partners must obtain the money from one of the following sources:

Personal Resources

Because they often reinvest profits back into the business, the surviving partners' personal assets are usually tied up in the business. As a result, in few instances will the surviving partners be able to finance the purchase out of their own funds. Even where they can, by financing the purchase with their own funds, they pay 100 cents out of their resources for every dollar of the deceased partner's interest. Under the life insurance plan, however, the purchase is made with discounted dollars to the extent that the premiums paid in do not equal the proceeds used in making the purchase.

Borrowed Funds

Borrowing the money to finance the purchase is usually a difficult task. Firm credit has been weakened with the death of a partner, since the original firm no longer exists. Often, firm credit is tied to the personal credit of the individual partners. Personal credit of surviving partners may be impaired because they are liable for business debts, and the business may now be in an uncertain and precarious position. Firm creditors will be looking to them for payment of firm obligations, especially if it appears that the estate of the deceased will be unable to bear its full share of those debts.

By borrowing, the survivors obligate themselves to pay interest and principal. In contrast, under the life insurance plan, they pay the premiums and never have to worry about the principal.

Other Sources

The partnership may wish to use firm assets to finance the agreement. However, when a partner dies, the former partnership, as such, no longer legally exists. Ordinarily the attempt to dispose of firm assets results in tremendous losses and curtailment of business activity.

Another possible source of financing is a reserve fund. Under this method, the partners begin building—through annual deposits—a fund that hopefully will be sufficient when the need arises to purchase a deceased member's interest. However, it will take years to build such a fund, and the need may arise in a matter of weeks.

Life insurance provides the only sinking fund plan that will be sure to furnish the required cash to the surviving partners, in full, on the death of a partner, regardless of whether death occurs tomorrow, a year from now or many years from now. (See Ill. 5.3.)

Provisions of a Buy-Sell Agreement

An attorney must draft a buy-sell agreement because it is a legal document. Nevertheless, you should have a working knowledge of its nature and scope and the issues it covers. This will be particularly helpful to you in making sure that all insurance phases of the agreement are properly attested. Following is a brief summary of important elements included in an insured buy-sell agreement.

All buy-sell agreements generally follow a similar broad pattern, consisting of the essentials that the agreement should cover. These usually take the form of seven definite commitments:

1. Each partner agrees not to dispose of a partnership interest during his or her lifetime without first offering it for sale to the other partners (or the partnership) at the agreed upon contract price.

2. The partners agree that the surviving partners (or the partnership) will buy— and the deceased partner's estate will sell to the survivors (or the partnership)—the interest of the deceased partner.

3. An agreed upon purchase price is set to be paid by the surviving partners (or partnership) for the deceased partner's interest, or a formula is established to be used at the time of death to determine a definite price.

4. The partners (or the partnership) agree to purchase and maintain life insurance in a stated amount for the purpose of financing the purchase of the deceased partner's interest.

5. An agreement is made as to the ownership and control of the life insurance policies and the manner in which the policies on the lives of the surviving partners, owned by the estate of the deceased, are to be disposed of.

ILL. 5.3 ■ *Financing the Partnership Buy-Sell Agreement*

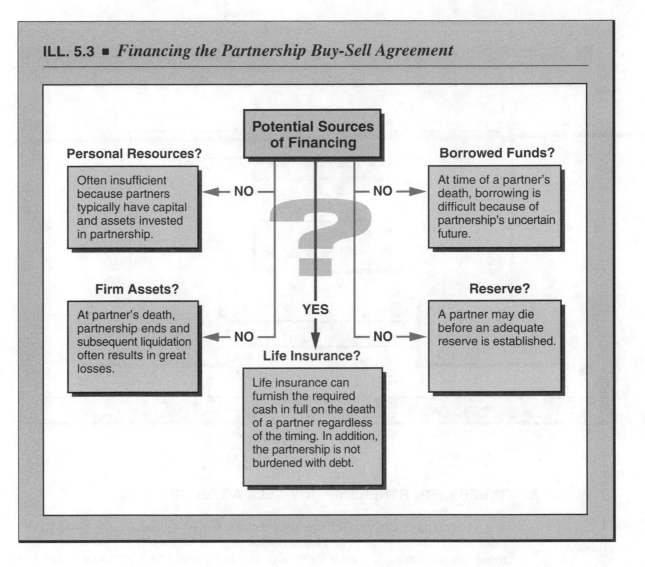

6. An agreement is reached as to the time and method of paying any balance of the purchase price in excess of the insurance proceeds. Conversely, the manner in which any proceeds in excess of the purchase price should be disposed of is established.

7. An agreement is made that the surviving partners will take over all debts of the partnership and release the deceased's estate from any obligation toward the same.

Once again, we should emphasize that a practitioner is not expected to draft a buy-sell agreement. This is the attorney's job. However, you should be able to discuss intelligently such an agreement with your partnership prospects.

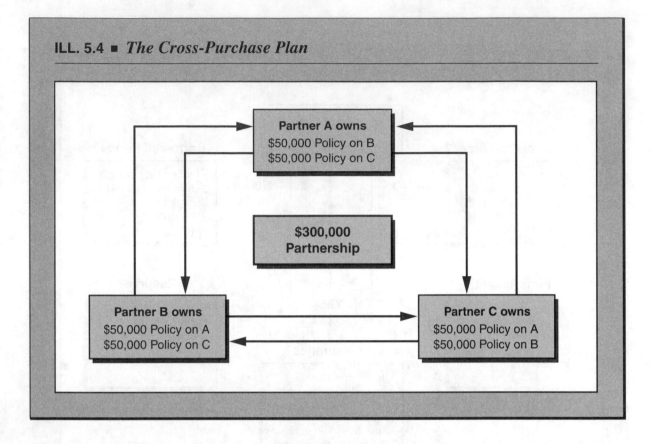

ILL. 5.4 ■ *The Cross-Purchase Plan*

Partner A owns
$50,000 Policy on B
$50,000 Policy on C

$300,000 Partnership

Partner B owns
$50,000 Policy on A
$50,000 Policy on C

Partner C owns
$50,000 Policy on A
$50,000 Policy on B

■ TYPES OF PARTNERSHIP BUY-SELL AGREEMENTS

A partnership insured buy-sell agreement can take two forms: the *cross-purchase plan* and the *entity plan*. A brief description of each follows. It should be kept in mind that the business owners themselves should select which plan to use. However, their attorney and accountant can be of help in providing advice. You will probably be called upon for assistance in those areas directly involving life insurance.

Cross-Purchase Plan

The *cross-purchase buy-sell agreement* is the more commonly used form. It is an agreement whereby the partners *individually* agree to purchase the interest of the deceased partner, and the representative of the deceased partner is directed to sell the interest directly to the surviving partners. The partnership itself is not a party to the agreement. Each partner owns, is the beneficiary of and pays for insurance on the life of the other partner or partners in an amount approximating the individual's share of the purchase price.

For example, assume a dual partnership worth $100,000 is owned equally. Under an insured cross-purchase plan, each partner insures the life of the other for $50,000. If partner B dies, partner A would have $50,000 of insurance proceeds with which to purchase B's interest under the buy-sell agreement.

What becomes of the policy B owned on A's life? A can buy the policy from B's estate for its cash value, or B's representative can surrender the policy, and its value at the time of death becomes a part of B's estate. The manner in which the policy is to be disposed of should be spelled out in the agreement.

Now let's assume there are three equal partners in a business worth $300,000. As shown in Ill. 5.4, A owns a $50,000 life insurance policy on each of B and C; B owns $50,000 on each of A and C; C owns $50,000 on each of A and B. A dies. B and C each receive $50,000 from the proceeds of the policies they owned on A's life. From A's estate, B purchases one-half of A's partnership interest, using these proceeds; C buys the other half of A's interest, also using the $50,000 proceeds. B and C now own one-half each, or $150,000 of the partnership, and A's estate has been fully compensated for its partnership interest.

Entity Plan

Under an *entity plan,* the partnership—rather than the individual partners—owns, pays for and is the beneficiary of the policies on the lives of the partners in amounts equal to each partner's interest. The partnership also becomes a party to the buy-sell agreement. This type of arrangement is used, for example, when the number of partners involved would make the cross-purchase plan too cumbersome. For example, in a four-way partnership the cross-purchase plan would require 12 different life insurance plans; the entity plan would require only four. The formula for the number of life insurance contracts required in a cross purchase plan is N (N-1), where N represents the number of partners. For example, if there were five partners, the

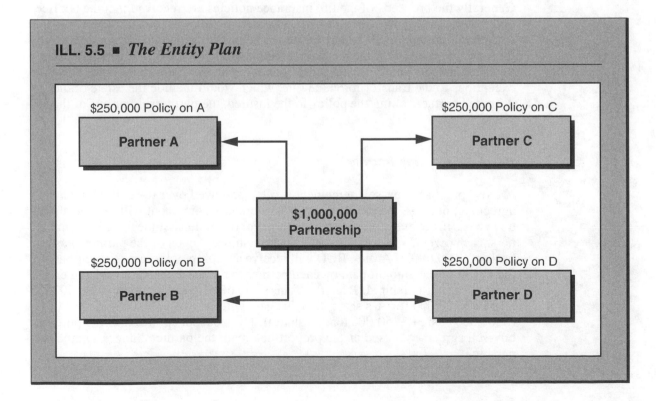

ILL. 5.5 ■ *The Entity Plan*

$250,000 Policy on A

Partner A

$250,000 Policy on C

Partner C

$1,000,000 Partnership

$250,000 Policy on B

Partner B

$250,000 Policy on D

Partner D

partnership would require 20 life insurance contracts to complete the buy-sell cross-purchase agreement.

With the entity plan, when a partner dies the partnership buys the deceased partner's interest from the estate. This interest is then divided among the surviving partners in proportion to their partnership interests.

Illustration 5.5 shows a four-way partnership worth $1,000,000. The firm purchases $250,000 of insurance on the life of each partner. If partner A is the first to die, the firm purchases his or her interest from the estate, and the interests of partners B, C and D increase from 25 percent to 33⅓ percent each. The firm immediately buys an additional amount of insurance on the life of each surviving partner to assure the availability of the full purchase price upon the death of the next partner.

One last point concerning the entity plan is that most life insurance companies offer a quantity discount known as banding. This means that one $500,000 policy purchased under the entity plan may cost less than four $125,000 policies under the cross purchase plan.

Income Tax Considerations

The insurance premiums paid by to fund a buy-sell agreement are not tax deductible because the premium payors are directly or indirectly beneficiaries of the policies. This is true whether the premiums are paid by the individual partners or by the partnership.

Transfer for Value

Generally the proceeds of the life insurance policies are received income tax free under both plans. However, if the ownership of a policy was transferred for valuable consideration, the proceeds may be subject to ordinary income tax under the transfer for value rules. The income taxed amount would be the difference between the proceeds and any amounts paid for the contract plus total premiums paid. There are exceptions to the transfer for value rule, which would include the estate of the deceased partner selling the policy to the insured, the partnership or one of the surviving partners.

Basis of Surviving Partner

A cross-purchase buy-sell agreement is often preferred over the entity buy-sell agreement because the partners in a cross-purchase agreement will receive a step-up in basis in the event of a partner's death. For example, assume there are four partners, each owns 25 percent of ABCD partnership and each of the partners has a basis of $100,000. If A dies, BCD will receive a step-up or increase to their basis to the extent of the amount paid by each partner to purchase the deceased owner's share of the partnership. If B later sells his share of the partnership for $700,000 and he paid $250,000 for A's share, then his gain will only be $350,000. ($700,000 – ($100,000 basis + $250,000 for A's share)). This concept applies to entity purchase buy-sell agreement based on the proportionality of the partners' interest in the partnership.

■ ADVANTAGES OF AN INSURED BUY-SELL AGREEMENT

It is imperative that you become totally familiar with the following sales points. If properly presented, they can have a tremendous impact. If the partners are sincere in their desire to continue the business upon the death of the first partner, they will find these sales arguments irrefutable. They are the crux of the sale.

Continuation of Partnership Assured

The insured buy-sell agreement assures continuation of the partnership business without interruption. Business momentum is not lost because the agreement to buy and sell has already been established, the price, or method for determining the price, has been established and the purchase money is immediately available. Consequently, everything moves forward with smoothness and dispatch. The surviving partners take over a going business, goodwill is preserved, customers are retained. The business continues free and clear of debt to the deceased partner's estate.

With the continuation of the business assured, the careers of the surviving partners are also assured. They need not experience the danger of a lifetime of hard work and dedication being wiped out due to the death of a partner. The insured buy-sell agreement enables them to control their own destiny, instead of destiny controlling their careers.

Liquidation Losses Avoided

As previously noted, the liquidation of a going business usually results in severe monetary losses; the forced sale of partnership assets invariably brings distress prices. But the most severe loss of all—and it is usually total—is that of goodwill. *The buy-sell agreement, which guarantees an uninterrupted, uncontested continuation of the business, protects partnership assets including the goodwill built up by years of effort and service.*

Role of Liquidating Trustee Eliminated

Without a plan for the continuation of the partnership made while all the partners are living, the surviving partners become liquidating trustees for the purpose of winding up the partnership. This places them in a fiduciary capacity. As such, they are restricted in their conduct and are strictly accountable for every asset of the partnership in closing out the business. Not only is this responsibility time consuming and burdensome, but it is loaded with risks.

There are many court cases dealing with the fiduciary relationship of surviving partners. Some of these cases have been extremely costly affairs, dragging out for years. Others have cropped up years after the death of a partner. All place the burden of proof of good faith and conduct squarely on the surviving partners.

With a buy-sell agreement, instead of becoming liquidating trustees, the surviving partners become purchasers backed up by a legally binding contract.

Unfavorable Reorganization Plans Averted

With an insured buy-sell agreement, the surviving partners are not forced to choose between liquidation or a new partnership with the heirs (or incompatible outside interests). They will not have to take in the surviving spouse of the deceased partner as an inactive partner contributing nothing, yet sharing in the profits. They will also not find it necessary to borrow the purchase price from an outsider on the condition that the lender be admitted into the business. They will not be forced to sign an agreement prohibiting them from competing if the heirs, or other interests, agree to buy them out.

The insured buy-sell agreement guarantees to the survivors that the only reorganization plan they will face is one they blueprinted while all the partners were alive— an automatic new partnership embracing the surviving partners.

Value Set for Estate Tax Purposes

Another advantage of a buy-sell agreement is that it may be used to set the value of an interest in a partnership for federal estate tax purposes. This is important because in the absence of such an agreement, the interest in a partnership is often valued at an unrealistically high figure for federal estate tax purposes (the IRS, of course, seeks to appraise the business at the highest value possible). The value of a partner's interest may be difficult to ascertain and, in the absence of an agreement, it is often necessary to resort to expensive litigation in the courts to resolve valuation controversies.

A suit between the representative and the government over the value of the partnership's interest will prove a costly affair. A bona fide and properly arranged buy-sell agreement will avoid this and will be valuable to the representative in settling the deceased partner's estate.

There have been instances in which binding buy-sell agreements have failed to establish the value of a partnership interest for estate taxes. Therefore, the guidelines under Code §2703 must be closely followed. Section 2703 requires that the purchase agreement must:

- be a bona fide business arrangement;

- not be a device to transfer the property to members of the decedent's family for less than full or adequate consideration; and

- have terms comparable to those entered into by persons in an arm's-length negotiation.

Establishing the value of a partnership interest for estate tax purposes is known as a *partnership freeze*. Freezing the value of a partnership interest limits the increase in value paid by the surviving partners and also limits the increase in the deceased partner's gross estate for federal tax purposes. Special care, however, must be taken to comply with the valuation rules specified under Code §2701. IRS Code Sections 2701–2704 govern the process of asset valuation with regard to transfers of certain interests in corporations or partnerships.

The Partnership Business Is Enhanced

An insured buy-sell agreement will also enhance the business. Customers or clients of the partnership, knowing that the death of a partner will not destroy the continuity of the firm, will not be hesitant about entering into long-term contracts or business dealings.

Employees of the partnership, aware that a death will threaten their jobs, are more prone to remain loyal, efficient and productive employees.

Lending institutions, knowing that a partnership buy-sell agreement backed up by the life insurance exits, will be much more receptive toward extending a favorable line of credit over the years.

Finally—and most importantly—the partners themselves know where they stand. Each is aware that if fate decrees him or her a surviving partner, continuance of their business and career is assured. All the partners can thus give their full attention and best efforts to the job at hand, secure in the knowledge that, come what may, plans have already been established for the firm's future.

These four factors—solid customer relations, stable employment, a strong credit position and peace of mind—spell out additional profits for the partners while they are all living.

■ SUMMARY

In this chapter we have discussed the legal, tax and social issues regarding partnerships. From our discussion, we have concluded that the most efficient way to transfer ownership interests at the death of one of the partners is an insured buy-sell agreement created while all partners are living. The plan should enable the surviving partners to acquire the deceased partner's interest and continue the business. The estate, on the other hand, should receive cash for the agreed upon value of that interest in lieu of participating in the business. The plan should be definite, certain and binding on all parties concerned, so that the rights of each are fixed. It must also be adequately financed to guarantee that the surviving partners will have the funds to carry out the agreement. The only plan that achieves all these objectives is a buy-sell agreement funded by life insurance. It is the ideal solution to the problems of both the surviving partners and the heirs.

■ CHAPTER 5 QUESTIONS FOR REVIEW

1. The definition of *partnership* includes all of the following EXCEPT
   A. voluntary association
   B. two or more members
   C. engaged in for profit
   D. limited liability for all members

2. All of the following are characteristics of a general partner EXCEPT

A. shares in control and management

B. contributes capital

C. shares in profits

D. shares in liability only to the extent of capital contribution

3. In a two-member partnership, when one partner dies the survivor becomes

A. sole owner of the partnership

B. a partner with the heirs of the deceased partner

C. the liquidating trustee

D. the executor of the deceased partner's estate

4. What two choices concerning the business face the surviving partner after the death of a partner?

A. Liquidate or dissolve

B. Reorganize or incorporate

C. Liquidate or reorganize

D. Dissolve or incorporate

5. In an entity purchase plan, who buys the interest of a deceased partner?

A. The partnership

B. The other partners

C. The heirs of the deceased

D. Employees of the business

6. In a cross-purchase plan, who buys the interest of a deceased partner?

A. The partnership

B. The other partners

C. The heirs of the deceased

D. Employees of the business

7. A partnership with five partners will require how many life insurance contracts to complete an insured cross-purchase buy-sell agreement?

A. 5

B. 6

C. 10

D. 20

6

Close Corporations

T he third major form of business entity to be examined is the close corporation. The advantages and disadvantages of the corporate form are discussed, along with a consideration of the S corporation. The closely held corporation is one in which the owners are often actively involved in the management of the business. As a result, planning for the deaths of the major stockholders has much in common with planning for the death of a partner or sole proprietor. In this chapter, we will focus both on what is similar to these other entities and what is unique. The practical problems faced by heirs and surviving shareholders are addressed, along with the role of insurance in resolving these difficulties.

We have seen that sole proprietorships are one form of business organization and partnerships are another. Next we're going to look at a third form, one where life insurance sales and other opportunities abound—*close corporations.*

Unlike the sole proprietorship and partnership, a corporation is a *legal and taxable entity,* separate, distinct and apart from its shareholders. Unlike the sole proprietorship and the partnership, a corporation is not automatically dissolved at the death one of its shareholders. One of the principal advantages of the corporate form is continuity of life beyond that of the original shareholders.

The term *close corporation* refers to the fact that the company is closely held by a limited number of owners; contrast that with the open—or publicly held—corporation with an unlimited number of owners. Shareholders of publicly held corporations usually buy their stock on a recognized exchange or through the NASDAQ system. They may have a vote at shareholder meetings but normally do not have much to do with the day-to-day operation of the business.

Which type of corporation offers a better market for you as a life agent or financial advisor? Let's look at it this way. It is the close corporation that usually has the owners as active managers of the business, probably making up the firm's board of directors as well. It's a closeness that resembles a partnership in many ways. The death of an owner can have a much greater impact on the closely held corporation and its other shareholders than on a publicly held corporation. That's why our emphasis in this chapter will be on the close corporation and the opportunities this market presents to you.

■ ■ ■ ■ ■

■ CORPORATIONS IN GENERAL

Both publicly held and closely held corporations have three important characteristics that set them apart from other business organizations. One is their existence as *separate legal entities* apart from their owners, another is *limited liability* for the owners themselves as shareholders and the third can be termed *shareholders' rights*.

Separate Legal Entity

A corporation is a separate legal entity, distinct from the individuals who own its stock. Thus when an owner dies or transfers his or her stock ownership, the business is not legally affected. In other words, it is not automatically dissolved as in the case of a partnership. On the contrary, its span of life is limited only by its charter and state law. Usually, the corporation's life is perpetual.

Limited Liability

Limited liability means that shareholders are not personally liable for the corporation's debts beyond their own investments. They can lose what they have invested in the firm, but they are not individually liable to the extent of all of their personal assets as well, as they are with a proprietorship or partnership.

Shareholders' Rights

Another important characteristic of corporations is the rights that belong to their shareholders. Unlike general partners, corporate shareholders do not automatically share in the management of their corporation. However, they do have rights by virtue of their ownership. The most important of these rights are:

1. *The right to dividends.* Shareholders have a general right to share in any surplus profits of the corporation in proportion to the amount of stock they own. They receive their share of profits in the form of dividends declared by the board of directors. Dividends, which are corporate funds derived from earnings and profits, are distributed at the *discretion* of the board of directors.

   As a general rule, dividends are paid only from corporate surplus. *Surplus* is the amount by which the value of total assets of a corporation exceeds the sum of its liabilities and capital stock. Normally, surplus is derived from profit earned by the corporation. Thus, if the corporation does not earn a profit, dividends will not usually be paid.

   On the other hand, the fact that the corporation may enjoy a profit in any given year does not mean that dividend payments will automatically be declared. For example, the directors may prefer to pour the profits back into the business for expansion or other business purposes.

2. *The right to inspect books and records.* Shareholders have the right to inspect the books and records of the corporation, without regard to the number of shares they own. This can be an especially valuable privilege for shareholders owning minority shares, because it can enable them to determine whether or not their investment is being properly managed.

3. *The right to attend shareholders' meetings and vote.* Shareholders have the right to attend shareholders' meetings and to vote on certain matters at these meetings. More important, these voting rights entitle the shareholders to participate in the election of the corporation's board of directors. While not all shares of stock carry voting rights, *common stock* usually includes this privilege. We'll assume in this chapter that all stock under consideration carries voting privileges.

4. *The right to transfer stock.* Shareholders have a general right to dispose of their stock at will. In open or public corporations, this privilege is constantly being exercised. Millions of shares of stock are bought and sold every day on stock exchanges or through dealers. This general right, however, may be restricted by the corporate charter or by a contract between the shareholders. This is common in close corporations. Frequently, the corporation or the other shareholders must first be given the opportunity to buy the stock of a shareholder who wants to sell.

■ CLOSE CORPORATIONS

The legal characteristics of corporations and shareholders' rights generally apply to both open and close corporations. But some of them take on new—and limiting—dimensions when applied just to close corporations. Let's look at the distinctions.

Limited Liability

Close corporation shareholders often choose incorporation over partnership because of limited liability. Bear in mind, however, that the shareholders typically are directors and officers as well. Therefore, for practical purposes, the protection of limited liability often takes on a minor role if the corporation is relatively new, or if its financial standing is somewhat shaky. Creditors and lending institutions might hesitate to enter into transactions based strictly on the financial strength or assets of the corporation. Creditors frequently require the personal guaranty of the shareholders before extending credit. Thus, shareholders in close corporations often must obligate themselves personally in order to carry on their businesses. Such outstanding personal obligations can affect all parties concerned when a close corporation shareholder dies.

Dividends

The shareholders of a close corporation—as active employees of the firm—usually receive most of the profits in the form of salaries. This is as it should be, since profits usually are attributable to the experience and skills of the shareholder executives. However, some profits inevitably must be retained in the business if it is to grow and flourish.

Thus, dividends may be declared only occasionally, and often in modest amounts. The full impact of a nonexistent or limited dividend policy is usually not realized until a shareholder dies and subsequent dividends distributed to heirs who receive the decedent's stock do not come close to replacing the salary he or she was earning.

Transferability of Stock

While shareholders normally may sell their stock at any time, the market for shares of close corporation stock is severely limited. It is not sold on an exchange or through dealers. Often, the only individuals interested in purchasing the stock—or the only persons to whom the stock may be sold by contract—are the other shareholders of the corporation. Additionally, there is a question as to whether other shareholders have the money and the inclination to buy the decedent's shares. Thus, the advantage of being able to sell or transfer the stock may not be much of a practical benefit in a close corporation.

Management of the Corporation

Shareholders, as such, have no authority to participate directly in the management of the corporation. However, as stated earlier, they do elect a board of directors who manage the corporation. No director can individually act for the corporation in his or her capacity as a director, but can act only collectively with fellow board members.

The day-to-day affairs of the corporation are run by the *officers* of the corporation. The officers are usually the president, vice president, secretary and treasurer. These officers are appointed by the board of directors and are responsible to the board.

A shareholder can be a director and/or an officer of the corporation. As a matter of fact, most top officers of corporations own stock in their companies. This is particularly true in close corporations, where the shareholders, directors and officers are usually one and the same.

S Corporations

It is appropriate at this point to mention and describe a certain type of close corporation known as an *S corporation.* An S corporation is a corporation whose shareholders have elected, under IRS Code 1361, to be treated for federal income tax purposes essentially as a partnership, with all income, gain, loss, credits and other income tax attributes passed through to the shareholders in much the same manner as a partner receives an allocatable share of partnership tax attributes. However, not all corporations are eligible to elect S corporation status. A corporation must meet certain requirements regarding the number and kind of its shareholders, its classes of stock and its sources of income. The significance of S corporation status will be clarified below, in our discussion of corporate taxation.

■ TAXATION OF CORPORATIONS

Though a thorough treatment of corporate taxation is beyond the scope of this course, a brief overview is warranted. As a practitioner, the ability to market your sales and services to close corporations requires a working understanding of the tax issues corporate business owners face.

To begin with, because a corporation is a distinct legal entity, it is taxed as a distinct entity. The federal government imposes income taxes on corporations just as it does on individuals. Currently, corporate income tax rates are as follows:

Taxable Income	Tax	Tax Rate on Excess
$0–$50,000	$ 0	15%
$50,001–$75,000	$ 7,500	25
$75,001–$100,000	$ 13,500	34
$100,001–$335,000	$ 22,250	39
$335,001–$10,000,000	$ 113,900	34
$10,000,001–$15,000,000	$ 3,400,00	35
$15,000,001–$18,333,333	$ 5,150,00	38
Over $18,333,333	$6,416,667	35

A 5 percent surtax is charged on income over $100,000 until the benefit of the 15 percent and 25 percent rates is canceled; as a result, taxable income between $100,001 to $335,000 is taxed at 39 percent. Also, income over $15,000,000 is subject to an additional tax of the lesser of $100,000 or 3 percent of the excess over $15,000,000; thus, taxable income between $15,000,000 and $18,333,333 is taxed at 38 percent. Most *personal service corporations,* those performing services in the fields of health, engineering, architecture, accounting, actuarial science, performing arts or consulting, pay a flat 35 percent rate on corporate taxable income.

Double Taxation

A significant tax issue facing closely held corporate owners is *double taxation.* Double taxation arises from the tax imposed *first* on the corporation and *second* on the corporation's shareholder-owners to the extent of dividends they receive. In most cases, shareholders must report dividends received on their individual income tax returns and pay taxes on them. Since dividends must generally be paid from the corporation's earned surplus, the company pays an income tax on the amount of dividends when earned and the owners pay a second income tax when dividends are received. Consequently, dividends are double taxed.

One of the benefits to shareholders under an S corporation is the avoidance of this double taxation. (This is also available to members of some limited liability companies—see Ill. 6.1.) Because all income or loss is passed through to the shareholder-owners individually and taxed as individual income or loss, there is essentially no taxable income at the corporate level. As a result, where individual rates for shareholder-owners are lower than the applicable corporate rate, a decision to adopt Subchapter S treatment (if the corporation qualifies) can result in significant income tax savings since S corporations generally pay no federal income tax at the corporate level.

You can see that the rights of shareholders differ in many respects from those of partners. The problems created by the death of a shareholder are somewhat different from those created by the death of a partner. Let's examine next the problems created by the death of a close corporation shareholder.

▪ WHEN A SHAREHOLDER DIES

When a shareholder dies, the corporation does not come to an end. Remember that a corporation is an entity, separate and distinct from its shareholder-owners. The death of a shareholder does not have any legal effect on the life of the business. The deceased shareholder's interest in the corporation passes to the heirs and there is no legal disturbance to the corporation or to its business affairs. Notice the emphasis on the word *legal*. Practically speaking, the death of a close corporation shareholder *will* affect the business, to one degree or another, and will affect the surviving shareholders *unless plans are formulated while all of the shareholders are living.*

For all practical purposes, many shareholders of a close corporation conduct themselves and their business affairs as though they were partners. For example, they work together as a team and their shareholder and director meetings resemble informal business sessions rather than formal gatherings. Decisions are usually reached quickly and unanimously. Unfortunately, this situation can change quickly when a shareholder dies.

Management Disrupted

Remember that the corporation usually loses an important member of the management team, regardless of whether the deceased shareholder held a majority or minority interest. This loss can be a serious blow to the corporation because of the deceased's role as a key member of management. While the business continues legally, it can suffer financially until the surviving shareholders can restore a balanced management team.

Heirs Acquire Interest

At the very moment that the surviving shareholders are faced with internal management problems, their difficulties are compounded by a more serious external problem. The deceased shareholder's interest is now owned by his or her family. In many situations, family members will not have been active in the corporation before the shareholder's death and may be unqualified to take part in the everyday management of the corporation. This does not, however, prevent the heirs from demanding a voice in corporate affairs, even though they lack the experience and skill to contribute toward its profits and earnings.

Let's examine the effect of shareholder-heirs on the surviving business owners.

If the Survivors Are Majority Shareholders

Surviving majority shareholders must remember that the heirs of minority shareholders have certain legal rights that cannot be ignored. These rights can be used to harass and frustrate the corporation unless the minority shareholders are treated more liberally than good business judgment might otherwise dictate.

ILL. 6.1 ■ *Limited Liability Companies: The Best of Both Worlds?*

The *limited liability company* (LLC) is a relatively new form of business entity created by state statute. As the LLC's name suggests, this business form generally provides limited liability for its members. The "members," those who will be equity holders in the LLC, can be individuals, corporations, partnerships, trusts, estates, other LLCs or other business entities. Typically, an LLC must have two or more members, although some states allow for one member LLCs. All members may participate in the LLC's management. While the statutes vary from state to state, generally an LLC is created by drafting documents called articles of organization and filing these documents with the appropriate state agency.

What makes the LLC form so attractive is that while it provides the limited liability usually associated with the corporate form, it may also offer the pass-through tax advantages associated with partnerships. (While an S corporation can provide these benefits, the LLC is not subject to the ownership restrictions that apply to S corporations.) The Tax Code does not address LLCs explicitly but Revenue Rulings have established guidelines regarding the taxation of an LLC. Whether an LLC will be taxed as a corporation or a partnership depends on whether the LLC possesses the following corporate characteristics: (1) continuity of life; (2) centralization of management; (3) limited liability; and (4) free transferability of interest. If the LLC possesses three or more of these characteristics, it will be taxed as a corporation. Otherwise, it will be taxed as a partnership.

A detailed discussion of these corporate characteristics and how they are analyzed in the LLC context is beyond the scope of this text. We should note that creating an LLC that will be taxed as a partnership is easier in some states than in others. Certain states have LLC statutes referred to as "bulletproof statutes." These statutes are drafted in such a way that all LLCs that meet the statute's requirements will qualify for partnership tax treatment. In other words, LLCs created under a bulletproof statute will lack at least two of the characteristics set out above. Other states have "flexible" or "check the box" statutes that allow more freedom in determining the characteristics of the LLC. However, an LLC created under a "flexible" statute is not assured treatment as a partnership for tax purposes. It may be taxed as a corporation or a partnership depending upon the provisions of the LLC's operating agreement and the provisions contained in the state statute. In states with flexible statutes, it is not enough to meet the state statute's requirements; careful attention must be paid when drafting the organizing documents and operating agreements in order to assure partnership taxation.

Heirs have as weapons at their command the right to vote at corporate meetings, to take part in the election of directors and to demand information concerning the management of the corporation. To compound the problem, majority shareholders who are directors and officers also have responsibilities to the new minority interests.

As directors, the survivors must exercise the highest degree of care and good faith in all business dealings. Otherwise they will be liable to the minority shareholders for any losses that result. As officers, they are personally liable if they exceed or abuse their authority—or are guilty of neglect or mismanagement in the discharge of their duties—to the injury of any shareholder of the company.

Inactive minority shareholders are sometimes sensitive to any action by the directors or controlling shareholders that they feel is against their own interests. Surviving majority shareholders are fortunate if they can avoid unpleasantness and bickering in every shareholders' meeting. At worst, a hostile, expensive and time-consuming shareholders' suit could be brought by the heirs against the survivors.

If the Survivors Are Minority Shareholders

Surviving minority shareholders are in an even more precarious position than are surviving majority shareholders. The heirs of the deceased majority shareholders—as new owners of the controlling interest of the corporation—are now actually in a position to determine corporate policy while survivors are left to do all of the work.

Such heirs have the power to select a board of directors that is suitable to them and to their purposes. Through this power to elect directors, the majority shareholders also have the power indirectly to select the corporate officers. Thus, the surviving shareholders—who may be officers of the corporation—may have their jobs at stake if they do not conform to the policies set forth by the heirs. Keep in mind that ownership of minority stock is no guarantee of a continuing job as an officer—or even an employee—of the corporation.

The heirs also have the power to force a declaration of dividends regardless of any long-range growth program that the survivors, as executives of the corporation, deem essential for the corporation. Accustomed to a standard of living based primarily on the salary the deceased majority shareholder received from the corporation, the heirs may want to "take up the slack" by instituting a much more liberal dividend policy, even to the extent of reducing the surviving shareholders' salaries.

Heirs who exercise their legal right to a controlling voice in the corporation are usually not making a deliberate attempt to destroy the surviving minority shareholders. On the contrary, it more often represents an honest effort to accomplish what the heirs think is best for the business. The difficulty, of course, arises because their ideas as to what is good for the business may differ substantially from those of the surviving minority shareholders.

Surviving minority shareholders can easily find themselves the victims of innocent and honest intentions of heirs whose lack of business ability and desire for dividends can ultimately spell an end to the business and to the jobs of the surviving shareholders.

If the Survivor Is an Equal Shareholder

There are many close corporations carried on by two people who are equal owners of the stock. Many started out as partnerships incorporated because of tax considerations and the advantages of limited liability and perpetual existence. But the owners still run the business as partners, who work together informally and harmoniously. In this sense, such businesses may be thought of as *incorporated partnerships* since the workload and the profits are divided equally.

When an equal shareholder dies, the survivor is faced with the prospect of carrying the full burden of work while taking on a new equal, but inactive, partner (the surviving spouse, for example). This is only half the story, however. Each shareholder votes one-half the stock, but neither actually controls the corporation. In most cases, this new arrangement has little chance of succeeding. The inevitable conflict of interests as to dividends and company objectives between parties having equal ownership and voting power will frequently bring about an irreconcilable deadlock that can be resolved only by liquidating the corporation and the surviving shareholder's career as a business owner.

▪ ACQUIRING THE DECEASED SHAREHOLDER'S INTEREST

From your study of partnerships, remember that surviving partners face the alternatives of reorganization or liquidation of the partnership. In a close corporation, the threat of liquidation is minimized because the business does not automatically dissolve when a shareholder dies. But the corporation is faced with reorganization when the interest of a deceased shareholder passes through the individual's estate to his or her heirs. A management reorganization takes place because the heirs have a voice in the affairs of the corporation.

Heirs of a deceased shareholder may fit in a close corporation if someone in the family has been trained to take the deceased's place. Such an individual must be competent, compatible with the surviving associates and able to make a contribution toward the stability, growth and success of the corporation. In the majority of close corporations, an heir with these qualifications does not exist. We will study the situations where the corporate stock should be retained in the family later. Here, we will assume that the surviving shareholder should acquire the decedent's stock.

Unless there are restrictive contractual provisions to the contrary entered into while all the shareholders were alive, corporate stock is freely transferable. The heirs, therefore, are not obligated to sell to the surviving shareholders. There are a number of conditions under which they—or the deceased's representative—might sell to outsiders, even though the survivors would be the logical purchasers.

What can the surviving shareholders do to keep the heirs out of the business? Obviously, the sensible course of action is to buy the deceased's stock from the heirs. The logical decision for the heirs is to sell their stock if they are not qualified to contribute actively toward the earnings and profits of the business.

However, in the absence of proper plans made while all the shareholders are living, a buyout is loaded with obstacles. These obstacles are similar to those confronting the surviving partners in attempting to buy a deceased partner's interest. Let's briefly examine the major hurdles facing the surviving shareholders.

The Heirs Can Sell to Anyone

Under any one of the following situations, the stock of the deceased shareholder can be sold to an outsider:

- The representative may be forced to sell the stock promptly in order to raise cash for administration expenses, estate obligations and death taxes.

- The heirs themselves may have a desperate need of cash.

- The heirs may have no desire to own the stock and wish to dispose of it as quickly as possible to anyone who has the immediate cash.

In these situations, surviving shareholders with insufficient funds may find themselves confronted with the menacing possibility that the deceased's interest in the corporation can be sold to outsiders who have the cash to satisfy the representative's or heirs' desire for immediate sale of the decedent's stock.

This threat is particularly acute where the deceased shareholder owned the controlling interest in a successful close corporation. Here the survivors may find themselves bidding against business competitors who are eager to acquire a successful, going business on the one hand and to eliminate competition on the other. Many close corporations have been acquired by outside interests because the surviving shareholders could not come up with a satisfactory price within a reasonable time after the majority shareholder's death.

The Survivors Must Raise the Money

The heirs may recognize the surviving shareholders as the logical purchasers and prefer to sell to them rather than to outsiders. Therefore, they may be willing to make financial arrangements to enable the survivors to purchase the stock. However, the heirs also expect a fair price for the stock. Thus, the surviving shareholders face the same financial barriers that confront surviving partners in attempting to buy out a business interest.

Assuming they do not have the ready cash, the survivors have two choices: they can (1) borrow the money or (2) buy the stock on an installment plan. As we have discussed, these are both undesirable alternatives.

Borrowing Plan

An attempt to borrow the purchase price comes at the most inopportune time. The chances are that the corporation's credit has been impaired by the death of the shareholder. This is especially true where the deceased shareholder owned a controlling interest or where his or her personal credit provided the bulwark for a substantial portion of the firm's financial backing. As mentioned earlier, the limited liability concept is somewhat weakened in a close corporation because the corporation's credit is often tied to the personal credit of one or more of the shareholders. Where the deceased was a majority shareholder, death may dry up the firm's credit.

Another factor often precludes borrowing. Lending institutions are not eager to make loans when the management of the business is in a state of uncertainty after the loss of a key executive. Moreover, lenders know that any substantial loans to a close corporation—or to its shareholders for the purpose of buying out a business interest from the heirs—may put a severe financial strain on the borrowers for years to come. This in itself often makes such loans a poor risk.

Installment Plan

If they are unable to borrow the purchase money from a third party—or if they prefer not to—the surviving shareholders or the corporation itself might arrange an installment purchase plan with the deceased shareholder's heirs. The financial problems inherent in an installment plan are the same for shareholders as those for surviving partners. The surviving shareholders of the corporation will start out with additional debt at a time when its management and financial positions are at their shakiest. Moreover, installment payments must be met with previously taxed dollars.

■ PROBLEMS FACED BY THE HEIRS

Close corporation stock in many instances does not belong in the hands of the heirs. Legally, of course, the heirs are entitled to the stock. But when stock falls into their hands, adverse consequences often follow. Next we will discuss some of the major problems the heirs face if they receive the decreased shareholder's stock.

A Poor Investment

A person who becomes a shareholder in a close corporation usually takes on a full-time career as well as an investment. Income is chiefly in the form of salary for personal services rendered. This is natural and proper, for in most cases much of the close corporation profits are attributable to the shareholder's management skill rather than the earnings on the shareholder's invested capital. Also typical of close corporation shareholders is that the shareholder's stock interests constitute the bulk of their estates. At death, these factors create problems that make their business interests poor investments for the surviving heirs. Following are some of the reasons why.

Need for Income

Heirs need income but as inactive shareholders who are not providing services or contributing to profits, their income from the corporation comes only from dividends. The surviving shareholders, called upon to conduct the business alone, feel that the profits should either go to them in the form of salary increases or be reinvested in the business for future growth and development. This conflict of interests usually results in unsatisfactory income for the heirs.

On the other hand, if the heirs' stock ownership is great enough to demand a continual and sufficient amount of dividend income, the financial strain may drive the corporation under or, at the least, drive the surviving minority shareholders out of the business. If the heirs are minority shareholders, they can expect little or no dividend income from their stock interest.

No Ready Market

Learning the hard way that their stock interest will not produce the necessary income, the heirs have no alternative but to sell the stock. Obviously, the ideal buyers are the surviving shareholders or the corporation itself. Rarely, however, does either have the necessary funds with which to buy the stock. The heirs must then look for an outside buyer.

Finding a buyer for a closely held stock interest can be an exceedingly difficult task. Anyone contemplating such a purchase would want reasonable assurance that credit has not been impaired by the shareholder's death. Unfortunately, this is often the time when credit is impaired. The prospective buyer would also want to be compatible with his or her new associates, but, under many circumstances, the surviving shareholders may resent new interests. Finally, the buyer would want the purchase to be a profitable venture.

If the heirs find an interested outside buyer in spite of these obstacles, they run headlong into their toughest problem—obtaining a reasonable price for the deceased's stock. It is always a shock when the sale of close corporation stock to outside interests does not bring the price the heirs assume it would. Yet, most outsiders who buy in are not willing to incur a disproportionate risk. They will normally accept only a bargain price. Hence, a distress sale usually results—at a distress price.

Lack of Estate Liquidity

The legal representative may be forced to sell some or all of the deceased's stock for an entirely different reason. Often, the principal asset of a typical close corporation shareholder is his or her business interest. This often creates a lack of estate liquidity. If other property in the estate is insufficient to pay debts, death taxes and funeral and administration expenses, some portion of the stock will have to be sold to raise money for estate settlement costs. If the stock must be sold at a sacrifice price—not an unlikely occurrence—further losses result.

▪ THE SOLUTION

The death of a close corporation shareholder can create serious problems for both the surviving shareholders and the heirs of the deceased. What is needed to overcome these problems is a *buy-sell agreement*—funded with life insurance—which has been set up by all of the original shareholders before a death occurs. This is the only available plan that guarantees that the survivors will acquire full ownership and control of the firm at the same time it bestows benefits on the heirs.

The Insured Buy-Sell Agreement

Just as in partnerships, the corporate insured buy-sell agreement takes two forms: the *cross-purchase plan* and the *entity plan* (in corporate situations the entity plan is often referred to as a *stock redemption plan*). In recent years, there has been a move toward a "wait and see buy-sell plan," which is a hybrid of a cross-purchase plan and an entity plan. It is worth repeating that the type of plan is up to the shareholders. In turn they should rely on the advice of their attorneys and accountants. From your personal standpoint it does not really matter which plan is selected. A buy-sell agreement is necessary in either case and each plan must be supported by the same amount of life insurance.

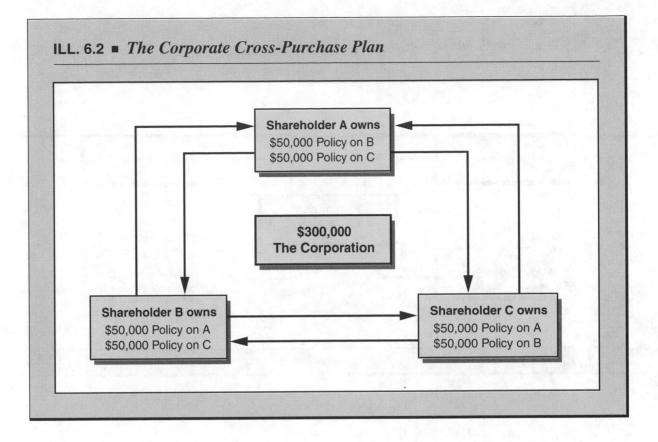

ILL. 6.2 ■ *The Corporate Cross-Purchase Plan*

The Cross-Purchase Plan

The cross-purchase plan in a close corporation is similar to that in a partnership. Under the buy-sell agreement the shareholders individually agree to purchase the interest of the deceased shareholder, and the estate of the deceased shareholder agrees to sell the interest directly to the surviving shareholders. The corporation is not a party to the agreement.

Each shareholder owns, is the beneficiary of and pays for insurance on the life of each of the other shareholders in amounts totaling the individual's share of the purchase price. When a shareholder dies, the surviving shareholders' life insurance on the decedent provides them with the purchase price to carry out the terms of the agreement. The deceased's estate then usually sells to the survivors the policies it owns on their lives. In rare instances, the estate may surrender the policies if the survivors do not have a need for them. (See Ill. 6.2.)

The Entity Plan

The entity plan also operates in much the same fashion in a corporation as it does in a partnership. The corporation—rather than the individual shareholders—owns, pays for and is the beneficiary of policies on the lives of the shareholders in amounts equal to each shareholder's interest in the corporation. Under this arrangement, the corporation becomes a party to the buy-sell agreement. When a shareholder dies,

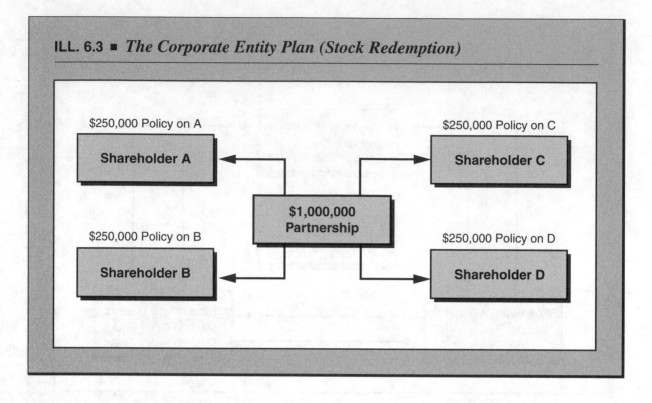

ILL. 6.3 ■ *The Corporate Entity Plan (Stock Redemption)*

$250,000 Policy on A
Shareholder A

$250,000 Policy on C
Shareholder C

$1,000,000 Partnership

$250,000 Policy on B
Shareholder B

$250,000 Policy on D
Shareholder D

the life insurance proceeds are paid to the corporation that in turn uses them to buy the deceased's stock from the estate.

As in the partnership context, the insurance premiums are not tax deductible regardless of whether they are paid by the shareholders individually or by the corporation. This is more than offset, however, by the tax-free receipt of the proceeds. (See Ill. 6.3.)

The Wait and See Plan

The wait and see buy-sell agreement is a relatively new plan that carries the characteristics of both the cross-purchase plan and the entity plan. As the name implies, the specific purchaser of a shareholder's business interest remains uncertain until the death of the shareholder. The typical wait and see buy-sell agreement would give the corporation the first option to purchase stock from the deceased shareholder's estate. If the corporation does not exercise this option, then the individual shareholders would have the second option to purchase this stock. Finally, if the shareholders themselves decide not to exercise their option, the corporation *must* purchase the deceased shareholder's stock. While the wait and see buy-sell agreement may seem like the best of both worlds, there may be family attribution problems in the event of redemption under the first option or the mandatory purchase provision.

Income Tax Considerations

The insurance premiums paid to fund a buy-sell agreement are not tax deductible because the premium payors are directly or indirectly beneficiaries of the policies. This is true whether the premiums are paid by the individual stockholders or by the corporation.

Transfer for Value

Generally, the proceeds of the life insurance policies are received income tax free under both plans. However, if the ownership of a policy was transferred for valuable consideration, the proceeds may be subject to ordinary income tax under the transfer for value rules. The amount subject to income tax would be the difference between the proceeds and any amounts paid for the contract plus total premiums paid. There are exceptions to the transfer for value rule, which would include the sale or transfer of the policy to the insured, or to the corporation in which the insured is an officer or shareholder. Please note that these exceptions *do not* include transfers between individual stockholders.

Basis of Surviving Shareholder

A cross purchase buy-sell agreement is often preferred over the entity buy-sell agreement because the shareholders in a cross-purchase agreement will receive a step-up in basis in the event of a fellow shareholder's death. For example, assume there are four shareholders that each own 25 percent of ABCD Corporation and each of the shareholders has a basis of $100,000. If A dies, BCD will receive a step-up or increase in their basis to the extent of the amount paid by each shareholder to purchase the deceased shareholders interest in the corporation. If B later sells his shares of the corporation for $700,000 and he paid $250,000 for A's shares, then his gain will only be $350,000 ($700,000 – [$100,000 basis + $250,000] for A's shares).

In an entity buy-sell agreement the value of each surviving shareholders stock will be increased proportionately to his or her stock interest. Unfortunately, the cost basis of each survivor's stock *will not* be increased, thus making the future sale by a surviving shareholder potentially less tax efficient than with a cross-purchase plan.

Provisions of the Buy-Sell Agreement

As you learned in our discussion of partnership buy-sell agreements, it is the function of an attorney to draft the stock buy-sell agreement because it is a legal document. Your function is to have a working familiarity with the important points of such agreements, particularly those relating to the life insurance policies, ownership of policies and the exercise of policy rights.

An insured buy-sell agreement must be tailored by an attorney to fit the particular needs of the close corporation in question. Nevertheless, all agreements deal with similar problems to the extent that the contents of various agreements follow a broad general pattern consisting of the following six commitments. As you study these commitments, bear in mind that any or all of them provide you with excellent sales points when talking to the prospect:

1. the shareholders' agreement not to sell their stock without first giving the other shareholders, or the corporation, an opportunity to buy at a stipulated price;

2. the surviving shareholders', or the corporation's, agreement to buy, and the agreement that the estate of the deceased shareholder will sell, the shares of stock of the deceased shareholder;

3. the agreed upon purchase price to be paid by the surviving shareholders or the corporation, or a definite method or formula for determining the price at the time of death;

4. an agreement by the shareholders, or the corporation, to buy and maintain stated amounts of life insurance with which to finance the purchase of the stock;

5. an agreement as to who will have ownership and control of the policies, and, under a cross-purchase plan, the disposition of the policies on the lives of the surviving shareholders owned by the deceased's estate; and

6. an agreement as to the time period and method of paying any balance of the purchase price in excess of the insurance proceeds; alternatively, the method of disposing of insurance proceeds in excess of the purchase price.

Life Insurance: The Only Realistic Funding Vehicle

A close corporation prospect who initially questions life insurance as the method for funding a buy-sell agreement probably does not understand its numerous advantages over other funding vehicles. Once the individual is aware of the true costs and headaches inherent with other financing arrangements, an appreciation of life insurance to back up the buy-sell agreement will result.

Cost Efficient

Funding the agreement with life insurance eliminates the necessity—next week, next year or some time in the future—of purchasing the stock for one hundred cents on the dollar. Even for that rare group of shareholders or close corporations with the funds immediately available to carry out the agreement, the insured plan is a much less expensive way of financing the agreement.

For the majority who would not have the funds available, the alternatives of borrowing the money or buying the stock in installments are not only expensive but, in many cases, unavailable.

Accumulating the purchase price through advance savings is also unrealistic for two reasons: (1) the obstacles to accumulation from competing uses for funds and (2) the inability to ascertain how long the savings period must be, since it is impossible to predict when death will occur.

Life insurance, on the other hand, is ideal for funding a buy-sell agreement because the *death that creates the need for cash simultaneously creates the cash to meet the need.*

Life insurance makes it possible to amass the necessary purchase money with discounted dollars. The premium payments rarely equal the face amount because the plan is self-completing for the full amount at death. In addition, because permanent insurance involves a plan in which compound interest is generally earned and credited tax-free each year to the policies' cash values, the annual premium may amount to only 3 percent or 4 percent of the purchase price.

Funds Corporate Surplus

These general life insurance advantages apply to partnerships and close corporations. In addition, there is another advantage that relates strictly to an entity plan in the close corporation.

Most states will allow a corporation to redeem its own stock from a deceased shareholder to the extent that the purchase dollars are available in its surplus. But few close corporations will have $100,000, $200,000 or $500,000 or more of available cash in surplus for purchasing a shareholder's interest at death. Life insurance will fund corporate surplus with the required amount of purchase dollars exactly at the time they are needed.

By funding the agreement with life insurance, the surviving shareholders are assured of total ownership of the corporation.

■ ADVANTAGES OF BUY-SELL AGREEMENTS

We have examined the purpose, types and general provisions of corporate buy-sell agreements. We have also reviewed a number of reasons that life insurance is an excellent source of funds for the agreement. Now, let's take a look at the two in combination. Working together, they provide you with some extremely powerful sales points.

Advantages to the Survivors

First, let's look at the advantages such a plan can provide for the surviving shareholders. They include eliminating inactive interests, guaranteeing the purchase of a deceased owner's stock, guaranteeing funds for the purchase and stabilizing the corporation.

Inactive Interests Are Eliminated

Ownership of shares in a close corporation usually belongs in the hands of the active shareholders. When a block of stock is separated from the active management, the spirit of harmony and cooperation that prevailed among all the shareholders before one of them died can be impaired. Active management and ownership in a close corporation must be kept together for the corporation to thrive.

By acquiring ownership of *all* the shares under an insured buy-sell agreement, the surviving shareholders have the opportunity to continue the business free of conflicting interests.

Opportunity to Buy Stock Is Guaranteed

In the absence of a buy-sell agreement, the survivors have no assurance that they will be able to acquire the decedent's interest. If the stock passes to the heirs, they are not obligated to sell. If the decedent in his or her will has instructed the representative to sell the shares, the survivors must outbid all other offers.

The insured buy-sell agreement makes both ownership and the purchase price definite and timely.

The Purchase Funds Are Guaranteed

Without funds available to execute the plan, the buy-sell agreement becomes meaningless. Financing through life insurance eliminates the possibility that the surviving shareholders or the corporation would not have the purchase price on hand when death occurs. It also provides the survivors with the most convenient and economical method for obtaining the necessary funds.

The Corporation Is Stabilized

An insured buy-sell agreement also offers advantages to the shareholders while they are living. This fact cannot be emphasized too strongly. An insured buy-sell agreement has a strong stabilizing effect on all parties directly or indirectly concerned with the corporation.

Employees, knowing that the business will continue in the hands of the survivors among the present shareholders, can concentrate on their jobs, secure in the knowledge that their careers will not be disrupted by an owner's death. Expensive employee turnover is reduced to a minimum.

Bankers, knowing of the existence of the insured buy-sell agreement, will think more favorably about extending a line of credit for business expansion or other needs.

Suppliers and customers, aware that plans have been made for the orderly continuation of the corporation, will be more willing to enter into business dealings on a long-term basis.

And, most important, *the shareholders,* confident that their futures are more assured by the existence of the insured buy-sell agreement, can devote their full time and energies to making their close corporation a successful, profitable organization.

Advantages to the Heirs

We have learned that stock in a close corporation is normally a poor investment for inactive heirs. Yet its very existence creates an estate that is high in value but low in cash. An insured buy-sell agreement will overcome these two serious problems and provide other advantages as well.

Prompt and Full Payment Is Guaranteed

With an insured buy-sell agreement, the representative does not have to haggle with the survivors or other interested buyers over the price of the stock. The heirs receive a price for the stock considered satisfactory to the shareholders while they were living.

Cash Certainty Substituted for a Poor Investment

Stock in a close corporation usually belongs to the active shareholders who have the talent and initiative to meet the challenges and risks in a business venture. By the same token, this type of investment may not be best for the heirs. The insured buy-sell agreement substitutes certainty for uncertainty.

"Freezing-Out" Process Avoided

In the absence of a buy-sell agreement, the surviving shareholders probably won't relish doing all the work and dividing the profits with the heirs. The result may be an attempt to *freeze out* the heirs by raising salaries and lowering or eliminating dividends. While the spouse may have an outside chance to force dividends in court, the costs of litigation are high and the likelihood of success is low because there must be evidence of actual fraud.

Cash Provided for the Estate

Every estate has obligations that must be met before assets can be distributed to the heirs. Funeral and administration expenses, debts and death taxes can range from 10 percent to 50 percent or more of the total assets. Cash to meet these expenses is uncommon in the estate of the close corporation shareholder who, through the years, has poured available cash back into the business. An insured buy-sell agreement provides the money necessary to meet all estate obligations.

Value Set for Estate Tax Purposes

As with partnerships, a buy-sell agreement may be used to set the value of an interest in a closely-held corporation for federal estate tax purposes. To achieve this purpose, the agreement must be a bona fide business arrangement and have terms comparable to those entered into by persons in an arm's-length negotiation. The agreement may not be a device to transfer the property to members of the decedent's family for less than full or adequate consideration.

This feature is important because, in the absence of such an agreement, the stock of a close corporation often is valued for federal estate tax purposes at an unrealistically high figure. Because close corporation stock is not listed on an exchange or sold over the counter, its value is difficult to ascertain or appraise. In the absence of an agreement, it is often necessary to resort to expensive litigation in the courts to

ILL. 6.4 ■ *Business Valuation by the Courtroom Method*

Title of Case	Estate	Value Per Share IRS	Court	IRS: Estate	Court: Estate
Anderson, Est. of J. Macfie v. Comm T.C.M. 1972-125	$2,500.00	$3,000.00	$2,500.00	120%	100%
Bader v. U.S. 3 AFTR 2d 1824	$521.83	$1,250.00	$643.00	240%	123%
Baltimore National Bank v. U.S. 136 F. Supp 642	$1,509.64	$2,500.00	$2,300.00	166%	152%
Bartol, Exr. v. McGinnes 6 AFTR 2d 6123	$84.00	$87.00	$84.00	104%	100%
Braverman, Est. of Morris v. Comm. T.C.M. 1962-21	$2,058.25	$4,000.00	$2,724.92	194%	132%
Brush, Est. of Marjorie Gilbert v. Comm. T.C.M. 1963-186	$3.00	$7.38	$5.50	246%	183%
Burda, Est. of L.J., 2 T.C.M. 497	$3.00	$20.00	$5.00	667%	167%
Damon, Est. of Robert Hosken v. Comm. 49 T.C. 2914	$3.00	$6.00	$3.75	200%	125%
Ewing, Est. of Anna C. v. Comm. 9 T.C.M. 1096	$2,400.00	$6,530.00	$4,750.00	272%	198%
Garrett, Est. of Jessie Ring v. Comm. 12 T.C.M. 1142	$50.39	$285.65	$285.65	567%	567%
Gessel v. Comm., 41F. 2d 20	$310.00	$475.00	$475.00	153%	153%
Hanscom, Melville, 24 B.T.A. 173	$50.00	$100.00	$100.00	200%	200%
Heinhold, Est. of Matthew, 363 F.2d 329	$3.17	$10.00	$8.00	315%	252%
Huntington, Est. of Henry E., 36 B.T.A. 698	$10,638.35	$16,559.67	$16,100.99	156%	151%
Katz, Est. of Sidney L. v. Comm. 27 T.C.M. 825	$290.00	$800.00	$300.00	276%	103%
Kuhn, Est. of Harold L. v. U.S. 28 AFTR 2d 6239	$1,290.43	$1,700.00	$1,355.00	132%	105%

ILL. 6.4 ■ *Business Valuation by the Courtroom Method (continued)*

Title of Case	Estate	Value Per Share IRS	Court	IRS: Estate	Court: Estate
Levenson, Est. of David J. v. *Comm.* 18 T.C.M. 535	$252.85	$1,033.00	$900.00	409%	356%
Leyman, Est. of Harry Stole v. *Comm.* 40 T.C. 100	$536.00	$700.00	$630.00	131%	118%
Louis, John J. Jr. Exr. v. *U.S.* 18 AFTR 2d 6318	$3.25	$20.00	$5.34	615%	164%
Luckenbach, Est. of Edgar F. v. *Comm.* T.C.M. 1958-38	$114.75	$229.52	$175.00	200%	153%
Maxcy, Est. of Gregg v. Comm. 28 T.C.M. 783	$9,984.95	$11,747.00	$9,984.95	118%	100%
Maxcy, Est. of Hugh G. v. Comm. 28 T.C.M. 783	$7,018.68	$9,358.24	$7,018.68	133%	100%
Miller, Est. of Mary K. v. Comm. 18 T.C.M. 1127	$500.00	$1,150.00	860.00	230%	172%
Mitchell, Est. of Julian v. Comm. 256 F. Supp. 913	$700.00	$980.00	$800.00	140%	114%
Obermer, Nesta v. U.S. 238 F. Supp. 29	$3,350.00	$5,921.67	$3,947.78	177%	118%
Perlick, Est. of Hilbert R. v. U.S. 31 AFTR 22	$38.00	$66.19	$39.17	174%	103%
Reynolds, Est. of Pearl Gibbons v. Comm. 55 T.C. 172	$316.67	$2,637.50	$1,600.00	833%	505%
Ridgely, Est. of Mabel Lloyd v. U.S. 20 AFTR 2d 5946	$106.00	$115.00	$115.00	108%	108%
Righter, Est. of Jessie H. v. U.S. 27 AFTR 2d 1691	$424.00	$1,000.00	$700.00	236%	165%
Rothgery, Est. of Bernard Anthony v. U.S. 31 AFTR 2d	$60.72	$582.00	$582.00	958%	958%
Russell, William E. Exr. v. U.S. 18 AFTR 2d 6278	$1,360.00	$2,100.00	$2,100.00	154%	154%
Schneider-Paas, Est. of Alfred Johannes v. Comm. T.C.M. 1969-21	$4,761.90	$38,500.00	$23,809.00	808%	500%
Snodgrass, Est. of John Milton v. U.S. 23 AFTR 2d 1834	$53.00	$65.00	$53.00	123%	100%

ILL. 6.4 ■ *Business Valuation by the Courtroom Method (continued)*

Title of Case	Estate	Value Per Share IRS	Court	IRS: Estate	Court: Estate
Thompson, Est. of Barbara F. v. Comm. 18 T.C.M. 801	$225.00	$535.00	$283.50	238%	126%
Tompkins, Est. of Lida R. v. Comm. 20 T.C.M. 1763	$834.00	$12,725.85	$5,500.00	153%	659%
Wallace, Est. of Marvin R. v. U.S. 31 AFTR 2d 1395	$64.23	$147.00	$91.50	228%	142%
Worthen, Exr. (Stone) v. U.S. 7 AFTR 2d 1801	$100.00	$175.00	$104.00	175%	104%
Yeazel, Gilbert A. Exr. v. Coyle 21 AFTR 2d 1681	$304.11	$450.00	$400.00	148%	132%

solve the problem. If the Internal Revenue Service maintains that the stock should be valued at a higher figure than that proposed by the estate, the court usually will accept the IRS determination of value or fix a value of its own, unless the estate can support its valuation by legally admissible evidence.

As you can see from Ill. 6.4, court dockets are full of disagreement over business valuation. In this sample, the court averaged 211 percent higher than the estate's value, but the IRS valuation was even higher at 279 percent of the estate value! This is in addition to the estate spending substantial sums of money for attorneys, accountants and expert appraisers.

In addition to the valuation disagreements, the length of time to close an estate can become protracted in many instances. The average time delay in Ill. 6.5 is 7½ years. A buy-sell agreement might have averted this problem.

Illustration 6.6 tells a different story than the previous illustrations; namely that the court's decision was the exact duplicate of the valuation provided for in the buy-sell agreement. Buy-sell agreements can save valuable time and money to the deceased owner's heirs and surviving business owners, not to mention the inherent advantages to the practitioner who was instrumental in setting up the agreement.

In any event, a suit between the representative and the government over the value of the stock will prove a costly affair. A bona fide buy-sell agreement can avoid controversy and litigation and prove of valuable assistance to the representative in settling the deceased shareholder's estate.

ILL. 6.5 ■ *Delay in Closing Contested Estates*

Title of Cases	Time Elapsed Between Date of Death and Decision		
	Years	Months	Days
Atkins, Estate of Charles H.M. v. *Commissioner* 10 T.C.M. 997	3	6	4
Bader v. *U.S.,* 172 F. Supp. 833	7	9	24
Bendet, Estate of Louis, 5 T.C.M. 302	4	1	23
Bank of Calif. v. *Commissioner* 133 F. 2d 428	6	9	15
Brush, Estate of Marjorie Gilbert v. *Commissioner* 22 T.C.M. 900	5	3	2
Damon, Estate of Robert Hosken v. *Commissioner* 49 T.C. 2914	7	10	11
Ewing, Estate of Anna C. v. *Commissioner* 9 T.C.M. 1096	7	6	24
Fitts, Estate of Cora Russell v. *Commissioner* 14 T.C.M. 1065	6	7	20
Garrett, Estate of Jessie Ring v. *Commissioner* 12 T.C.M. 1142	6	6	16
Goodall, Estate of Robert A. v. *Commissioner* T.C. Memo 1965-154	11	7	13
Gould v. *Gronquist* 3 AFTR 2d 1788	2	10	28
Harrison, Florence M. et al v. *Commissioner* 17 T.C.M. 776	5	7	3
Heinold, Estate of Matthew I. v. *Commissioner* T.C. Memo 1965-6	6	4	2
Houghton, Albert B. v. *U.S.* 15 AFTR 2d 1359	8	11	25
Laird, Mary Du Pont 38 B.T.A. 926	10	10	29
Louis, John J. Jr. Exr. v. *U.S.* 18 AFTR 2d 6318	7	8	26
Luckenbach, Est. of Edgar F. v. *Commissioner* T.C. Memo 1958-38	14	10	11
Maxcy, Est. of Gregg v. *Commissioner* 28 T.C.M. 783	8	11	21
Miller, Est. of Mary K. v. *Commissioner* 18 T.C.M. 1127	7	0	29
Moore, Anna H. 13 B.T.A. 864	6	10	22
Nathan's Estate, In re, 166 F. 2d 422	7	4	11
Patton, Estate of Walter L., 10 T.C.M. 1066	7	3	16
Perlick, Est. of Hilbert R. v. *U.S.* 31 AFTR 22	6	11	9
Reynolds, Est. of Pearl Gibbons v. *Comm.* 55 T.C. 172	7	10	22
Ridgely, Est. of Mabel Lloyd v. *U.S.* 20 AFTR 2d 5946	4	8	9
Righter, Est. of Jessie H. v. *U.S.* 27 AFTR 2d 1691	9	10	25
Rothgery, Est. of Bernard Anthony v. *U.S.* 31 AFTR 2d	10	10	0
Russell, William E. Exr. v. *U.S.* 18 AFTR 2d 6278	6	6	5
Schneider-Pass, Est. of Alfred Johannes v. *Comm.* T.C. Memo 1969-21	11	1	19
Snodgrass, Est. of John Milton v. *U.S.* 23 AFTR 2d 1834	5	5	6
Tomkins, Estate of 20 T.C.M. 1763	8	10	24
Wilber National Bank 17 B.T.A. 654	7	2	15

Average time delay in above cases 7½ years; a buy-sell agreement might have averted this problem.

ILL. 6.6 ■ *Buy/Sell Agreements Can Fix the Value*

Type of Business	Name of Case	Value Per Share		
		Value as Provided in Agreement	IRS Challenge	Court's Decision
Advertising Agency	Mitchell, Estate of John T.H. 37 B.T.A. 1	$123.45	$348.63	$123.45
Coal Wholesaler	May et al., v. McGowan 194 F.2d 396	$ 0.00	$100.00	$0.00
Electrical Parts Wholesaler	Salt, Albert B. 17 T.C. 92	$ 20.00	$ 60.00	$ 20.00
Mental Hospital	Slocum v. U.S. 256 F. Supp. 753	$100.00	$1,108.62	$100.00
Newspaper	Littick, Orville B. 31 T.C. 181	$298.50	$384.94	$298.50
Optical & Lens Manufacturer	Lomb v. Sugden 82 F. 2d 166	$69.44	$100.00	$69.44
Real Estate Developer	Fieux's Estate 149 N.E. 857	$100.00	$200.50	$100.00
Shoe Store	Third National Bank v. U.S. 64 F. Supp. 198	$100.00	$150.00	$-100.00
Soft Drink Bottler	Strange, Estate of John Q. 42,247 P-H Memo T.C.	$250.00	$5,953.16	$250.00

■ THE ORDERLY RETENTION OF A SHAREHOLDER'S INTEREST

Thus far we have examined why shareholders, in most cases, should contractually agree to sell their business interest to the surviving shareholders at death. Now we turn to a second situation—the shareholder of a close corporation who justifiably wants this business interest to be retained for his or her family's benefit at death.

Usually this situation will arise where the close corporation is controlled by one family. In such corporations, factors are often present that indicate the prospect's stock should be retained in the family.

The following five factors are important when determining whether a corporate interest should be retained by the family:

1. *Commercial corporation.* The corporation should have a going-concern value separate from the personal services of the shareholder. Typical of this type is a manufacturing or mercantile corporation that has capital assets in the form of real estate, machinery, inventory, fixtures and other equipment essential to the operation of the business. When the shareholder dies, these assets are not lost to the corporation.

2. *A controlling stock interest.* We have discussed at length the disadvantages of a minority corporate interest in the hands of the heirs. If stock in a close corporation is to be retained in the family after the shareholder's death, it is usually desirable that the stock interest be of sufficient size to guarantee that control will rest with the heirs.

3. *Capable successor management.* Unless this factor is present at the shareholder's death, the interest should be sold. It would be ill-advised to retain a business interest for the family's benefit if there is no suitable successor management to manage it. There is no such problem, of course, when a capable and experienced family member will succeed to the management of the corporation. If such a family member does not exist, however, the corporation must have competent, salaried successor management ready and willing to stay on after the shareholder's death to run the business for the family.

4. *Adequate working capital.* The corporation should have adequate working capital to stabilize the business during the transition period following the controlling shareholder's death. In line with this, it should have little or no long-term debt that would drain substantial earnings away from the family. If inactive family members, such as the surviving spouse, are expected to derive future income from the business, the corporation must continue a reasonable policy of dividing profits between that portion retained for growth and dividends to be paid to shareholders.

5. *Adequate estate liquidity.* We now come to the crux of our story. As you will learn shortly, planning for the retention of a family corporation is futile unless effective plans are also made to supply the deceased shareholder's representative with adequate estate liquidity.

While the practitioner cannot control factors one, two or three, you can make factors four and five possible through corporate-owned life insurance. If the first three factors exist—a commercial corporation, a controlling stock interest and capable successor management—you can demonstrate how life insurance, working in combination with a specific federal tax provision, can conserve the estate and make an individual's dreams for perpetuation of the family corporation come true. The

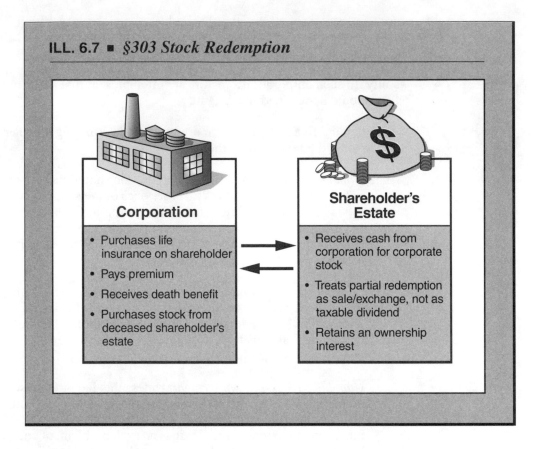

ILL. 6.7 ■ *§303 Stock Redemption*

Corporation

- Purchases life insurance on shareholder
- Pays premium
- Receives death benefit
- Purchases stock from deceased shareholder's estate

Shareholder's Estate

- Receives cash from corporation for corporate stock
- Treats partial redemption as sale/exchange, not as taxable dividend
- Retains an ownership interest

balance of this chapter will explore a plan that is tailor-made for this type of corporation.

§303 Stock Redemptions

As a rule, the bulk of a controlling shareholder's estate consists of business interest. At death, for estate tax purposes, stock is valued at its current market value. Hence, a prosperous business often brings about an estate that is high in value but lacking in liquidity needed to pay the costs of estate settlement. Therefore, the controlling shareholder who is satisfied that the company could continue to operate successfully after his or her death should arrange for sufficient liquidity to pay estate settlement costs. Without such liquidity, a representative would be forced to dispose of a substantial amount of the stock to pay debts and expenses of the estate. Such stock disposition might destroy the shareholder's hopes for retention of the business with the family.

Since accumulating sufficient estate liquidity is a difficult task—and because the average business owner pours a lot of excess earnings back into the business—such liquidity normally must come from outside sources if a business interest is to be retained. Fortunately, today this can be done if proper action is taken. This action is a §303 stock redemption plan.

A Former Dilemma

In the past, the estate of a typical sole or controlling owner of a close corporation faced a tax squeeze that often made retention of the business impossible. Consider the dilemma that formerly existed.

On the one hand, if the estate considered selling some of its stock to outside interests to raise cash, family control of the corporation would have been jeopardized because normally only a controlling interest was salable. A minority interest in a close corporation has little appeal to outsiders.

On the other hand, if the corporation itself had sufficient cash surplus to buy enough of the deceased's stock to provide the representative with funds to pay the costs of estate settlement (which is exceedingly rare in close corporations), the purchase price of the stock usually was considered a *dividend* and *taxable* as ordinary income to the estate. (Only by selling *all* of the deceased's stock to the corporation was the representative certain of avoiding a taxable dividend.) This placed the estate in the unhappy position of paying both estate and income taxes on the stock the representative was forced to sell to the corporation in order to raise cash. Since this meant losing most of the money to taxes, this plan was usually rejected.

All too often the representative had no choice other than to sell the stock to outsiders or liquidate the corporation. This meant not only a severe shrinkage in the estate, but the end of a going business as far as the deceased's family was concerned.

The Solution

Congress recognized the particular dilemma of the shareholders anxious to retain control of the business within the family. It enacted §303 of the Internal Revenue Code specifically as a relief measure. Section 303 permits an estate, under certain conditions, to sell stock to the corporation and treat the cash received for the stock as a *capital gain* rather than as *ordinary income*. The proceeds of this sale can then be used to pay death taxes and funeral and administration expenses.

While this is a helpful piece of tax legislation, particularly for family corporations, it does not in itself provide the corporation with the funds necessary to buy the permitted amount of stock from the controlling shareholder's estate. Remember, while Congress, attorneys and accountants can offer help from the legal and tax standpoint, only the practitioner is in the position to deliver a check to the deceased owner's heirs.

Cash funds available in close corporations sufficient for partial stock redemption generally are as rare today as they were before the enactment of §303. Without ready cash in the corporation to redeem the permitted amount of stock in the deceased's estate, §303 is of little value. But corporate-owned life insurance and §303, working together, can be a logical solution to the problem of retaining a going business within the family.

The advantages of life insurance in conjunction with §303 will be discussed later, but first let's examine this significant tax provision.

The Mechanics of §303

As we indicated, §303 permits under certain conditions an estate to redeem stock that is includable in the decedent's gross estate to provide estate settlement costs and to treat the redemption as a sale or exchange rather than a fully taxable dividend. Under sale or exchange treatment the redemption proceeds are taxable only to the extent that proceeds exceed the basis of the stock in the estate.

For this treatment to apply, certain conditions must be met. The significant conditions are as follows:

- The value of the deceased's stock must exceed 35 percent of the adjusted gross estate (the gross estate less estate settlement costs and liabilities).

- The redemption must be from a shareholder whose interest in the estate is reduced by payment of death taxes and funeral and administration expenses.

- The redemption cannot exceed the expenses incurred for death taxes and funeral and administration expenses.

In arriving at the more than 35 percent determination, stock in two or more corporations will be treated as stock in a single corporation if the decedent owned more than 20 percent of the total outstanding stock by value in each corporation. The stock, to qualify for §303 redemption treatment, must be included in the gross estate.

The amount of stock redemption proceeds qualifying for §303 treatment is limited to death taxes (with interest, if any) plus funeral and administration expenses of the estate that are deductible for federal estate tax purposes. Any generation-skipping transfer tax imposed on the value of the decedent's stock is treated as an estate tax for purposes of §303.

Provided these conditions are met and the stock is redeemed within the time limits set in §303, the tax treatment accorded by §303 will generally apply. It may not be a totally tax-free redemption since appreciation of the stock's value may result in a capital gains tax. Still, the combined tax will generally be less than if the redemption were subject to ordinary income taxation as a dividend distribution rather than as a sale or exchange.

Life Insurance and §303

Life insurance goes hand in hand with a §303 redemption. A corporation seldom has sufficient cash in its surplus to redeem the permitted amount of stock. It is organized to make money. If it tied up working capital for redemption purposes, the ordinary progress of the business would suffer.

Insurance on the stockholder's life, owned by and payable to the corporation, will supply the funds necessary to acquire the amount of stock permitted under §303. Life insurance releases, rather than ties up, needed working capital. Only the annual premium—a small fraction of the total amount needed at death—must be set aside each year. The first annual premium will automatically create the entire sum necessary.

Thus, through life insurance, a shareholder is able to provide liquidity for his or her estate and retain the corporation in the family with corporate dollars rather than personal funds.

While adequate estate liquidity is the first prerequisite to preserving a close corporation, another factor runs a close second. Typically, the majority or sole owner of a close corporation is also its chief executive officer. Death takes away the knowledge, the vision, the driving force, the experience, the sales ingenuity and the individual's administrative skill. All those traits that molded the corporation into a profit-making enterprise are gone.

A shareholder who is sincere in the desire to leave a going business must recognize that providing adequate estate liquidity does not in itself guarantee the future success of the business. Further, the individual must consider what effect the loss of management ability will have on corporate profits. Death can bring these consequences:

- less liberal terms from suppliers—anxiety on the part of creditors as to the corporation's future without this key leadership;

- a tightening of financial assistance—the tendency of bankers to adopt a wait-and-see policy with respect to company stability; and

- a slowdown in company business—the hesitancy of customers concerned about future production.

Without funds to absorb the shock of the principal shareholder's death, many close corporations have failed to survive. Life insurance is the most practical offsetting factor. While it does not replace the abilities of the controlling stockholder, death proceeds can make the business strong enough financially to see it through the adjustment period.

Over and above the amount of life insurance needed to buy stock from the deceased's estate under §303, the corporation should insure the shareholder's life to protect itself against the loss of this management ability. This portion of the total becomes key-executive life insurance. (Chapter 9 is devoted to an extensive examination of key-executive life insurance.) With the corporation in a strong financial position, the family can continue the business as a going concern.

Advantages of §303 Redemptions

Let's review the advantages of an insured §303 stock redemption plan. These six advantages are actually selling points for you.

1. The corporation will have the funds necessary to redeem the permitted stock under §303.

2. The estate will have the cash necessary to pay death taxes and funeral and administration expenses.

3. The money received by the estate for the stock that is redeemed will not be a dividend fully taxable as ordinary income.

4. If the value of the deceased's stock should increase during life, the existence of corporate-owned life insurance assures the estate that the corporation will have funds to absorb an increase in the stock's value.

5. The deceased is able to accomplish estate objectives without spending personal (after-income tax) funds.

6. Life insurance proceeds exceeding the amount needed to redeem the permitted amount of stock can act as key-executive insurance to indemnify the corporation for the loss of management ability. The family will inherit a corporation that is financially strong enough to tide them over a difficult period.

Section 303 of the Internal Revenue Code has created a tailor-made sale for you. When your prospecting efforts among close corporations uncover a family corporation, be on the alert immediately for a §303 sale. If family and corporate circumstances dictate a retention of the business after the controlling shareholder's death, and the estate qualifies for a §303 redemption of stock, the need for life insurance to fund the plan should become readily apparent to the controlling shareholder and his or her financial advisors.

■ SUMMARY

The close corporation refers to an incorporated entity whose ownership resides with a limited number of owners. While similar in legal characteristics to publicly held corporations, close corporations differ in many respects regarding issues such as limited liability, dividend payments, stock transferability and corporate management. The owners/shareholders of a close corporation are faced with the dilemma of double taxation arising from the taxes imposed both at the corporate and personal level. However, the owners may elect S status or incorporate as an LLC, which allows pass through of all income, gain, loss or credits directly to the owners themselves. When a shareholder dies, the corporation continues in existence, although there are numerous issues and problems faced by both the surviving shareholders and the heirs. Some of these issues and problems are a disruption in management, heirs selling their interest in the corporation to outsiders and the lack of liquidity in the decedent's estate.

The solution to these issues and problems is a properly drafted insured buy-sell agreement. This agreement can transfer ownership of the business, provide liquidity to the decedent's estate and set a value of the business for estate tax purposes, all on a cost-efficient basis. There is and always will be a needed demand in the business community for the competent and conciliatory practitioner who aids the owners of closely held corporations in achieving their business continuation goals.

■ CHAPTER 6 QUESTIONS FOR REVIEW

1. Which of the following is NOT a characteristic of a corporation?

   A. Separate legal entity from the owners
   B. Death of an owner dissolves the business
   C. Limited liability
   D. Usually separate taxable entity from its owners

2. Which of the following does NOT describe the typical close corporation?

   A. Dividends seldom paid
   B. Owners usually officers
   C. Limited market for the transfer of its stock
   D. Shareholders have unlimited personal liability

3. What type of corporation is taxed similarly to a partnership?

   A. C corporation
   B. S corporation
   C. Close corporation
   D. Public corporation

4. How does the highest marginal corporate tax rate compare to the highest marginal individual tax rate?

   A. Lower
   B. Higher
   C. The same
   D. Depends on the type of corporation

5. Which of the following statements about §303 stock redemptions is correct?

   A. The value of the deceased's stock must equal 50 percent of the adjusted gross estate.
   B. The redemption is treated as a dividend.
   C. The stock is purchased by the corporation.
   D. The proceeds from the redemption may not be used to pay death taxes.

6. If a $900,000 close corporation with three equal owners has a cross purchase agreement, how much life insurance would shareholder A have on either shareholder B and C?

   A. $75,000
   B. $150,000
   C. $300,000
   D. $600,000

7. If the same corporation had an entity plan, the corporation would own how much life insurance on each shareholder?

   A. $75,000

   B. $150,000

   C. $300,000

   D. 600,000

8. All S corporations begin as C corporations who then elect S corporation status under IRS Code section

   A. 1361

   B. 361

   C. 415

   D. 761

9. Without a prior agreement, the stock of a deceased shareholder can be sold to an outsider

   A. to pay for estate obligations and/or estate taxes

   B. because the heirs need the cash

   C. the heirs have no desire to hold the stock

   D. all of the above

10. How much would a close corporation with $335,000 in taxable income pay in federal income tax?

   A. $22,250

   B. $52,500

   C. $113,900

   D. $136,150

..... *Section Three*

Planning Opportunities with Business Entities

7

Business Disability Plans

I n previous chapters, we looked at financial consequences that can result from the death of a business owner or shareholder. Now we turn to another equally serious hazard—disability. For many individuals, the chances of disability prior to retirement age may be two or three times greater than that of death. Business disability plans for both partners and corporate shareholders are examined, along with a discussion of the role of disability buyout plans.

So far in your study you have been examining the financial consequences that can occur at the death of a business owner or shareholder. You now know that insurance on the lives of these individuals can prevent financial hardship.

In this chapter the subject will be a little different. It introduces an equally serious hazard—*disability*. We're talking about a serious, incapacitating disability that takes a person off the job, possibly permanently.

We'll be looking at how a business organization can protect itself, its owners and its employees against the economic hardships created by a serious disability that prevents the individual from earning a living. We'll see how various forms of disability insurance can help mitigate the financial impact when an individual is disabled—an impact which in some ways can be more severe than the kind resulting from death or retirement.

In many ways, the same disability income problems are faced by all businesses whether they are proprietorships, partnerships or close corporations. But there are some differences as well. As we will see, the income tax treatment of disability insurance premiums and benefits differs somewhat, depending upon the type of business organization.

■ DISABILITY: THE IGNORED HAZARD

While disability is not inevitable, it is too common to be ignored. Actuarial data from a report by the Society of Actuaries suggests that the chances of a man age 37 being disabled for 90 days or longer is 5.5 times greater than the likelihood of death, while for a man age 47 the likelihood of disability over death is 3.5 times. Clearly the risk of disability is greater than the risk of death. So how would a business fare if the owner was disabled for a long period? How long could the organization carry a nonproducing owner during a long-term disability?

Even where competent help is available to fill in for the disabled owner, he or she still has a voice in the business. To keep income sufficiently high during the period of disability, the owner, to the extent it is necessary, may direct the business down the road of high current yield, making little provision for the future. This is a course a business owner would probably avoid if given a choice. But the circumstances of a disability may leave no other alternative.

From a financial standpoint, disability should be feared more than death. A disabled person continues to be an expense to his or her family. Let's look at some of the expenses facing a self-employed business or professional person who is disabled even temporarily.

Expenses of Disability

When disability strikes, self-employed people face a burden of expenses much greater than that of salaried employees. They have the usual expenses connected with any sickness or injury—doctor and hospital bills, nursing care and continuing family expenses. Mortgage payments still must be met, children educated, utility bills paid and food purchased during the period of disability. In addition to these personal expenses, other expenses arise simply because they are business owners.

Businesses must continue operating; business overhead also continues. The office lease is not suspended because of the business owner's disability; rental payments continue. Telephone and other utility services must continue to be available and paid for. Employees must remain at their jobs, and they must be paid. All of the other fixed expenses normal and customary in the operation of the business continue to accrue and must be met.

What we obviously are leading up to is a discussion of the methods of insuring against the hazards of disability. Fortunately, they *can* be successfully insured against. Why insure? Basically, self-employed owners must insure against the expenses of disability because, typically, they cannot afford to cover these costs during a period of disability.

Let's turn now from the reasons *why* self-employed owners should provide against the consequences of disability to *how* this can be done.

■ DISABILITY INCOME INSURANCE

The disability of self-employed business or professional people takes its gravest toll in reducing the income available to meet ever-present family expenses. When self-employed persons list their family's monthly expenses and combine them with the expense of running their businesses they soon realize that if they are disabled, their savings probably will be insufficient to cover everything. Furthermore, even after they have recovered and are back to work, the consequences of a disability may continue to be felt in the form of depleted savings and huge debts.

The most practical way for self-employed owners to protect themselves against such losses is to purchase disability income insurance. This insurance replaces income lost during periods of disability.

There are four ways that disability income insurance is sold:

1. as riders to life insurance policies;

2. as individual disability income policies;

3. as association-sponsored insurance through a professional or trade association; and

4. as part of an employee group insurance program.

Disability Income Insurance Riders

The *disability income rider* available on some life insurance policies provides for the payment of a specified monthly income during the continuance of total disability. Typically, the disability must have existed for at least six months and commenced prior to age 55 or 60. The monthly disability income is fixed according to the face amount of the life insurance policy. For instance, some companies will write $100 of monthly disability income for each $10,000 of life insurance, with a maximum monthly income of $500 or, in some cases, $750.

The disability income rider is not a widely sold benefit, even though the extra insurance premium charged is reasonable when compared to the premium for other forms of disability income insurance. This probably is due to its limited coverage. The maximum monthly income benefit is small when compared to income needs of today. Furthermore, the benefit in many instances is not available past age 55 or 60, when so many total disabilities occur. Finally, many insureds could not wait six months for the first payment.

For these reasons, this method of providing disability income usually is inadequate for self-employed business owners. Because of business overhead expense, in addition to their living expenses, they require larger incomes—dollars not tied to a life insurance policy's face amount. Furthermore, a plan that is not available past age 55 or 60 is unrealistic. One satisfactory answer to their needs is the individual disability income policy.

Individual Disability Income Policies

The *individual disability income* policy is the most widely used method today for self-employed business or professional people to hedge against the hazards of disability. The amount of the monthly disability income is related to the current income of the insured; however, the amount of disability income available to the insured is never 100 percent of earned income. The reason is that a disabled person who could replace total income by insurance would in theory lose the incentive to return to work promptly. Disability insurance is designed to replace *after-tax* income rather than *before-tax* income. As a result, most insurance companies will insure a person for no more than 60 percent of monthly earned income with a lesser percentage applicable to income in excess of a given amount. Companies also generally limit the total amount of disability insurance they issue, regardless of the insured's income.

With individual disability policies there are as many policy options as there are types of policies. Some of the key issues surrounding these policies are the definition of disability, residual disability and continuance provisions.

For a business owner, the disability policy should protect him or her in the event that they cannot continue to remain gainfully employed in their chosen profession. A policy with an "own-occupation" definition of disability should be purchased to insure the disabled owner is allowed an adequate amount of time to recuperate without being forced back to the workplace under the less favorable "any occupation" definition.

If the insured returns to work on a part-time basis, and the policy does not include a provision for residual disability, the benefits payments will terminate. Residual disability provides an incentive for the insured to return to work while keeping the benefits payments albeit at a reduced amount. The typical formula for a residual disability clause is:

$$\text{Benefit amount} = \frac{\text{Loss in Net Income}}{\text{Base} - \text{Period Net Income}} = \frac{\text{Maximum Full}}{\text{Disability Amount}}$$

The continuance provisions of the policy address the length of policy term, policy renewability, and the option to cancel or change premium rates. The best policy is a noncancelable policy, which usually provides that the insurance company cannot cancel the policy prior to age 65 and that the policy will continue in force as long as premiums are paid with no increase in premium.

A critical consideration relating to individual disability income insurance is the length of the insured disability period. Does the self-employed person, for example, need lifetime coverage for sickness and accident hazards?

There is no one answer to this question. The situations of individual business owners vary so much that no rule of thumb could apply to all of them. Nevertheless, self-employed business owners can assess their own needs if they keep in mind the relevant factors. For example, according to the National Council of Compensation Insurance, among those between the ages of 35 and 44 who become disabled, 74 percent will return to work. However, of those between the ages of 45 and 54 who become disabled, only 52 percent will return to work. Age is but one factor to be considered in this decision.

The extra premium required to obtain lifetime payments, or payments to age 65, is not large. The length of coverage is a choice individuals must make depending on the risk they are willing to assume and the premium they are willing to pay.

In considering the purchase of a disability income insurance policy, many self-employed business or professional people have a source available to them not open to the general public: the coverage available through trade and professional associations.

Association Disability Income Insurance

More and more *professional and trade associations* today offer disability income insurance coverage to their members. Because this coverage is becoming such an important aspect of the disability income market, we should recognize some of the distinctive characteristics and limitations of this coverage.

The initial annual premium for association insurance is quite low; this is its chief selling point. The association through which the insurance is purchased serves as the medium to bring the insurer and the insured together. It promotes the sale of the insurance to members and in return the association receives some income. This can be in the form of a nonaudited expense reimbursement or a percent of sales as an incentive to use a particular insurer's policy.

There are drawbacks, however, that limit the effectiveness of this coverage. First of all, there can be a long waiting period after disability occurs before benefits begin. In some instances benefits do not start until after a full year. Also, the coverage extends only to members of the association while in the active practice of their particular trade or profession. Thus loss of membership in the association, or a change in one's trade or profession, could result in loss of coverage. As a result, this coverage cannot be relied upon as a primary source of disability insurance. Yet it is equally evident that it can be a most valuable source for "backup" coverage in conjunction with an individual disability income policy.

There is, of course, one other method of obtaining disability income insurance, one that plays an important role in the businessperson's search for economic security: group insurance.

Group Disability Income Insurance

Group disability income coverage is offered by insurance companies, generally, as part of an insurance package. Such a package usually includes life insurance and medical expense protection as well as income replacement. Self-employed business or professional people with a specified minimum number of workers—including themselves and any partners—may qualify on a nonmedical basis for group disability coverage. Thus insurance from this source is limited to those self-employed owners with a sufficient workforce to meet the minimum group requirements. For those who can qualify, it is worthwhile coverage for both self-employed persons and their employees.

The Business Owner's Employees

The emphasis to this point has been primarily on the disability expenses of business owners, but business owners are employers, and their employees also may become disabled. Employees, too, have medical care expenses, house payments and food bills. They, too, must meet living expenses in the event of their disability. The typical employer generally feels some sense of responsibility to employees, but the ability to help is, in most cases, limited. Larger payrolls make the employee disability problem more acute in the corporate setting than for the sole proprietor or the partnership. Consequently, we have deferred a more detailed examination of this subject to our discussion of corporations later in this chapter. At this point it merely should be noted that disability income insurance can solve the problems for the employee as efficiently as it does for business owner-employers themselves.

We have seen the various methods of providing disability income through insurance and the scope of benefits available. Now let's take a look at the tax principles applied to this insurance.

■ TAXATION OF DISABILITY INCOME INSURANCE

There are tax consequences arising from the payment of disability income insurance premiums, as well as from the receipt of the benefits. These consequences are not the same for the self-employed as they are for employees.

ILL. 7.1 ■ *Taxation of Disability Benefits*

Taxation benefit results when premiums are employee paid vs. employer paid

	Employee-Paid Premium		Employer-Paid Premium	
Monthly Benefit	$5,500		$6,500	
Annual Premium	$2,000		$2,400	
	$2,780	Gross earnings required in 28 percent tax bracket to pay premium personally	$1,584	Net cost to corporation in 34 percent tax bracket
		Results When Disabled		
Annual Benefit	$66,000		$78,000	(gross)
Federal Tax	– 0		– 11,027*	(net)
Net Income	$66,000		$66,973	
Cost to Obtain	$ 2,780	(gross)	$ 2,400	(gross)
	$ 2,000	(net)	$ 1,584	(net)

In every instance, calculations will vary depending upon the prospect's personal and corporate tax brackets. Individual counseling on the part of the practitioner is very important.

* Assumes $20,000 deductions (mortgage interest, real estate taxes, etc.), reducing the $78,000 disability benefits received to $58,000, net, resulting in a 28 percent joint return tax bracket, and federal tax in the amount of $11,027.

Premiums

Self-employed business or professional people who are sole proprietors or partners can deduct as a business expense premiums paid for disability income insurance covering *only their employees*. It makes no difference whether the policies are of the group or individual type. Furthermore, the premiums will not be considered income to the employees for income tax purposes.

Premiums that proprietors or partners pay toward *their own* disability income insurance *cannot* be deducted as a business expense. This rule also applies regardless of whether the policies are group or individual. Further, the premiums may not be deducted as a medical expense, for they fail to qualify under the tax law as an expense for medical care.

Benefits

Generally, disability benefits paid to an employee under a wage continuation plan are treated as taxable income if the employer paid the premiums. There are exceptions to this if the employee has retired on a disability pension prior to age 65 because of a permanent and total disability. But the general rule is that if the employer pays the premium in an employer-sponsored plan, the benefits must be included in the employee's gross income.

Premiums that individuals—whether self-employed or employees—pay for their own personal disability income insurance are not deductible; however, these individuals gain on the other end, since all of the disability benefits they receive are tax free. (See Ill. 7.1.)

With the foregoing discussion in mind—why self-employed business owners should insure against the hazards of disability, the different types of coverage available and the tax treatment of disability income plans—we can now turn to another key area where disability can have a significant impact in a business setting. That is the disruptive effect a disability will have in a partnership when one of the partners becomes disabled.

■ DISABILITY PLANS FOR THE PARTNERSHIP

We saw in Chapter 5 that, in the absence of an adequately funded buy-sell agreement, the death of a partner can raise nearly insurmountable problems for the surviving partners and the family of the deceased partner. We saw further that many, if not all, of these problems could be eliminated by having a buy-sell agreement supported with life insurance covering the partners.

As far as the partnership is concerned, there is little distinction between the actual physical death of a key partner and a permanent disability. Obviously, a business agreement that provides only for the purchase of a deceased partner's interest has not covered all possible hazards. A disabled partner could hamper the business operations of the partnership seriously. He or she creates a double liability for the partnership. It owes this person a share of the partnership profits yet in many cases it will have to hire a suitable replacement.

Business or professional partners should make some arrangement for the purchase or readjustment of the interest of a partner disabled with a long-term ailment.

The partnership can accomplish this by doing two things:

1. having its partners personally purchase as much *short-term* disability income insurance as possible under maximum limits and

2. arranging in the articles of partnership or in a separate agreement for the purchase of a disabled partner's interest after some predetermined period of *long-term* disability.

Short-Term Disability Income

First, the partners purchase short-term individual disability income insurance policies on themselves. Each partner would be the owner and beneficiary of the contract on his or her own life. Any disability income payments should go directly to the disabled partner and not flow through the partnership. While the premiums each partner pays for disability coverage are nondeductible personal expenses, the disabled partner would receive any disability payments tax free.

To avoid tax complications, it is best for the individual partners personally to own the disability income contracts. If the partnership wants to assure itself that insurance premiums are paid on time, it could have the premium notices mailed to the partnership address. Then it could pay the premiums and debit each partner's drawing account.

Advantages of Short-Term Disability Income

If a partner becomes disabled, his or her desire is to receive a share of the partnership profits, or another sum equal in amount. There should be relatively little difficulty in accomplishing this, provided the disabled partner has purchased the disability income insurance as suggested. Under the policy, the partner would receive a monthly income equal to, let us say, 60 percent of average monthly income. By prior agreement, the partnership would be committed to pay only the remaining 40 percent of his or her normal share of the profits.

Such a plan has advantages for all parties concerned. The disabled partner receives a regular income, and the individual's family can make the mortgage or rent payments and meet other continuing financial needs. On the other hand, the partnership no longer faces the distasteful task of eliminating the disabled partner's draw. The partnership is assured that the disabled partner will have adequate income. Yet it has reduced its commitment to this person and is in a position to hire a competent replacement if necessary.

Effective as this plan is, however, it often answers only the problem of relatively short-term disability that lasts less than two years. What about the long-term disability that lasts two years, five years or even longer?

ILL. 7.2 ■ *If Disability Has Continued for Two Years*

	At the end of two more years			At the end of five more years		
Age When Disabled	This % Will Still Be Disabled	This % Will Have Died	This % Will Have Recovered	This % Will Still Be Disabled	This % Will Have Died	This % Will Have Recovered
Age 25	64.7	5.3	30.0	46.2	9.7	44.1
Age 35	69.9	6.8	23.3	53.7	12.3	34.0
Age 45	74.6	10.4	15.0	58.6	19.9	21.5
Age 55	78.0	14.1	7.9	59.7	28.5	11.8

The Mandatory Buyout

Actuarial data from the report by the Society of Actuaries mentioned earlier reflects a significant statistic regarding long-term disability. That is, the older a person is when he or she becomes disabled, the chance of a disabled partner's returning to work becomes more and more remote. A partnership can arrange a suitable disability income plan through insurance and a partial sharing of the partnership profits. However, even a 40 percent sharing to a nonproductive, disabled partner can become burdensome to the partnership over the period of a long-term disability of two, five or more years. This is especially true for personal service partnerships.

The best solution in these cases is for the partners to agree to a mandatory purchase of a disabled partner's interest over a predetermined period of disability. Most agreements include the following general provisions:

1. an agreement for the purchase of disability income insurance covering each partner—the benefit to be a specified percentage of the partner's regular draw—the premium to be paid either by the individual partner, or the partnership, but with the partners owning their own individual policies;

2. a provision that the difference between the insurance benefit and the partner's regular draw would be made up by the partnership;

3. a provision that spells out the period of time during which partnership payments would continue—such as two years or some other stipulated period. If the disability continues after this period, the disabled partner's interest would be purchased under terms and conditions set forth in the agreement; and

4. a provision that includes a formula for valuation of a partner's interest—one which is realistic, yet flexible enough to reflect changing circumstances.

This provides a brief outline of the provisions generally included in a buyout agreement. There are, in addition, some other factors that should be taken into consideration. We will discuss two of the most common factors that the partners should consider providing for in the agreement.

The Disabled Partner's Recovery

What happens if the disabled partner recovers and wants to return to work? In the first place there is nothing to prevent the other partners from agreeing to halt the purchase upon the recovery of a disabled partner. The agreement itself could contain a provision for this eventuality.

However, while it is possible for such a recovery to occur, the probability is that a person disabled two years or longer stands small chance of recovery. This is especially true of individuals in the 35-to-55 age class—the most common age when businesspeople consider the problems of disability. This statement is borne out by actuarial data from the Society of Actuaries. (See Ill. 7.2.)

The sole proprietorship and the partnership are particularly susceptible to the ravages of disability. These forms of business organization generally distribute profits immediately. As a result, both insurance and personal expenses continue to mount, and some source must be found to supply the income necessary to meet these expenses. Furthermore, in a partnership, the partners must consider the probable effect of a long-term disability on the partnership, and the desirability of purchasing or adjusting a partner's interest after such an event.

Funding the Purchase Price

Once an individual has applied for and purchased a disability income insurance policy up to 60–70 percent of average personal income, additional disability income insurance may not be available. In this event, other arrangements must be made to accomplish the mandatory purchase.

One method would be to purchase a disability buyout policy as a separate contract from a disability income policy. Another method would be to spread the purchase payments over a considerable period of time. This would permit the partnership to make its payments out of current operating income. Still another method would be to defer purchase until the disabled partner dies. The purchase of the decedent's interest would be mandatory at that time and would be arranged in the fashion described in Chapter 5. The partners' lives would be insured by those having the duty to purchase. At death, the insurance proceeds would simply be exchanged for the partnership interest. Illustration 7.3 explains the disability buy-sell agreement.

■ DISABILITY PLANS FOR CLOSE CORPORATIONS

Disability income planning is obviously as important for corporation employees as it is for the self-employed and their employees. Insofar as individual employees are concerned, problems caused by disability are the same whether they work for small close corporations or large, publicly held corporations. Because of the nature of the problem, however, our concern here is primarily with the closely held corporation—a corporation owned by a small group of shareholders, all of whom generally are employed by and participate actively in the management of the corporation.

Disability Income and the Corporate Employee

As previously noted, in many respects the owners of close corporations face disability income problems almost identical to those of sole proprietors or partners. All need to provide for both personal and business expenses in the event of their own disabilities. In addition, all have responsibilities to their disabled employees.

This latter aspect of the disability problem is more pronounced in the case of small corporations, that often employ many people. Yet their ability to help, in many cases, is limited. The close corporation is in no better position to meet the medical costs and family living expenses of employees on an out-of-pocket basis than is the sole proprietor or partnership. Furthermore, the close corporation must also compete in the labor market for the better employees. Good people are often attracted by fringe benefits, including disability income plans.

We saw in the chapter on close corporations that one of the distinguishing characteristics of a corporation is its existence as a separate entity, apart from those who own the stock. As a result of this separation, a shareholder is viewed as both employer and employee. Here lies the real distinction between disability income plans for the corporate employees and those designed for businesses that are not incorporated.

The Shareholder-Employee in General

Disability income for shareholder-employees can be provided through a plan similar in most respects to the one we outlined in the discussion on partnerships—that is, individuals are covered by disability income insurance. Again, the amount of coverage available normally is limited to a percentage of their salaries. The corporation may provide the difference between these insurance benefits and the disabled employee's regular salary through a salary continuation plan.

The plan need not cover all employees. It may be selective in deciding who will and who will not be covered, but it may not discriminate between shareholder-employees and common-law employees. Finally, to make this arrangement a valuable tool in competing for the better employees, it should be defined in a written plan and announced to the employees.

Taxing Corporate Disability Income Plans

The tax consequences arising under a corporate plan are, with one notable exception, exactly like those arising under the plan we described for partnerships. Benefit payments to the employee are generally included as gross income if the employer pays the premiums. The same exception applies for employees under age 65 who retire early as a result of total and permanent disability.

Likewise, premiums paid by the corporation on employee disability income insurance are *not* considered income to the covered employee, but *are* deductible by the corporation as a business expense. The corporation enjoys the added advantage

ILL. 7.3 ■ *How the Disability Buy-Sell Works*

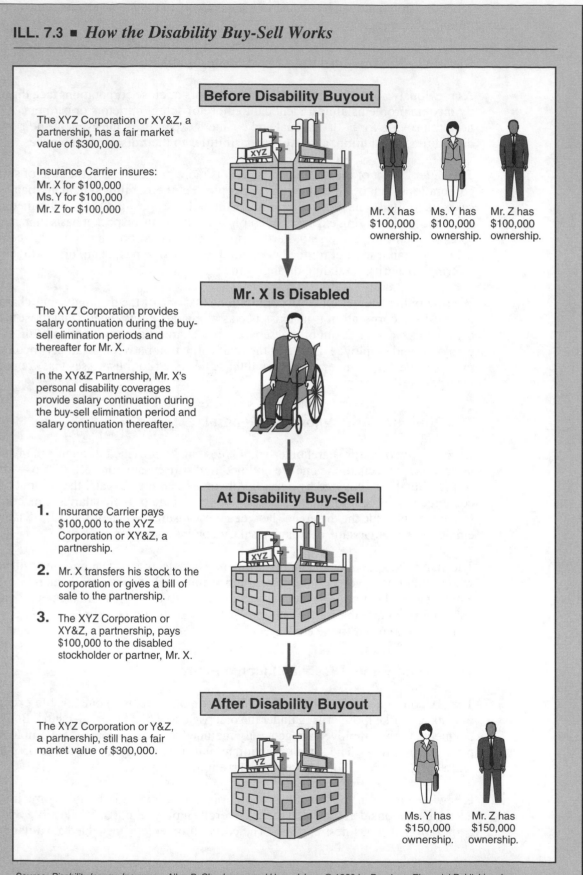

Before Disability Buyout

The XYZ Corporation or XY&Z, a partnership, has a fair market value of $300,000.

Insurance Carrier insures:
Mr. X for $100,000
Ms. Y for $100,000
Mr. Z for $100,000

Mr. X has $100,000 ownership.
Ms. Y has $100,000 ownership.
Mr. Z has $100,000 ownership.

Mr. X Is Disabled

The XYZ Corporation provides salary continuation during the buy-sell elimination periods and thereafter for Mr. X.

In the XY&Z Partnership, Mr. X's personal disability coverages provide salary continuation during the buy-sell elimination period and salary continuation thereafter.

At Disability Buy-Sell

1. Insurance Carrier pays $100,000 to the XYZ Corporation or XY&Z, a partnership.

2. Mr. X transfers his stock to the corporation or gives a bill of sale to the partnership.

3. The XYZ Corporation or XY&Z, a partnership, pays $100,000 to the disabled stockholder or partner, Mr. X.

After Disability Buyout

The XYZ Corporation or Y&Z, a partnership, still has a fair market value of $300,000.

Ms. Y has $150,000 ownership.
Mr. Z has $150,000 ownership.

Source: *Disability Income Insurance,* Allen B. Checkoway and Harry J. Lew, © 1989 by Dearborn Financial Publishing, Inc.

that *all* premiums are deductible, *including those paid to cover its shareholder-employees.*

The Shareholder-Employee and Long-Term Disability

While the corporate form of doing business assures the legal continuity of the firm, it does not guarantee that the corporation will continue to function as a going concern. To small closely held corporations, the death or long-term incapacity of key shareholder-employees can be as fatal as if the same tragedy had occurred in a partnership.

On the one hand, shareholder-employees face a continuing need for income to meet medical and doctor bills. Furthermore, their daily living expenses continue without interruption. On the other hand, the corporation has lost the disabled shareholder's productivity and contribution to the corporation. In addition, it may have to hire a replacement for the employee, thus doubling the corporate expense.

An insured corporation disability income plan covering shareholder-employees is a big step toward keeping the corporation's sick-pay expenses within bounds. Thus the continuity of the corporation is more nearly assured, despite the disability of a key executive. Yet even this does not solve satisfactorily the problems arising in event of death or a long-term disability.

One solution, as in the partnership setting, is a formal plan for the mandatory purchase of a disabled shareholder's interest. A corporation should assure itself that the *death* of a shareholder will not disrupt corporate operations. Many close corporations have done this through a buy-sell agreement funded by insurance on the lives of the shareholders. Unfortunately, too few corporations have protected themselves against the equally tragic circumstances that can arise as a result of the long-term disability of these same shareholders.

The Mandatory Purchase Plan

The mandatory purchase plan is most advantageous in small corporations. It is especially beneficial to personal service corporations. Such corporations have continuing obligations to pay a portion of disability income benefits. Quite often corporate resources are severely limited and continuing payments can tax these resources sorely. Yet the corporations have to survive and grow. They have to continue to provide services to their clients. To do this, new associates may be needed to take up the client or patient workload.

It may be wise—or even necessary—to sell new employees an interest in the business. If this is the case, where would the shares representing their interest come from? Whose shares would it be best to sell? Obviously, it would be best to sell new individuals the shares owned by disabled shareholders, who after long periods of disability are not likely to return to work. These shares would become available through the operation of the stock purchase plan.

The Stock Redemption Agreement

The purchase or redemption of a disabled shareholder's stock should be provided for in a formal, written agreement, signed by all shareholders and the corporation through its duly authorized officers. Such an agreement should contain the following general provisions.

1. *An employee salary continuation plan.* Shareholder-employees are assured of their regular incomes for a specified period of time. Payments to them would consist partially of disability income insurance and partially of additional payments from the corporation.

2. *Period of time during which benefits are to be paid.* The time during which corporate payments will continue is spelled out in the agreement. If after passage of this period of time the disability still continues, disabled shareholders' business interests would be purchased under such terms and conditions as are set forth in the purchasing agreement.

3. *A valuation formula.* The method of valuing the business interest must be definite and realistic. Yet it should be flexible enough to reflect changing circumstances.

4. *Funding.* Definite plans for providing the necessary cash to buy the stock should be outlined in detail. Providing for funding is as troublesome in the corporate setting as it is in partnership arrangements.

Other Considerations

As discussed earlier, a business must continue to operate while the disabled owner is convalescing. A business overhead expense disability insurance plan (BOE) is designed specifically to provide coverage for those expenses normally paid by the insured in the ordinary course of business. Typically, these expenses include rent, property taxes, utilities, cleaning services, professional dues, accounting costs and employee salary and fringe benefit payments. The coverage is usually for periods between 6 and 24 months and is limited to a percentage of the insured's income.

The typical excluded expenses are new business purchases, owner salary and depreciation. The premiums for a BOE plan are deductible by the insured as a business expense and taxable income to the insured. Of course, regular business expenses paid by the insured would be a deductible expense to the business.

There are other considerations when arranging the disability buyout plan. One is the question of what to do if a disabled shareholder recovers and wants to return to work. The answer is the same as under the partnership plan. In the first place, the odds are against a person's recovering after being disabled for a long period of time. However, if he or she does recover, there is nothing to prevent the active shareholders from agreeing to halt the buyout. The agreement itself could contain a specific provision allowing this.

This still leaves the serious problem of finding adequate cash to fund the purchase of a disabled shareholder's interest—the difference between the purchase price and the insurance coverage. The problem and its solution are identical to those discussed previously in the partnership setting.

The payments to disabled shareholders could be spread over a period of years, thus reducing the immediate burden to the corporation. Another answer would be simply to defer the purchase until a shareholder's death. At this time, the corporation would redeem the individual's stock, using the proceeds of life insurance purchased to fund the buyout agreement.

■ SUMMARY

Both employees and employers alike often overlook the issues of business disability planning. This is unfortunate because the chances of a disability occurring during a working career are about two or three times greater than the occurrence of death. When disability strikes the proprietor, partner or shareholder of a close corporation, these individuals face the various medical bills associated with the disability, while the usual expenses of running the business continue to be due and payable. Disability income policies are sold as individual policies, as riders to life insurance, as part of an employee group benefit or through a professional or trade association. As a general rule, if premium payments are deductible, the benefit payment is taxable income. Likewise, if the premium payments are not deductible, the benefit payment is income tax free.

A disability buy-sell agreement is similar in many respects to life insurance buy-sell agreements in that each owner's interest would be purchased according to the agreement. As mentioned at the start of the chapter, disability insurance plans are an overlooked area of insurance coverage. This presents ample opportunity to the enterprising practitioner to serve this needed market and in doing so benefit the business owner and the practitioner at the same time.

■ CHAPTER 7 QUESTIONS FOR REVIEW

1. Which of the following is NOT an expense typically faced by a disabled self-employed person?

    A. Continuing personal expenses

    B. Disability-connected medical costs

    C. Business expenses

    D. Estate settlement costs

2. Using disability income riders is NOT a common way of providing disability insurance because

    A. of the high cost

    B. of the limited coverage provided

    C. such riders are not available

    D. only short-term disability may be covered

3. Generally, premiums paid by a sole proprietor for disability coverage on employees are

   A. taxable to the employees

   B. treated the same as premiums paid for coverage on the owner

   C. deductible as a business expense

   D. deductible by the employee

4. If the employer paid premiums on the coverage, disability benefits paid to an employee under a wage continuation plan are

   A. deductible by the business

   B. taxable to the business

   C. taxable to the employee only if unreasonable in amount

   D. treated as taxable income to the employee

5. What is the major difference between the tax treatment of disability income plans of a corporation and those of a partnership?

   A. Premiums paid on coverage for shareholder-employees of a corporation are deductible.

   B. Payments to corporate employees are taxed if the business paid the premiums.

   C. Premiums paid by the corporation are taxed to the covered employee.

   D. There is no difference.

6. A group disability income insurance plan usually includes all of the following EXCEPT

   A. life insurance

   B. medical expense insurance

   C. income replacement

   D. an investment account

7. A business overhead expense plan (BOE) includes all of the following EXCEPT

   A. office rent payment

   B. employee salaries

   C. utility payments

   D. life insurance on the owner

8. Disability income insurance plans are sold as

   A. individual policies

   B. an employee group benefit

   C. as riders to life insurance policies

   D. all of the above

8

Key-Executive Life Insurance

T he primary function of life insurance is to offset the economic loss resulting from an individual's death. In other words, to compensate for the human value that disappears with death. You may be aware from our other insurance studies how life insurance acts to indemnify a family against the loss of an income-earning parent. The key-executive experience is similar. In this chapter we'll be talking about human life values, but we'll emphasize how life insurance protects an individual's human life value to a *business,* rather than for a family. It can do so through a key-executive life insurance plan.

■ ■ ■ ■ ■

■ WHAT IS KEY-EXECUTIVE LIFE INSURANCE?

Key-executive life insurance is insurance on the life of an individual whose particular skills make a significant contribution to the organization for which he or she works. The organization is owner, premium payor and beneficiary of the policy. In other words, it is insurance that a business purchases to indemnify itself against the economic setbacks resulting from the loss of a key contributor to the firm's profits.

Because the business has complete control of the policy, other benefits are available as well. Insurance is often considered a company-owned asset not earmarked for any specific purpose, thus the policy proceeds or cash values may be used for virtually any purpose. It is this versatility that makes key-executive life insurance so popular with business owners and such a strong sale for you.

The Human Factor in Business

Virtually all businesses accept without question the wisdom of protecting the firm against the loss of its property values. They take care to insure the physical assets against loss from fire, storm damage and other hazards. Yet, protection against the loss of *human life values,* insurance on the *people assets* of the business, may be a far more vital need.

The danger of a business being disrupted and sustaining serious losses by reason of the death of a key executive or valued employee may be eminently greater than the danger of a fire loss. In fact, about one out of every three people dies during the working years of their lives. This often results in a financial loss to the business a key executive owns or for which he or she works.

The late Dr. S. S. Huebner, dean of insurance educators, said: "Judged by the number of times it happens within the working period of life, and within a given total of risks, the striking power of death is thirty times as great as the striking power of fire." Dr. Huebner further pointed out that the average fire loss does not exceed 10 percent of the property value insured, while the loss from death is always 100 percent.

Losses suffered from the death of key executives are likely to be far more permanent and disastrous than are those resulting from any physical hazard. A plant destroyed by fire or flood can be rebuilt. The new building will be an improvement over the old one: more efficient, sounder, representing the latest in engineering developments. The new building is likely to be more useful and more valuable than the old. But what about the new manager or employee?

The executive or employee lost through death may have possessed some unique ability or a combination of talents that will be tremendously difficult to duplicate in any other person. He or she may have had experiences and knowledge unique only to him or her. This loss may be irreparable and a complete replacement impossible. In most instances, *any* person who steps into the shoes of the deceased will be far less useful to the business until he or she becomes familiar with duties and problems that were routine matters for his or her predecessor.

Our purpose in this discussion is to emphasize the flexibility—and thus the many sales opportunities—of key-executive life insurance by examining its usefulness in two specific areas. These two areas, which work together to make key-executive insurance a sound financial arrangement, are:

1. as an indemnification vehicle; and

2. as a business reserve and credit vehicle.

Then we will discuss an approach and questions that might be used in the fact-finding interview to put the subsequent key-executive presentation on the strongest possible track.

If you are already working in the key-executive field, some of the following ideas should increase your effectiveness, or at least give you added insight and appreciation as to the flexibility of key-executive insurance. If you have not worked in this field, this discussion should give you practical sales ideas and a broad picture of the sales potential of key-executive insurance. This discussion may also provide you with a stimulus to give this profitable market a try.

▪ KEY-EXECUTIVE INSURANCE AS AN INDEMNIFICATION VEHICLE

The fundamental purpose of key-executive life insurance is to *indemnify a business organization for the monetary loss brought about by the death of a valuable key employee.* In other words, key-executive life insurance insures management brainpower in the same manner that property insurance insures against physical damage.

The Need for Key-Executive Insurance

Whether a company is making money or losing money, its success or failure can normally be traced to the human factor. Profits, for the most part, result from managerial skill applied to physical assets. Given identical resources, some companies will succeed while others will fail. Human skill is the difference.

Dun & Bradstreet, Inc. publishes an analysis each year covering business failures that points out the importance of the human factor in business. Business failures in this study included businesses involved in court proceedings or voluntary actions that include losses to creditors.

The underlying causes of business failures are as follows:

Finance Causes	47.3%
Economic Factors	37.1
Disaster	6.3
Neglect Causes	3.9
Fraud	3.8
Strategy Causes	1.0
Experience Causes	.6

All of these factors except disaster are influenced by human factors. It should be noted that among the finance causes, the leading cause for business failure was heavy operating expenses. Among the economic factors causing failure were insufficient profit and inadequate sales. Such factors as these can be influenced heavily if the business has the proper people in place.

The sales value of emphasizing the Dun & Bradstreet report is to emphasize the all-important fact that the human element is the dominant and controlling factor in any business organization. Therefore, just as the human element must be held accountable for business failures, it must be given proper credit and recognition for business successes.

Educating the Prospect

Despite the overwhelming importance of the human element, when it comes to protecting a business against a human loss or the loss of a physical asset, the latter still receives far greater emphasis by the vast majority of business organizations.

Thus the Dun & Bradstreet report is a powerful third-party piece you can use with business owner prospects who tend to downgrade the importance of their own contributions—and the contributions of their key people—to company profits.

Another tool you can use to help educate your prospect is to clip stories from your local paper or from business periodicals citing how a company was affected by the death of its owner or a key executive. To help your business prospect understand how valuable their key person is, ask them to remember how tough it was on their business when the key executive was on vacation or jury duty. You should ask them to imagine how tough it would be if he or she was never coming back, could not check in for messages and could not give any notice about his or her departure.

■ WHAT HAPPENS WHEN A KEY INDIVIDUAL DIES?

There are two types of key-executive prospects:

1. active proprietors, partners and stockholders; and

2. nonowner employees of proprietorships, partnerships and close corporations.

The death of either type of prospect may result in irreparable financial loss to a business if it is not protected by adequate key-executive life insurance.

Key Owners

In most cases, active business owners will be the company's most valuable executives. In partnerships and close corporations, keep in mind that partners and stockholders usually start a business together because their combined talents give them an opportunity to make more money than each would realize from working alone. One owner might be an expert in sales, another a topflight financial authority, the third outstanding in production, the fourth a creative genius. They joined forces so that their combined talents could be used for the mutual benefit of all.

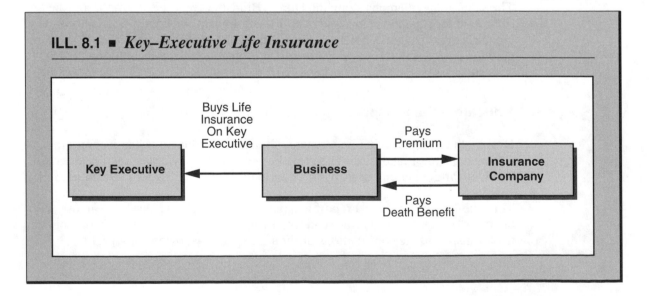

ILL. 8.1 ■ *Key–Executive Life Insurance*

Obviously, if one should die, a smooth working team would be disrupted. When an active business owner dies, his or her knowledge, vision, driving force and experience disappears. All of those traits that helped mold the company into a successful, profitable enterprise are lost completely for all time.

The death of a business owner key executive also can have the following effects on company profits from outside sources:

- Less liberal terms from suppliers—creditors are anxious about the company's future without the owner's contribution to its leadership.

- A tightening of financial assistance—bankers tend to adopt a wait-and-see attitude with respect to the stability of the company.

- A slowdown in company business—customers concerned about future production and service are hesitant to buy.

- An actual loss in company business—valuable accounts, formerly retained because of a close relationship between the business owner and the customer, may go elsewhere.

- Possible raiding by competitors of nonowner key individuals—employees are doubtful of their future with a company struggling from the effect of the owner's death.

Thus, a business can suffer a serious financial blow unless provisions have been made to offset the monetary loss brought about by a business owner's death. The company should insure the life of every business owner in the firm to protect itself and the surviving business owners against this serious financial contingency.

Key Managers and Employees

Many companies' key people are not limited to the business owners. Many will have nonowner employees whose authority extends to the policy-making level and others who are experts in specialized areas. Those people who guide a particular phase of the business are vital to its overall success. They contribute toward company profits. The death of any of them will reflect on these profits.

It should be emphasized to the employer that the company would almost inevitably face one or more of the following problems if a nonowner key person should die:

- the cost of finding, and then attracting at the right salary, an adequate replacement at a time when there may be a dearth of management material;

- the cost of delays during the time required to find and train a replacement;

- the cost of training a new employee; and

- the cost in inexperience and mistakes until the replacement attains, if ever, the same degree of skill as the deceased predecessor.

ILL. 8.2 ■ *Corporate Earnings Required to Equal Insurance Proceeds*

| | Corporation Must Earn | | |
If Key Person Is Worth	In 15 Percent Tax Bracket	In 34 Percent Tax Bracket	Life Insurance Required
$ 50,000	$ 58,820	$ 75,760	$ 50,000
75,000	88,240	113,640	75,000
100,000	117,650	151,515	100,000
150,000	176,470	227,270	150,000
200,000	235,300	303,035	200,000

The death of a key-executive business owner or nonbusiness owner can hurt a company more financially than almost any other factor. This is the reason so many companies have failed, sold out or merged in recent years. Without key-executive life insurance to sustain them after an executive's death, some companies simply have not made the grade. Of course, the majority survive—but not without substantial loss of earnings.

■ ADVANTAGES OF KEY-EXECUTIVE INSURANCE

Key-executive life insurance offers many benefits to businesses, all of which you should stress in your sales presentations. Let's summarize these benefits and then review another significant advantage: favorable tax treatment.

Benefits to the Business

Key-executive life insurance will provide the business with cash for all the following purposes:

- to keep the business running

- to assure creditors that their loans are safe

- to assure customers that the business will continue

- to cover the special expenses of finding, attracting and training a successor

- to cover the mistakes that the deceased's successor will make until the things the deceased knew from experience have been learned

- to carry out long-range development programs

Thus key-executive insurance permits the business to protect itself against one or more of the serious financial reverses—temporary or permanent—that inevitably

ILL. 8.3 ■ *Unincorporated Earnings Required to Equal Insurance Proceeds*

If Owners' Effective Tax Rate Is	Firm Must Earn to Net $50,000	Firm Must Earn to Net $75,000	Firm Must Earn to Net $100,000
15%	$58,820	$ 88,240	$117,650
28	69,440	104,170	138,890
31	72,460	108,700	144,930
36	78,120	117,190	156,250

comes with the loss of the services of an active business owner or a valuable person in the organization.

Favorable Tax Treatment

Favorable tax treatment is the other factor that makes key-executive life insurance particularly attractive. Premiums paid on a key-executive policy are not deductible for income tax purposes. However, in most cases, key-executive life insurance reimburses a company for the loss of an executive's ability *with income tax-free dollars.* This is about the only way a business organization can receive nontaxable money. With a substantial portion of profits going to taxes, every business enterprise faces obstacles accumulating cash for future needs.

Because virtually all employers are tax conscious, the tax-free character of key-executive insurance proceeds cannot be emphasized too strongly. Let's see what this can mean to different types of business organizations.

Corporations

As we learned in Chapter 6, corporations are taxed at rates from 15 to 39 percent, depending on their taxable incomes. Now take a look at Ill. 8.2. This illustration compares, in round figures, the amount of corporate earnings required to replace a key person to the amount of key-executive insurance required to accomplish the same job.

As you can see, to offset the monetary loss of a $100,000 key person, a corporation taxed at 15 percent must earn for this purpose, $117,650 over a period of years, and a corporation whose top income is taxed at 34 percent must earn $151,515. In either case, key-executive life insurance of $100,000 will effectively and immediately cover the loss.

It should be noted that larger corporations could have an alternative minimum tax on the life insurance proceeds received on a key executive's death. Alternative minimum tax is only applicable for C types of corporations; if the corporation's annual gross receipts for the last three years have not exceeded $5 million it is exempt from the alternative minimum tax.

Unincorporated Businesses

Now let's look at the tax-exempt implications of key-executive life insurance from the standpoint of unincorporated businesses. Partnership and proprietorship earnings are taxed to the owners individually rather than to the business itself. The more the firm earns, the higher the incremental income tax of the individual owners. If a valuable key employee should die, it would require higher earnings to replace his or her value.

Illustration 8.3 shows in round figures how much a firm must earn at its *owners'* effective tax rate to offset the loss of key people valued at $50,000, $75,000 and $100,000 respectively. Of course, the same purpose would be served by a life insurance policy of $50,000, $75,000 or $100,000.

■ AMOUNT OF INSURANCE NEEDED

Once you have sold your prospect on the need for key-executive insurance, you probably will be called upon to help the employer determine the necessary amount of life insurance. Because human factors are involved, no one formula can place a monetary value on a key individual's life. However, the following are common yardsticks that you can suggest to the prospect.

The Discount Approach

A common method of calculating the economic effect of the loss of a key employee is the "discount approach." this technique applies a percentage discount to the fair market value of the business.

The discount approach requires an appropriate discount factor. Some advisors believe that if the business will survive the loss of the key employee, and in time, will hire a competent replacement, an appropriate discount factor is 15 to 20 percent.

If the business will fail at the death of the specified key executive, or will be placed in jeopardy from the loss of the key employee, an appropriate discount factor is 20 to 45 percent.

The officers of the business and the firm's accounting and legal advisors, however, should determine the appropriate discount factor to use in each situation.

The Key Person's Worth in Net Profits

A true key employee is one who makes a definite contribution to the company's success and is accountable for some portion of its *profits*. This is easier to ascertain in cases where the key individual performs a specialized function, the results of which are easily identifiable on a dollar and cents basis. In any event, the employer usually has a fairly good idea who is contributing how much to company profits each year. For example, assume that the employer determines that Brown, a key salesperson, is directly responsible for $100,000 of company profit each year.

ILL. 8.4 ■ *Determining the Amount of Insurance Needed with the Discount Method*

Fair Market Value of Business with Key Executive	$750,000
Discount Without Executive	20%
Value Without Key Executive ($750,000 × .80)	$600,000
Life Insurance to Replace Key Executive	$150,000

The employer anticipates that this contribution to profit would be totally lost the first year following Brown's death, and that the amount would be regained at the rate of 20 percent a year thereafter. Thus the amount of key-executive insurance the company should have on Brown would be determined as follows:

	Loss to Company
First Year	$100,000
Second Year	80,000
Third Year	60,000
Fourth Year	40,000
Fifth Year	20,000
	$300,000

A $300,000 key-executive insurance policy would make up for the anticipated loss in sales in this case. If the proceeds are paid in a lump sum, investment earnings generated over the five-year period can be used for other business purposes.

The Key Person's Present Salary

Using the key employee's *present salary* as a yardstick is another popular way to determine the amount of insurance needed because a person's salary obviously is an indication of what the employer feels the individual is worth. If this measure of loss is used, the employer usually determines how much insurance is needed by multiplying the salary by the number of years it will take a new employee to attain the same degree of skill. For this purpose, 3 to 10 times the key employee's salary has been used extensively. For example, assume that Green is making an annual salary of $85,000 and Green's employer anticipates that it would take another person three years to attain the same degree of skill that Green currently possesses. In this case, a $255,000 key-executive life insurance policy on Green's life would probably adequately protect the company.

The Cost of Replacing the Key Person

The cost of *replacing* the key employee is most important in cases where the key person has scarce talents. There are several software programs available to help calculate the amount needed on a key executive's life. However, such costs as the time involved to recruit the successor employee and the salary level required must be considered. In addition, the cost of training the replacement should be taken into consideration. For example, White works in the research department of a small drug company. The company figures that its net cost in replacing White with an employee of equal ability and experience would be $100,000. Thus, the company takes out a $100,000 policy on White to indemnify itself in the event of White's death.

Additional Issues

Before concluding the indemnification function of key-executive life insurance, you should be aware of two additional important factors. Your prospect might ask a question regarding them and you should be prepared with a proper answer. These questions are:

1. "Is an agreement necessary?"

2. "What happens if the key person leaves the company?"

Is an Agreement Necessary?

When key-executive life insurance is being carried by a company on the life of an active owner or nonowner employee to indemnify the business for losses that result from the death of the insured, *no accompanying agreement is needed.* The insurance is simply carried by the firm on the key individual involved, just as the firm carries insurance on its property values. However, maintenance of the insurance and payment of its premiums should be authorized in a proper meeting under proper resolutions. Of course, the key individual would have to be willing to sign the application for the insurance.

A sample resolution appears in Ill. 8.5. Such a resolution should be prepared by the firm's attorney.

What Happens If a Key Person Leaves?

There is always the possibility that an insured employee may terminate employment, particularly if he or she is not an owner of the company. Some prospects may be concerned about this and will ask about the disposition of the policy should the insured quit the company.

Assuming the policy is a cash value policy, the company has many options:

1. The company can surrender the policy for its accumulated cash value.

2. The cash values can be used to purchase paid-up life insurance of a reduced amount for the benefit of the business.

ILL. 8.5 ■ *Sample Resolution for Key-Executive Insurance*

RECITALS

1. _____ (Key Executive) is now and for many years has been the President of the Corporation, and by reason of his or her unusual ability as its chief executive officer, it has consistently earned profits for the stockholders well above the average for the industry.

2. The termination of _____ (Key Executive) by reason of his or her death would result in the loss of his or her managerial skill, experience and profit-making ability to the Corporation.

3. The Corporation desires to make secure its financial position in the event of the death of _____ (Key Executive), and to indemnify itself against losses to its earning power which his or her death would occasion.

RESOLUTION

THEREFORE, IT IS RESOLVED: That the _____ (officer) be authorized and instructed to secure a policy or policies of life insurance in the _____ (company or companies) on the life of _____ (Key Executive), having a total face value of $ _____, with the Corporation to be named beneficiary of the policy or policies and to be owner of same, the policies so obtained shall be of the _____ type. The Treasurer is instructed to pay all premiums on such policy or policies as the become due.

---

3. The company can continue the policy in force even though the insured is no longer an employee. The policy may be of an age where the cash value is increasing at a greater rate than its annual premium; thus, the policy becomes an excellent accumulation vehicle for the company. When the insured dies, the proceeds will come to the company income tax free.

4. The key employee, upon leaving the company, may be permitted to buy the policy from the company for its cash or replacement value. The insured will not run afoul of the federal income tax transfer-for-value rule in this transaction, because of an exception to the rule where the purchaser of the policy is the insured. Thus at the insured's death, the beneficiary would receive the entire proceeds free of federal income tax.

5. An insurance exchange rider permits the company to continue the policy by transferring it to another key employee who must medically qualify for the policy.

The Internal Revenue Service has ruled that if a business utilizes the exchange option and there is any gain in the policy (cash surrender values are greater than total premiums paid) at the time of the exchange, the business will recognize the gain as income.

These alternatives regarding the disposition of the policy when a key employee terminates employment will further demonstrate to the prospect the amazing flexibility of the key-executive life insurance plan.

As you can see, key-executive life insurance as an indemnification vehicle is an outstanding solution to a problem that haunts hundreds of thousands of business organizations; it is a concept easy for the prospect to grasp; it is a plan that is relatively simple for you to install. Now let's turn to a second way in which insurance on the life of a key individual can effectively serve a business organization.

■ KEY-EXECUTIVE INSURANCE AS A BUSINESS RESERVE AND CREDIT VEHICLE

While the death benefit generated by a term insurance policy can provide cash for a business organization at the key executive's death, when a business organization buys a cash-value life insurance policy, it automatically acquires a versatile financial vehicle that can perform a variety of valuable services for the business itself while the insured is an active employee. In other words, the key-executive policy has "living values" in addition to providing protection in case of death. The company is the owner of a constantly increasing asset—the policy's cash value, reflected as an asset on the company's balance sheet.

Cash Values as Assets

The balance sheet is a statement of the financial position of a business organization at a given date, generally at the end of the fiscal year when the books are balanced and closed. The balance sheet reveals the financial strength of the business.

The company's properties are represented on the balance sheet under the term "Assets." Balance sheets sometimes classify assets that do not belong in any of the regular categories under such headings as "Investments" or "Miscellaneous" or "Other Assets." The cash value of company-owned business life insurance is a case in point. Most authorities agree that a policy's cash value should not be listed as a current asset, even though the funds are readily accessible, because it is not a part of working capital. Thus it may be shown under "Other Assets" (although it is not an "Investment" in the strictest sense of the word) or "Miscellaneous Assets." Yet you may encounter balance sheets that list cash values as current assets.

Illustration 8.6 is a typical balance sheet for a business organization that includes under "Assets" the cash value of a company-owned life insurance policy. Note that in this case the cash value is classified as "Other Assets."

The business owner who can point to life insurance cash values on a balance sheet can also point to a number of advantages that accrue to the business because of the existence of company-owned insurance. These advantages give you a number of excellent sales points to emphasize in your key-executive life insurance sales presentation.

ILL. 8.6 ■ *The XYZ Corporation Balance Sheet, December 31*

ASSETS

CURRENT ASSETS			
Cash on Hand and in Bank		$15,000	
Notes Receivable		10,000	
Accounts Receivable		15,000	
Merchandise Inventory		40,000	
Marketable Securities		5,000	
Total Current Assets			$85,000
FIXED ASSETS			
Land		$30,000	
Buildings	$200,000		
Less: Allowance for Depreciation	48,000	152,000	
Machinery and Equipment	60,000		
Less: Allowance for Depreciation	32,000		
		28,000	
Furniture and Fixtures	$ 25,000		
Less: Allowance for Depreciation	11,500	13,500	
Total Fixed Assets			$223,500
DEFERRED CHARGES			
Prepaid Interest		$ 300	
Prepaid Insurance		$ 400	
Total Deferred Charges			700
OTHER ASSETS			
Cash Surrender Value—Life Insurance			6,000
Total Assets			315,200

LIABILITIES

CURRENT LIABILITIES			
Notes Payable		$42,000	
Accounts Payable		15,000	
Notes Payable—Bank		34,000	
Accrued Interest Payable		100	
Dividends Payable		5,000	
Total Current Liabilities			$ 96,100
FIXED LIABILIITIES			
Mortgage on Building			120,000
DEFERRED CREDIT			
Interest Collected in Advance			200
Total Liabilities			$216,300

NET WORTH

Capital Stock			
Par Value, $75; Authorized and Outstanding, 1,000 Shares	$75,000		
CAPITAL SURPLUS	5,000		
EARNED SURPLUS	18,900		
Total Net Worth			$ 98,900
Total Liabilities and Net Worth			$315,200

Policy Creates Business Reserves

The accumulation of some portion of current business earnings in a liquid reserve fund for emergency purposes is a recognized business practice that is essential to long-term business success. Insurance on the lives of the key executives provides a safe, convenient and simple method for the gradual accumulation of a substantial reserve in the cash and loan values of the policies. The following are some of the business reserve advantages of key-executive insurance that should be stressed in an effective sales presentation.

Compulsion to Accumulate

Every business needs a method that will make the accumulation of a reserve fund automatic and incidental to its principal business activity. This is accomplished with key-executive insurance because the premiums are listed as a routine business cash expenditure (nondeductible) and paid like any other bill. The accumulation of the insurance reserve fund becomes a primary business obligation rather than a secondary consideration. This provides the necessary degree of compulsion so vital to the company's successful accumulation of the desired reserve.

Safety

With a nonvariable life insurance policy, the reserve fund accumulated in a life insurance contract is guaranteed by the entire assets of the life insurance company. The premiums are invested automatically with all other funds and represent a cross section of the real assets of the entire company. Diversification is obtained as to the type of investment, the territory in which investments are made, the number of different investment securities involved and the maturity dates. It's practically impossible to find such diversification in any other plan for accumulation of surplus funds.

Reserve Does Not Fluctuate

The problem of fluctuating values is a serious one in any other plan for accumulation of a business reserve. Reserve funds invested in normal channels may be at their lowest value to the business just at the time they are needed most—in a time of general financial and business turmoil. The reserve is worth only the market value of the investments that constitute that reserve, and the market is constantly changing. The firm has no real idea today what its reserve fund will be worth tomorrow if needed quickly. Marketability and liquidity of the assets making up this reserve enter into the problem.

Under the traditional fixed-premium permanent life insurance plan, the reserve values are guaranteed in advance. A guaranteed market, at a guaranteed price, is provided in the policy. The insurance plan assures the firm that the reserve fund it accumulates will be worth more in the year it is needed than it has ever been worth before. Its value will not be depreciated just when the need is greatest.

Reserve Fund Separated

To make certain that a business reserve fund will not be invaded for day-to-day operating needs, it should be separated from the reserve funds of the regular business assets. With key-executive insurance, the reserve accumulations are held by the insurance company and kept entirely apart from the firm's other assets. Although quickly available at any time, the insurance reserve fund is less accessible for general business use, since an attempt to use the fund indiscriminately will be a reminder that such other use can defeat its primary purpose of key-executive indemnification and the long-term advantages of the policy.

Readily Available

Perhaps most important from a company's standpoint—*the cash value reserve fund can be obtained quickly and without publicity when the firm has a real need for cash in a hurry.* Unexpected opportunities or sudden serious emergencies are examples. It can be obtained for an unlimited period of time at a guaranteed rate of interest. The fact that the loan is noncallable and that it can be obtained in secrecy without red tape is enormously appealing to every business organization. Policy loan values furnish a continuous, automatic, guaranteed source of dollars in time of stress. Regardless of any restrictions of general credit facilities, the company can depend on its own insurance reserve fund and borrow dollars when needed.

Additional Benefits

Use of key-executive life insurance as a reserve fund has other benefits as well. The life insurance cash value reserve fund grows substantially each year and the annual increases are generally not taxable income to the business organization. Also, the cash value reserve fund may be used as collateral for a bank loan. It is ideal collateral because it has a guaranteed market value that increases with the passage of time. This advantage cannot be overemphasized with your client.

Finally, accumulation of the reserve in life insurance policy values relieves the business managers of the problems of investment and reinvestment. These people are engaged in operating a business, not in the investment or accumulation of capital. With the life insurance company handling the investment problems, greater time is left for the effective management of the business.

Policy Enhances Business Credit

As you have already learned, the death of an active business owner or key employee may seriously impair a company's credit. Key-executive insurance can improve the firm's credit rating by assuring its continuity and solvency. Here are two major ways in which key-executive insurance helps a firm's credit picture.

Evidence of Business Character

The maintenance of key-executive insurance provides tangible evidence of business judgment. Creditors are obviously willing to look favorably upon a company that has insured its human assets. A commercial loan may be granted largely because of the creditor's confidence in the capacity and character of the firm's business owners and other executives. Company-owned life insurance indicates thrift and sound financial management. A key-executive insurance program also shows long-range planning and evidences the preservation of a stable business.

Guarantees Loan Repayment at Death

As stated previously, the accumulated cash values of key-executive insurance are available as supporting collateral for a loan, guaranteeing available cash in the event of default. However, with respect to credit purposes, the real value of key-executive life insurance lies in its ability to guarantee payment in the event of the insured's death. If the key individual lives, repayment of the obligation will come from earnings. The lender would not make the loan if he or she were not satisfied in this regard. But if the key employee should die, cash would be available from the life insurance itself. Or if the insurance proceeds were poured back into operating capital, the firm could adjust sufficiently to repay the loan through earnings. Thus the existence of key-executive life insurance enhances the firm's credit because cash will be available at the key person's death.

In addition to the multiple benefits accruing to the company or firm that invests in key-executive life insurance, the firm receives an income tax deduction for interest paid in connection with loans for the first $50,000 of life insurance coverage per key person. A "key person" is an officer or 20 percent owner of the corporation. The number of persons who may be treated as key persons is limited to the greater of (1) five individuals or (2) the lessor of 5 percent of the total officers and employees or 20 individuals. If the business is not a corporation, a 20 percent owner is any person who owns 20 percent or more of the capital or profits interest in the business. It may make sound business sense to acquire as much coverage as the officers or owners deem affordable. Illustration 8.7 summarizes all of the benefits of key-executive life insurance.

This completes our discussion of key-executive insurance. Now let's consider an approach to an employer and some questions that might be asked the prospect in the initial interview.

■ KEY-EXECUTIVE INSURANCE SALES PROPOSAL

Unless you have previously obtained reliable information about your company prospect from which you can build the most appealing key-executive presentation, you should attempt only to secure necessary facts on the first interview.

An Approach

To build interest in the prospect's mind, and to pave the way for subsequent questions, you might incorporate some of the following items in your fact-finding interview. Alternatively, these same items can be incorporated into a pre-approach letter used to obtain an interview.

- The human factor is a business organization's most important asset. Profits or losses—company successes or failures—result from human skill applied to physical assets.

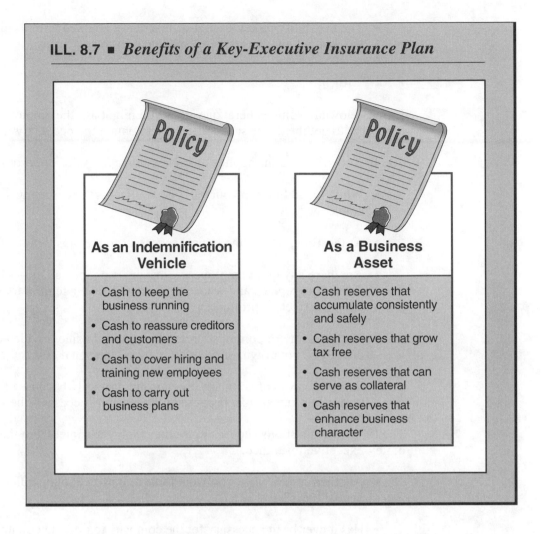

ILL. 8.7 ■ *Benefits of a Key-Executive Insurance Plan*

As an Indemnification Vehicle

- Cash to keep the business running
- Cash to reassure creditors and customers
- Cash to cover hiring and training new employees
- Cash to carry out business plans

As a Business Asset

- Cash reserves that accumulate consistently and safely
- Cash reserves that grow tax free
- Cash reserves that can serve as collateral
- Cash reserves that enhance business character

- A Dun & Bradstreet study showed that the human factor is involved in the majority of business failures. Thus, more and more companies are insuring key people—their human assets—to help offset the loss of a key individual's contribution to profits should death occur prior to retirement.

- Enclosed is a recent article from _____ illustrating how ABC Company coped with the loss of one of its key employees. Just imagine how you would cope if your key executive left you tomorrow without notice, could never call in to check messages and was never coming back.

- The existence of company-owned life insurance has provided over a million companies with emergency reserve funds in cash and loan values. *These same values are also the finest collateral available.*

- The very existence of key-executive insurance strengthens the credit position of a business organization in the eyes of financial institutions and other creditors.

- The flexibility of key-executive insurance, coupled with its tax advantages, has made it an unbeatable arrangement for many firms.

Fact-Finding

Listed below are some general questions you might ask the employer, after the approach, to get the discussion started and to obtain the necessary information.

The first set of questions applies to *key-executive life* sales opportunities:

- Who—in addition to yourself—do you feel is the company's most valuable employee?

- At this time, who is the logical successor to the presidency of the firm?

- Are there any other employees—managers or specialists—who would be difficult to replace and whose death would have a temporary or permanent adverse effect on profits?

- Are there any important sources of company business which can be traced directly to your own, or other employees', personal contacts?

- Do any sources of company credit result primarily because of your personal leadership, rather than because of the general success of the firm itself?

The following questions should arouse the employer's interest in the *living values* of key-executive insurance:

- Are there times when you would like to borrow money quickly on a confidential basis?

- Has it ever been necessary for the company to provide collateral in order to secure a loan?

Whenever possible, you should try to obtain as much information as you can about your prospect prior to the initial interview. You then will be able to come in with a specific sales presentation at that time. However, if this is not possible, the above questions will help you secure information to build an effective presentation. Equally important, such questions will help you emphasize the flexibility of key-executive insurance.

■ SUMMARY

The main purpose of key-executive life insurance is to protect a business against the losses associated with the death of an owner of key executive. Once the business has recognized the need, the next step is to work closely with the business to determine the appropriate insurance amount and to see that the appropriate documentation is put into place. As we have seen, besides protecting the business, a permanent cash-value life insurance policy can be a valuable business asset working to build reserves for a variety of business purposes. Almost all businesses are prospects for key executive life insurance and would benefit from the protection provided them with life insurance on their owners and/or key executives.

■ CHAPTER 8 QUESTIONS FOR REVIEW

1. Which of the following statements about human life values in a business is correct?

   A. They are more likely to be insured than physical assets.

   B. A loss of human values is never total.

   C. A loss from death is more likely than a loss from physical damage.

   D. The human element plays a very small role in business success or failure.

2. Generally, what is the tax treatment of proceeds received under key-executive life insurance?

   A. Tax free

   B. Fully taxable

   C. Taxable if the executive was an owner

   D. Taxable to the extent the proceeds exceed the cash value

3. Which of the following is NOT a common way to determine the monetary value to be placed on a key person's life?

   A. Worth in net profits

   B. Present salary

   C. Cost of replacement

   D. Ownership interest, if any

4. With regard to a key-executive life insurance policy, which of the following is NOT among the company's option if the key employee leaves the company?

   A. Continuing the policy in force

   B. Buying paid-up coverage with the cash value

   C. Selling the policy to the insured

   D. Surrendering the policy for its face amount

5. In addition to its use as an indemnification vehicle, what is the other major use of key-executive life insurance?

   A. As a business reserve and credit vehicle

   B. As a split-dollar funding vehicle

   C. As personal insurance for the key executive

   D. None of the above

6. Which of the following is NOT cited as a benefit to the business to having key-executive insurance?

    A. Keep the business running

    B. Assure creditors their loans are safe

    C. Keep the Internal Revenue Service from auditing the business

    D. Assure customers that the business will continue

7. Under a standard key-executive insurance arrangement, who has control of the policy?

    A. Insured executive

    B. Creditors of the business

    C. Business

    D. Independent government agency

8. Which of the following was NOT cited as contributing to business failures?

    A. Finance causes

    B. Disasters

    C. Government forces

    D. Economic factors

9

Key-Executive Incentive Plans

As we saw in Chapter 8, life insurance can protect a business from the loss associated with the death of a key executive. Life insurance can also be used to provide special benefits for key executives to adequately compensate them for their role in the success of the business. This can be a useful way of helping to retain excellent executives over the long haul. This chapter therefore focuses on the use of deferred compensation plans, split-dollar life insurance and executive bonus plans to provide incentives for key executives.

In the last chapter we saw how life insurance can compensate a business for the loss of a key owner or employee. Now let's look at how life insurance can also provide benefits for those key people themselves. We'll change our focus in this chapter to concentrate on solving certain financial problems of individuals first; then we'll see how a business organization can also profit from providing meaningful benefits for selected employees.

The job of adequately compensating key employees is a problem to which corporations have devoted increasing attention in recent years. It's faced by large and small companies alike, regardless of whether they are publicly or closely held. A variety of executive compensation—or key-executive incentive—plans have evolved. Our discussion will concentrate on three such plans that involve life insurance. They are:

1. deferred compensation plans;

2. split-dollar life insurance plans; and

3. executive bonus plans.

Note at the outset that these are only three plans from a large portfolio of key-executive incentive plans in use today. However, these plans are among the most popular. In addition, they represent plans in which the advantages of life insurance are easily understood and appreciated.

In addition, you should recognize that this chapter presents only an introduction to each of these plans. It will provide you with a basic understanding of the plans and point out the sales opportunities. From this discussion, you'll want to continue to build with actual selling experience and more advanced study.

■ ■ ■ ■ ■

■ BASIS FOR KEY-EXECUTIVE INCENTIVE PLANS

The development of key-executive incentive plans has been prompted in large part by two basic factors: (1) keen competition among business firms for existing and potential management talent and (2) the impact of federal income tax on high-income individuals.

First, there is strong competition today in the business world for men and women with specialized talents and general executive abilities. The competition is particularly intense because of a shortage of individuals who possess the rare capacity both to function effectively themselves and to lead others in important company operations. To attract and retain select individuals, corporations have developed incentive plans that involve more than just high salaries.

Second, as an employee's salary increases, so do income taxes. An awareness of this has prompted many corporations to pay increasing attention to compensation arrangements that minimize the income tax burden on the employee.

The first plan we will discuss here is *deferred compensation.*

■ DEFERRED COMPENSATION PLANS

Deferred compensation is an arrangement for a key employee to receive—instead of current salary increases or current cash bonuses—a guaranteed number of fixed payments beginning at retirement. In other words, dollars earned by the employee during working years are not actually paid until his or her retirement. Of course, the attraction of the agreement is that the employee is not taxed currently on the value of the deferred benefits. Instead, he or she receives the benefits after retirement when taxable income is generally less than during his or her active working years.

Many businesses differentiate deferred compensation plans from salary continuation plans. A salary continuation plan is a fringe benefit plan that does not involve the deferral of current compensation. It simply provides for the continuation of an employee's salary upon retirement or death, with payment to the employee's beneficiary if the employee dies while working for the employer before retirement. In the strictest sense, a deferred compensation plan involves the employee's money, while a salary continuation plan involves the employer's money. However, both deferred compensation plans and salary continuation plans may have employee and employer money and are subject to the same income tax rules.

Deferred compensation arrangements are usually instituted as a supplement to, or instead of, a qualified pension or profit-sharing plan. We will study these qualified plans in detail in the next chapter. The term *qualified* means that the plan is eligible for certain income tax advantages.

Nonqualified deferred compensation plans are simply retirement or other deferral plans for employees that are not eligible for the tax benefits of qualified plans. Nonqualified plans are often "discriminatory" in that employees are covered on a pick-and-choose basis. While nonqualified plans do enjoy tax advantages of their own, such advantages are less substantial than those for qualified plans.

The conditions that must be met to obtain favorable income tax treatment for a qualified plan are not particularly harsh; however, a plan meeting these conditions may not fit the specific needs or desires of the company. Basically, such a plan must benefit employees as a whole and may not discriminate in favor of selected employees (i.e., officers, stockholders or other highly compensated employees). This requirement prohibiting benefits in favor of key employees—the very ones an employer normally wants to favor—has prompted the use of nonqualified deferred compensation plans.

Benefits for Employer and Employee

Since the nonqualified deferred compensation arrangement requires no qualification with the IRS, it enables a company to provide substantial retirement benefits exclusively for top management. Such a plan has many advantages for both the employer and the employee.

Benefits for Employer

Since the employee's right to receive deferred payments is usually conditioned upon remaining with the employer until retirement—and refraining from working for a competitor after retirement—the employer can usually depend upon the continued services of a valuable (and sought-after) key employee. In this way, a deferred compensation plan may discourage a valuable employee from taking his or her executive talents and knowledge of the company's affairs to another employer.

By the same token, a deferred compensation plan is often the key to attracting a much needed executive. With competition for talented executives always keen, good people are forever in a bargaining position. A deferred compensation plan can be the determining factor in attracting as well as holding a top individual.

In either case—attracting or retaining a key person—the employer is in the favorable position of offering a deferred compensation plan. As we will see, such a plan may be less expensive to the company in the long run than increasing the executive's current salary. Furthermore, increasing an executive's current salary does little to solve the executive's problem of creating adequate retirement income.

Benefits for Employee

A deferred compensation plan may enable the individual to receive more "spendable dollars" for his or her years of service with the company. But even more important, it provides peace of mind for retirement and in many cases helps replace future earning power for his or her family should death or disability occur before retirement.

How the Plan Works

There are a great variety of deferred compensation plans in existence. Flexibility is one of their strong advantages. Generally, however, all plans follow somewhat the same pattern. A deferred compensation plan usually is arrived at after an arm's-length discussion between the employer and the key employee. As a rule, the discussion centers upon the amount and type of compensation and the conditions of employment.

Contract of Employment

After an agreement on compensation is reached that is mutually satisfactory to both parties, a contract of employment is prepared by an attorney. Some or all of the following main points are covered in the contract.

The employer agrees:

- to utilize the employee in a stated capacity, and to pay the current salary agreed upon;

- to pay the employee a specified amount of deferred salary for a stated number of years, commencing at a specific retirement date;

- to continue payment to the employee's spouse or some other beneficiary for a guaranteed number of years if the employee dies after retirement but before receiving all the guaranteed payments;

- to pay a specified amount to a spouse if the employee dies before retirement (one popular method is to pay the specified amount of deferred salary for each year the deceased employee was under the deferred compensation agreement); and

- to pay the employee a stated amount of income until retirement age if he or she becomes totally and permanently disabled.

The employee agrees:

- to remain with the company for a specified number of years (normally until retirement); and

- to refrain from becoming employed by, or in any way serving, competing companies for a reasonable time and within a reasonable geographic area during retirement.

The types and amounts of deferred compensation as well as the conditions of employment are, of course, always dictated by individual circumstances. Thus if more than one employee is to be covered under a deferred compensation plan, an individual contract of employment should be prepared for each.

Tax Advantages of Deferred Compensation

As noted earlier, one of the driving forces behind deferred compensation has been federal income tax. Because of the tax advantages discussed below, deferred compensation is probably the best way for the key employee to increase overall net earnings. These same tax advantages enable the employer, under certain conditions, to offer a key employee greater total benefits at less cost through deferred compensation than by current salary increases. Many times these benefits can be provided under circumstances where the company's cash position actually improves. The tax advantages are as follows:

- Deferred compensation actually paid by the employer to the employee, or sums paid to a spouse, constitute a business expense and, if reasonable in amount, can be taken as an income tax deduction by the employer.

- The key employee incurs no additional income tax before retirement where preconditions for deferral of income tax are satisfied (for example, the agreement must be entered into before the income is earned). After retirement, income tax liability occurs from year-to-year as the deferred compensation is received. The employee will probably have lower taxable income after retirement and will end up with more after-tax dollars.

- If the key employee dies before all obligations have been paid under the plan—either before or after retirement—the value of the future payments at the time of death will likely be includable in the estate for federal estate tax purposes. However, if the surviving spouse is to receive the payments, there will be no estate taxes due because of the unlimited marital deduction (see Chapter 11 on estate planning for more information on the use of the marital deduction).

■ FUNDING THE DEFERRED COMPENSATION PLAN

When a company establishes a deferred compensation plan, the firm takes on a future liability. It is a wise business practice, therefore, for the company to hedge its future obligation by establishing a systematic reserve fund and making sufficient annual deposits to the fund to produce the sum necessary to meet the obligation when it comes due. The best way to create this fund is through an annuity, mutual funds or a life insurance contract. (See Ill. 9.1.)

Deferred Annuity Contracts

Deferred annuities are often purchased by individuals to provide for their retirement. Employers also purchase deferred annuities to fund benefits under qualified pension, profit-sharing and stock bonus plans, as well as under nonqualified deferred compensation plans.

However, income in a newly purchased annuity held by a business entity, such as a corporation or a partnership, is currently taxable as ordinary income to the policyowner. Because there is no longer a tax advantage to using annuities to fund deferred compensation plans, they are rarely used for that purpose. Only the

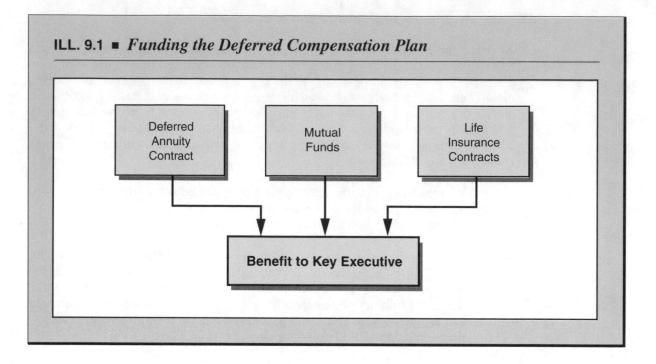

ILL. 9.1 ■ *Funding the Deferred Compensation Plan*

following annuity contracts, held by nonnatural owners, escape this tax treatment—an annuity contract that is:

1. acquired by an estate from a decedent;

2. held under a qualified plan, as a tax-sheltered annuity or as an IRA;

3. a qualified funding asset held by a structured settlement company or a property or casualty insurance company to fund periodic payments for damages;

4. purchased by an employer upon termination of a qualified plan and is held by the employer until the employee separates from service; or

5. an immediate annuity.

Mutual Funds

Mutual funds may also be used to fund deferred compensation plans—especially in those plans where the employee's deferred benefits depend upon the accumulations in the deferred account. In these plans, the earnings and gains benefit the employee, so he or she is interested in the best possible investment results. To satisfy the employee's investment desires, the employer may invest part or all of the deferred account in mutual fund shares. Despite the risks and absence of guarantees, funding by means of a diversified portfolio of securities may hold the best likelihood of long-term investment growth. Keep in mind that the employer will pay income taxes on any dividends/interest paid from the fund or capital gains passed through.

In addition, if the employer liquidates the mutual fund, it will pay income tax on the related gains.

Life Insurance Contracts

Another funding option is to use life insurance. In fact, life insurance is ideally suited for this purpose, and it has been generally accepted as a most practical method for funding a deferred compensation plan. What's more—in cases where death benefits are to be paid to a spouse if the employee dies before retirement (and most plans today include such benefits)—life insurance automatically creates the capital funds from which the payments can be made.

The concept of using life insurance to fund a deferred compensation plan is quite simple. Basically, the key employee's life is insured under the type of policy and in the amount the company feels most suitable to back up its liability under the plan. Since the employee has no interest whatsoever in the policy, the premium payments are not taxable income to the employee.

The life insurance is owned by and payable to the corporation. Its cash values become a part of general company assets. Its death proceeds are not earmarked for any specific purposes.

Tax Treatment for the Corporation

The employer makes all premium payments on the policy. The company cannot claim a deduction for the payments because a large portion of each premium payment represents accumulations as reflected in the policy's cash value. Those deposits, in essence, are simply a transfer of cash from one corporate account to another, with the policy's cash value shown as an asset on the company's balance sheet.

The remainder of each premium payment is allocated toward the risk portion of the life insurance. Although this portion is also not deductible, the proceeds of the policy are received by the company tax free at the employee's death. As stated in Chapter 8, it should be noted that larger corporations could have an alternative minimum tax on the life insurance proceeds received on a key executive's death. Alternative minimum tax is only applicable for C corporations; if the corporation's annual gross receipts for the last three years have not exceeded $5 million it is exempt from the alternative minimum tax. This is a most important factor, for proceeds received tax free will compensate many times over for the nondeductibility of the premiums paid.

Type of Policy

The type of policy to use usually depends upon the benefits the plan is intended to produce. Often, a whole life or universal policy is used because of their flexibility.

If the key employee lives to retirement, the whole life policy offers the company two alternatives:

1. the employer may use the policy's cash value to fund the deferred payments; or

2. if the employer's current earnings are sufficient to fund the deferred payments when the employee reaches age 65, the employer may keep the policy in force, usually without further premium payments and recoup the expense by receiving the proceeds tax free when the retired employee dies.

If, under this second alternative, the employer's earnings become insufficient to maintain the deferred payments, or if it puts an undue strain on earnings, the employer can call on funds from the policy's cash value to complete the contractual arrangement.

Treatment of Interest on Cash Value Loans

If the proceeds of a policy loan are used for business purposes, such as deferred compensation payments, deductibility of the loan interest depends on when the policy was purchased. For life insurance contracts issued or materially changed after June 8, 1997, no deduction is permitted for policy loan interest on any life insurance policy covering any individual who was financially interested in the business or who was an officer or employee. This rule also applies to any individual in whom the company has an insurable interest, including former officers, employees and individuals who formerly had a financial interest in the company.

The rules provide an exception to the interest disallowance for interest on indebtedness with respect to life insurance policies covering up to 20 key persons. "Key person" is defined as an officer or 20 percent owner. Under this exception, interest is deductible on the portion of a policy loan not exceeding $50,000 per employee.

Death Benefits

If the employee dies before retirement, or after retirement but before the completion of the deferred payments, the life insurance proceeds paid to the company assure the employer that it will be able to meet the death benefit provisions of the plan. Note again, in most situations these insurance proceeds are received tax free by the corporation.

If the employee dies before retirement, some of these same life insurance proceeds will also provide the company with dollars to compensate for the loss of valuable services. In other words, such a policy can double as key-executive life insurance for the corporation.

Advantages of Funding with Life Insurance

As discussed earlier, a deferred compensation plan funded by life insurance works to the mutual benefit of the company and the key executive. Let's review the advantages to each party, as they provide valuable sales points for the life underwriter.

To the Company

- Through the use of a deferred compensation plan, a business organization is able to offer a key employee attractive financial incentives to remain with the company. The same plan can also serve as an incentive for much needed talent to join the firm.

- By funding the plan with life insurance, the business organization creates a systematic fund to meet its future obligation.

- Life insurance enables the company to carry out its obligation with little or no cost to itself and, in many circumstances, with a substantial improvement to its cash position.

- If the employee dies before retirement, the company stands to receive insurance proceeds over and above its obligation, which can indemnify the company for the loss of the key individual's ability. Such proceeds are, in reality, an indemnity to the company financed by the insured's deferred income.

To the Key Employee

- With a nonqualified deferred compensation plan, the employee who abides by the employment contract is assured of a retirement plan that neither the company nor the employee alone could otherwise provide under a regular pension plan. The same generally holds true for disability and death benefits.

- By deferring a portion of this compensation, the employee is able to realize a much greater net financial return for the years of service to the company.

This concludes our study of deferred compensation. We are now ready to examine another popular key-executive incentive—split-dollar life insurance.

■ SPLIT-DOLLAR INSURANCE PLANS

The split-dollar insurance plan enables an employer and a select employee to share premium payments for life insurance on the employee's life. The key employee needs additional life insurance, but usually cannot pay all of the additional premiums. On the other hand, the employer has the funds to help finance the life insurance and has a special reason for doing so. There is practically no net cost to the employer, when compared with purchasing the same amount of life insurance independently of the plan.

The split-dollar plan is informal in nature; it requires no qualification with the Internal Revenue Service. Thus the employer can choose, without publicity within the corporation, those employees who will be given a chance to participate.

Benefits for Employer and Employee

The split-dollar plan, like deferred compensation, has become a popular employee benefit because of its obvious advantages to both the employer and the employee.

Benefits for Employer

The competition for junior executives—younger people with long-range potential—is keen. Business organizations have found that the split-dollar plan is an effective, economical way to emphasize the bright future within the organization for selected younger employees.

Like deferred compensation, a split-dollar plan also helps to discourage established executives from taking their talents and knowledge to a competitor. With a continued shortage of executive talent, experienced executives and those with specialized skills are in a powerful bargaining position. By helping these executives attain substantial amounts of much needed additional life insurance protection at bargain rates, their employers have taken an important step toward stabilizing their executive employment picture.

Benefits for Employee

The junior executive is typically one whose worth to—and salary from—the corporation is small in relation to what each eventually will become. But while present salary is modest, family responsibilities are high. Raising a family, buying a home and acquiring furniture and appliances often keeps the young executive strapped financially. Sometimes there is not enough current salary, after taking care of the absolute essentials, to provide the type of life insurance program necessary to capitalize fully on long-range earning power. Thus, while the executive is still young, income may not allow the purchase of enough life insurance when it is needed most.

The established executive is often in a financial bind despite a high income. A desire to provide his or her family with an above average standard of living cuts heavily into after-tax income. In addition, the heavy costs of educating children—or setting aside dollars for their future higher education—reduces available income even more.

At the same time, the need for additional life insurance protection becomes apparent as responsibilities increase. In the event of death, there must be sufficient life insurance to keep pace with the increased standard of living the family enjoys and to provide college educations for the children. In many cases, there may be an additional need for cash in the individual's estate to meet death taxes and other estate settlement costs brought about by an estate that has increased in size—perhaps substantially—over the past few years.

The established executive's need for additional life insurance protection on the one hand, and an inability to cope with its entire financial outlay on the other hand, are exactly the circumstances that set the stage for a split-dollar plan.

How the Plan Works

Under a split-dollar plan, the premiums are split between the employer and employee in a number of ways. The following three are the most popular:

1. The employer pays that part of the premium that always equals the annual increase in the policy's cash value. The employee contributes the balance of each year's premium.

For example, assume that in a certain year the cash value of a policy with a $2,000 annual premium increases by $1,300. In such a case, the employer contributes $1,300 toward the premium; the employee contributes the remaining $700.

This is the conventional method of premium splitting and is used in many instances. However, it does have one drawback in that the cash value increase in the first year is usually small; therefore, most of the first-year premium must be paid by the employee.

2. To minimize the financial impact to the employee in the first several years, the employer's contributions are leveled over the entire premium paying period.

   For example, assume a plan is adopted for an employee age 45 until retirement at age 65. Instead of paying the annual increase in the policy's cash value, the employer pays one-twentieth of what the policy's cash value will be at the end of the twentieth year, or the employee's age 65. The employee pays the balance.

3. If the plan is to be the most attractive, the employer will pay all the premiums every year with no contribution from the employee. This is often called an equity split-dollar plan.

   For example, assume a plan is established with annual premium payments of $5,000 for 20 years. The employer would pay the total premium with no premium contribution from the employee.

While we will discuss only these methods of splitting premiums, keep in mind that there may be other suitable arrangements that can meet the specific needs and desires of the employer and employee.

If the Employee Dies

If the employee dies under a plan in which the employer's contributions had been equal to the annual increase in the policy's cash value, the employer will receive the cumulative cash value and the employee's beneficiary will receive all death proceeds in excess of the policy's cash value.

If the employer's contributions had been leveled to reduce the initial outlay to the employee or if the employer had paid all the premiums, the employer, at the employee's death, will recover the total contribution to the plan. The employee's beneficiary will receive all proceeds in excess of the contributions made by the employer.

In either event, the employer is assured of getting back every dollar contributed to a split-dollar plan if the employee dies.

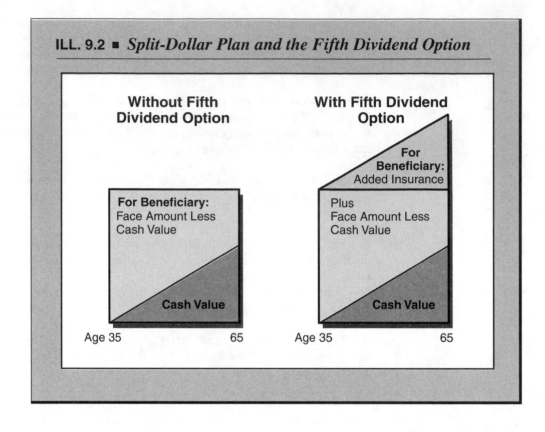

ILL. 9.2 ■ *Split-Dollar Plan and the Fifth Dividend Option*

Keeping the Death Benefit Level

Under the conventional split-dollar plan, the employee's death benefit decreases each year in direct proportion to the annual cash value increase, which also equals the amount paid by the employer. This is because the employee's beneficiary is entitled only to the difference between the policy's total proceeds and the policy's cash value at the date of death. In many instances, this results in a serious disadvantage to an employee whose need for life insurance protection remains level or increases for a number of years after the inception of the plan.

To overcome the adverse effect of a decreasing death benefit, many life insurance companies have developed methods for keeping the death benefit level. These are available on an optional basis.

Fifth Dividend Option

The most popular method offered by participating life insurance companies is the use of the so-called *fifth dividend option.* Under this method, a portion of each annual dividend is used to purchase one-year term insurance equal to the policy's cash value in that year.

To the extent that dividends are adequate to purchase the additional one-year term insurance, the death proceeds will always equal the initial face amount of the policy plus its cash value. Illustration 9.2 compares a split-dollar plan with and without the fifth dividend option. The contract illustrated is a straight life policy issued at age 35. The charts assume that the policy will remain in force until the employee's retirement at age 65, and that dividends during that period will be enough to purchase the one-year term insurance.

The charts make it apparent why the fifth dividend option enhances the appeal of the plan from the employee's standpoint.

Term Riders

A number of nonparticipating life insurance companies active in the split-dollar field have devised equally effective methods for keeping the death benefit level. These are either in the form of special term riders or policies that provide for increases annually in an amount equal to the policy's cash value or premiums paid.

Ownership of Policy

Under a split-dollar plan, the policy may be owned by either the employee or the employer.

Under the *employee-owned* method, the employee applies for the policy. He or she names a beneficiary and then assigns the policy to the employer as security for annual loans equaling the annual increase in the cash value. This approach is known as the *collateral assignment* method.

Under the *employer-owned* method, the employer is the applicant of the policy and is named beneficiary of that portion of the proceeds equal to the policy's cash value, or the employer's cumulative contributions, whichever is greater. The employer then names the employee's choice of beneficiary for the balance of the proceeds. This approach is known as the *endorsement method* since the beneficiary designation is protected by an endorsement and cannot be changed by the employer without the employee's consent.

The matter of policy ownership should be dictated by the circumstances of each case, and upon the advice of legal counsel. Generally speaking, many employers prefer to retain ownership of the policy because its cash value provides a steadily growing, readily available fund to call on for business needs and opportunities. However, if the plan is primarily meant to benefit the employee, the policy would be owned by the employee so he or she could have access to policy cash values that might accrue in excess of the employer's interest.

Separate Agreement

A separate agreement that spells out the rights of each party normally accompanies a split-dollar insurance plan. Usually, the agreements set forth the manner in which the premium payment will be split between the employer and the employee, and how the policy will be disposed of in the event the plan is terminated. In addition, under an employer-owned policy, the employer agrees to designate whomever the employee selects as beneficiary of the employee's share of the death proceeds.

Income Tax Treatment of Split-Dollar Plans

We will now consider the federal income tax treatment for each party under a split-dollar plan. The *employer* cannot deduct its share of the annual premium contribution; however, at the insured employee's death, the employer receives at a minimum—income tax free—every dollar contributed to the plan. The *employee* realizes an *economic benefit* from the employer each year; the value of this benefit must be reported as income in the year it is received.

Note that in 1996, the IRS ruled in a technical advice memorandum that in a collateral assignment arrangement, once policy cash values exceeded corporate premiums paid, the policyowner should recognize the excess as income. This ruling should be disclosed to any employer and executive considering a collateral assignment type of split-dollar plan.

Key-Executive Incentive Plans

This taxable economic benefit is measured by:

1. the value of the insurance protection payable to the insured employee's beneficiary under the basic policy

plus

2. the value of all policy dividends used for his or her benefit if the policy is participating

minus

3. any premiums paid by the employee.

Let's break this down step by step.

Value of the Basic Protection. The value of the basic insurance protection payable to the employee's beneficiary is computed on a year-to-year basis. The value is equal to the one-year term cost of the insurance protection. The cost of the one-year term insurance is determined by applying the lower of the government's P.S. 58 rates or the insurance company's published rates for individual one-year term policies. (See Ill. 9.3.)

The insurance company's published individual one-year term rates may be used for determining the employee's cost of insurance where lower than the P.S. 58 rates, provided that those lower published rates relate to *initial issue insurance.* The effect is to minimize the taxable benefit to the employee covered by the split-dollar plan sponsored by the employer.

The term rate is applied only to the *amount at risk.* The amount at risk is the basic policy's face amount minus its cash value or the employer's death benefit, whichever is the greater. Additional amounts payable under the previously described fifth dividend option, or any other dividend option, are not taken into consideration when computing the amount at risk. (The dollar value of the dividends used to purchase these additional amounts, however, is taken into consideration in the computation of the *value of the dividends,* discussed later.)

Here's an example of how to apply the P.S. 58 rates to determine the value of the basic insurance protection. Let's assume that a life insurance policy with a face amount of $25,000 has a cash value of $5,000. First, calculate the amount at risk by subtracting the cash value from the face amount:

$$\$25,000 - \$5,000 = \$20,000 \text{ (amount at risk)}$$

Next, look up the P.S. 58 rate for an insured employee at age 44. The P.S. 58 rate is $5.85 per $1,000 of insurance. Then multiply the P.S. 58 rate by the amount at risk. The result is the value of the basic insurance protection for that year:

$$\$5.85 \times \$20 = \$117$$

Value of the Dividends.   The actual dollar value of any dividends used for the insured employee's benefit is then added to the value of the basic insurance protection. That value includes any dividends:

1. paid to the employee in cash (or applied to his or her share of the premium);

2. used to purchase paid-up additional amounts of insurance where the employee controls the cash value of the additional insurance; and

3. used to buy additional term insurance under the fifth dividend option.

Employee's Premium Contribution.   The final step is to subtract the employee's share of the gross premium from the combined values of the basic insurance protection and the dollar value of the dividend used for the employee's benefit. The difference, if any, is the amount the employee must report as income in that year.

Thus, for example, assume that in a particular year the value of the basic insurance protection for an employee is $220 and that $250 in dividends is used to purchase term insurance under the fifth dividend option. Further assume that the employee's contribution to premiums in the year is $300. The amount the employee must report as income would be $170 ($220 + $250 − $300 = $170).

The Employee's Beneficiary.   Under the split-dollar arrangement, the part of the insurance proceeds payable to the employee's beneficiary at death is exempt from federal income tax.

Advantages of Split-Dollar Plans

Let's conclude our discussion of split-dollar plans with a summary of the advantages of such a plan to both the employer and the insured employee. These advantages are strong sales points in your presentation to prospective purchasers.

To the Employer

- *An incentive plan.* The employer is able to draw a key employee closer to the business by providing substantial assistance in the purchase of needed life

ILL. 9.3 ■ *P.S. 58 Table of One-Year Term Rates (per $1,000 of Insurance)*

Age	Premium	Age	Premium
15	$1.27	46	$ 6.78
16	1.38	47	7.32
17	1.48	48	7.89
18	1.52	49	8.53
19	1.56	50	9.22
20	1.61	51	9.97
21	1.67	52	10.79
22	1.73	53	11.69
23	1.79	54	12.67
24	1.86	55	13.74
25	1.93	56	14.91
26	2.02	57	16.18
27	2.11	58	17.56
28	2.20	59	19.08
29	2.31	60	20.73
30	2.43	61	22.53
31	2.57	62	24.50
32	2.70	63	26.63
33	2.86	64	28.98
34	3.02	65	31.51
35	3.21	66	34.28
36	3.41	67	37.31
37	3.63	68	40.59
38	3.87	69	44.17
39	4.14	70	48.06
40	4.42	71	52.29
41	4.73	72	56.89
42	5.07	73	61.89
43	5.44	74	67.33
44	5.85	75	73.23
45	6.30		

insurance. The employer's contributions are dependent upon the employee's remaining with the corporation.

- *May be selective.* The plan is informal, enabling the employer to be selective among employees and to keep it on a confidential basis.

- *No approval required.* The plan may be installed with a minimum of procedural detail and need not be submitted to the Internal Revenue Service for approval.

- *Creation of a business reserve.* When the employer is owner of the split-dollar policy, it is also owner of its cash value. Thus, the company has a growing and readily available reserve fund to call upon for business needs and opportunities. Remember though, that there is a $50,000 per employee limit for interest deductions for policy loans on corporate-owned life insurance.

- *No direct cost at death or retirement.* There is no cost to the employer other than the loss of earnings that might be earned if the money were invested elsewhere. If the employee dies, the company gets back its contributions income tax free. If the employee lives to retirement, the company gets back its share in the form of the policy's cash value. If desired, the employer can use the cash value to fund a special retirement plan for the employee.

To the Employee

- *Obtains low-cost insurance.* The employee obtains life insurance protection at the lowest possible cost. Although the *economic benefit* received must be reported as income, he or she nevertheless obtains insurance coverage on a very favorable cost basis.

  In the case of junior executives, they can obtain needed coverage at a time when they otherwise could not afford it.

- *Hedge against uninsurability.* The split-dollar plan represents a hedge against the employee's becoming uninsurable in the future. If disability should strike, and the acquisition of additional insurance becomes impossible, the employee nevertheless will be insured to a greater extent than otherwise might be possible.

- *Coverage beyond retirement.* The plan may permit the employee to continue coverage after retirement by repaying the employer for all company contributions. (If the employee lacks the resources, a loan could be obtained and the policy used as collateral.) This arrangement enables the employee to acquire a substantial amount of permanent life insurance with premiums based on his or her age when the policy was issued, rather than on the employee's age when the policy is purchased from the employer.

■ EXECUTIVE BONUS PLANS

Another commonly used benefit plan is the *executive bonus plan.* This plan meets a number of corporate and executive needs, is relatively simple to establish and is easy to understand. An executive bonus plan, also known as an "insured bonus plan" or a "Code §162 plan," is a nonqualified plan that provides benefits to both the employer and the employee.

Basically, an executive bonus plan is a simple life insurance fringe-benefit program in which an employee is given ownership of a policy on his or her life, with the employer paying the premiums, either directly or indirectly through a salary increase to the employee. The employee owns the plan from the very start and has control over the policy's cash values and the beneficiary designation.

An executive bonus plan benefits the employer because it chooses who will participate in the plan and may use the plan to attract, motivate and reward employees. In addition, the plan provides a simple way to buy personal life insurance for key executives (including owners) using tax-deductible business dollars. Finally, the employer can fix the costs of the plan in advance, which helps to assure proper cash management.

The executive benefits from an executive bonus plan because he or she receives permanent cash value life insurance at a very low personal cost. Though the premium payments made on the executive's behalf are considered a taxable benefit, his or her out-of-pocket cost is only the additional income tax generated on the bonus received. Furthermore, Code §162 plans are flexible so options may be selected at later dates to meet the executive's needs. For example, the employee could choose to take the policy's cash value at retirement under a payout option or leave the policy intact for its death benefit. Finally, the executive may feel rewarded by the company for his or her personal efforts.

Executive Bonus Plan Structure

Most executive bonus plans are designed to fit into the ERISA "safe harbor" for welfare benefit plans. By qualifying for "safe harbor" treatment, the plan is exempt from the participation, funding and vesting requirements of ERISA. The plan document can be as liberal or as restrictive as the employer desires.

The actual plan design is limited only by the imaginations of the life insurance professional, the attorney and the employer involved in its creation. Although it may be tempting to create a rather formidable document, a simple plan is easier to understand, administrate and amend at some later date.

An executive bonus plan may be funded by any form of permanent cash value life insurance. Annuity contracts are another popular funding alternative for a Code §162 plan. Although they lack the advantage of a preretirement death benefit, they can be issued to any executive, regardless of health. Also, annuity contracts may maximize future additional income when compared with some forms of permanent life insurance.

Income Taxation

An executive bonus plan is an employee welfare benefit plan under ERISA since it provides death benefits as well as other benefits. Code §162 sets out three requirements that must be met if an expense is to be deductible for the employer. The expense must be:

1. "ordinary and necessary" in the normal course of business and must be helpful in the business;

2. "paid or incurred" in the year it is deducted; and

3. "payment for services actually rendered" in the course of an employment relationship.

The executive has a single requirement: the amount of the premium payment or the bonus must be included in his or her gross income as "compensation for services." Even if the benefit is something other than cash, if it has a measurable value, it must be included as income.

The Market for Executive Bonus Plans

Executive bonus plans are especially appealing to new or struggling businesses with limited funds. The owner can select both the participants and the amount to be spent on each participant. The company can use tax-deductible business dollars to make modest premium payments to purchase substantial life insurance. Unlike the restrictions and "golden handcuffs" imposed by split-dollar or deferred compensation plans, executive bonus plans are portable. If a covered employee leaves the company, he or she may pick up the premium payment so there is no loss of coverage. This may be appealing to an employee since the employer's premium dollars and policy cash values built up to that point also go with the employee.

Plan Features	Split-Dollar Plans	Executive Bonus Plans
Employer Discretion for Employee Inclusion	Yes	Yes
Limitations on Plan Premium	No	No
Reduce Employee's Income	*	No
Employer Costs Deductible	No	Yes
Employer Costs Recoverable	Yes	No

* Employee is taxed on the term costs of the life insurance protection payable to a personal beneficiary less any employee premium contribution. The IRS has taken the position, in a collateral assignment arrangement, that cash values in excess of the employer's interest should be recognized as income by the employee.

Comparing Split-Dollar Plans to Executive Bonus Plans

The decision of which plan to utilize will vary by employer and employee situation. As a general rule, the executive bonus plan is utilized if the employer's income tax bracket is higher than the employee's bracket. If the employee's tax bracket is higher, the employer may want to consider a split-dollar plan. Also, degree of employer control and recovery of cost may be an important factor in plan design; in such a situation, an endorsement split-dollar plan may be favored.

Illustrating Key Executive-Incentive Plans

Almost every life insurance carrier that offers life insurance products in the business market can provide software to illustrate these various concepts with their particular products. Some carriers will provide the software free to all licensed agents, while others will charge a fee for access to their software. In any event, even if the software is not available, most insurance companies will develop the insurance proposal using one of these concepts from either the home office or a regional office.

■ SUMMARY

Almost every successful business has someone whose unique talent or experience is responsible for the success of that business. The business will suffer a material loss by reason of that person's death and the difficulties and expense inherent in securing and training a successor. The danger from loss or impairment of the human life values in the business is as serious, if not more so, as the danger from loss of the property values and the physical assets of the firm.

Deferred compensation, split-dollar life insurance and executive bonus plans offer you a vast potential market. With fringe benefits apparently taking an ever-increasing role in employee compensation, this market will undoubtedly continue to expand. We have covered the most popular forms of selective compensation strategies, deferred compensation, split-dollar insurance plans and executive bonus plans. Each has its unique strengths and weaknesses and can be used to solve a variety of compensation issues. This chapter should give you the confidence to meet with business clients and their key executives and discuss the various options available.

■ CHAPTER 9 QUESTIONS FOR REVIEW

1. Which of the following is an arrangement for an employee to receive, instead of current salary increases or current cash bonuses, a guaranteed number of fixed payments beginning at retirement?

   A. Split-dollar plan

   B. Key-executive life insurance

   C. Deferred compensation plan

   D. Employee indemnification plan

2. Which of the following statements about using life insurance with a deferred compensation plan is NOT correct?

   A. The company should own the policy.

   B. The company should pay all premiums.

   C. The policy should be specifically designated to fund the plan.

   D. The employee should have no rights in the policy.

3. The employer's share of the proceeds in a typical split-dollar plan is

   A. zero

   B. equal to the difference between the proceeds and the cash value

   C. 100 percent

   D. equal to the cash value

4. The fifth dividend option, when used with a split-dollar plan, is used to overcome what shortcoming?

   A. Taxation of the proceeds

   B. Decreasing death benefit for the employee's beneficiaries

   C. Large premium outlay for the employee in the early plan years

   D. Application of the transfer-for-value rule

5. Which of the following statements regarding executive bonus plans is correct?

   A. An employee covered by an executive bonus plan is taxed on the amount of the premium or bonus paid by the employer under the plan.

   B. An executive bonus plan is a qualified plan.

   C. The amount of premium or bonus paid under the executive bonus plan is never deductible by the employer.

   D. An executive bonus plan may not be funded by any form of cash value life insurance.

6. All of the following are split-dollar plan options EXCEPT

   A. the employer pays a premium equal to the annual increase in policy cash value

   B. the employer pays the entire policy premium each year

   C. the employer only pays the term costs policy each year

   D. the employer's contributions are leveled over the entire premium paying period

7. All of the following are benefits to an employer considering a split-dollar plan EXCEPT

   A. the plan is an incentive for key employees to stay with the employer

   B. the employer can be selective on which employees will participate

   C. the employer is given a tax deduction for its premium payments

   D. the employer can recover its costs from policy cash values or death benefits

8. For an employer to deduct the premiums paid under an executive bonus plan, all of the following must be true EXCEPT

   A. the premium is an ordinary and necessary business expense

   B. the premium was paid or incurred in the year deducted

   C. the employer owns the policy cash values

   D. the premium payment was for services actually rendered by the employee

10

Qualified Employer Retirement Plans

The business of selling and servicing tax-qualified retirement plans is challenging, exciting and profitable. Many practitioners make it their specialty and thousands of others make it a point to know enough about this highly specialized field to provide a valuable service to the business clients they have assisted with other plans covered in this course. Our purpose in this chapter is to give you a general introduction to the field of qualified retirement plans in the business arena.

■ QUALIFIED PLANS DEFINED

The term *qualified plan* means that a plan meets certain requirements for favorable tax treatment specified in the Internal Revenue Code. If these requirements are met, the federal government grants favorable income tax treatment for both the employers and employees. These provisions and the tax advantages are discussed in detail later in this chapter.

In contrast, *nonqualified* means that a plan does not meet the Code requirements. It may be that the plan purposely avoids such requirements because it provides benefits not permitted under a qualified plan. For example, a nonqualified deferred compensation plan enables an employer to select only those employees it wants to participate. Such individual selection is not permitted in a tax-qualified plan.

Qualified plans provide substantial benefits that make the Code requirements well worth meeting in many circumstances. Let's look at some of these advantages next. We'll focus our discussion in this chapter on qualified employer plans. In the next chapter our focus will be the qualified individual retirement plan.

■ QUALIFIED EMPLOYER RETIREMENT PLANS

Let's start our discussion of qualified employer plans by considering the reasons why these and other plans exist. Basically, there are two reasons:

1. They offer businesses a means to benefit their employees.

2. They provide advantageous tax incentives for businesses to adopt these plans.

Advantages for the Employer—A Sound Business Investment

From the employer's standpoint, a qualified retirement plan is a sound business investment. Among its advantages to the employer are the following:

- It increases the loyalty and stability of the workforce.

- The retirement benefits made available by a qualified retirement plan help motivate employees to increase productivity and reduce turnover.

- It encourages elderly workers to retire voluntarily, thus opening up the promotion channels for the younger employees.

The employer who realizes that Social Security provides only a minimum base for retirement can offer employees an attractive benefit by installing a qualified retirement plan.

Advantages for the Employee—A Problem Solved

Securing a comfortable retirement has become a problem of our social and economic way of life. The typical employee is in a particularly difficult position. He or she has achieved a standard of living considerably above the level that Social Security retirement benefits will provide. A satisfactory retirement for such an employee should be at least half of the income earned during the working years. This amount, coupled with reduced needs and taxes, may be enough to provide for basic necessities.

A properly implemented retirement plan may provide an employee with an adequate standard of living when earned income stops. This in turn can provide peace of mind that the future is taken care of and allow the employee to concentrate on present responsibilities.

■ TAX TREATMENT OF QUALIFIED EMPLOYER PLANS

One of the biggest advantages of a qualified retirement plan is the favorable tax treatment for both the employer and covered employees. The federal government encourages employers to help employees build adequate retirement incomes by extending favorable income tax treatment to qualified retirement plans. A qualified plan enjoys a number of federal tax advantages, which are discussed next.

ILL. 10.1 ■ *Qualified Employer Plans Benefit Employee and Employer Alike*

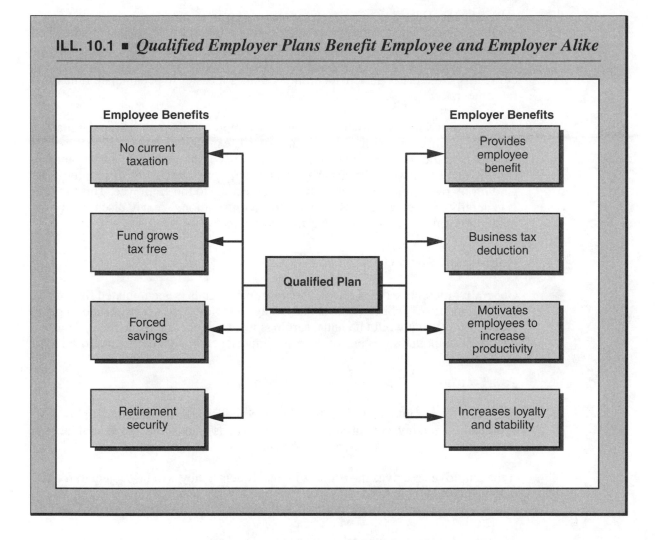

Employer Contributions Deductible

Employer contributions to a qualified retirement plan (not exceeding prescribed limits) are deductible by the business for income tax purposes, just as any other bona fide business expense. This is an extremely strong point in the eyes of a business prospect. If the business is in a 34 percent bracket, its cost is only 66 cents of each dollar paid into the plan.

Employer Contributions Not Currently Taxed to Employee

Deductible plan contributions made by the employer are not currently taxed to a participating employee. The employee's income tax liability is postponed until retirement benefits begin or until distributions are taken under the plan.

This deferral of current income tax represents the heart of the tax benefit for the employee under qualified plans. A significant factor accounting for their popularity in small-sized and medium-sized businesses is that highly paid owners and high salaried executives do not pay current income taxes on amounts contributed for their benefit (subject to some special rules and limitations discussed later). They do not have to set aside funds on an after-tax basis, unless they elect to do so under a plan that accepts voluntary nondeductible contributions. Other employees, too, enjoy this same tax benefit that definitely makes it easier to accumulate funds for retirement.

An exception does exist to this income tax exemption. Where a retirement plan is funded with insurance contracts offering some life insurance protection in the event a participant dies before retirement, the annual cost of the *pure* insurance protection (the difference between the cash value and the face amount of the death proceeds) paid for by the employer is currently taxable income to the employee. This tax cost is generally quite small compared to the total contribution. We will discuss the computation of this insurance cost later in this chapter.

Retirement Fund Grows Tax Free

Generally, income realized on invested retirement funds is accumulated free of current income taxes. This income tax advantage enables the retirement fund to grow much faster than it would if annual earnings were subject to income taxes. This tax-deferred compounding is one of the most important advantages of a qualified plan.

Tax Treatment at Retirement or Death

In general, the employer's contributions to a qualified retirement fund—plus any appreciation and investment earnings on those funds—are subject to federal income tax *when the employee receives the benefits.*

If the employee receives the benefits in installments, they will be subject to federal income tax when received. However, the employee's lower taxable income after retirement should reduce the tax.

The retired employee who takes the accumulated retirement funds in a lump sum within a single taxable year (assuming the plan permits this) may be able to elect favorable tax treatment.

Case Study: Tax Advantages to Business Executives

The fact that employer contributions within prescribed limitations and retirement fund earnings are not currently taxable to actively employed owners and other highly paid executives (subject to special rules and limitations) has tremendous sales significance. This is illustrated in the following example, which compares a tax-free accumulation under a qualified retirement plan to a comparable pay increase subject to current taxation.

Two key executives of the Ajax Corporation have their top dollars taxed at 28 percent. One, Mr. Jones, receives a salary increase of $2,000. The other, Ms. Smith, is to receive a pension benefit that requires an annual deposit of $2,000. Assume both are age 35 and the money is accumulated at the rate of 8 percent to age 65.

ILL. 10.2 ■ *Cash Accumulation in a Qualified Retirement Plan*

Number of Years	Cumulative Employer Payment		Cumulative Amounts After Taxes		Accumulated Retirement Fund at Age 65 (8% Interest)	
	For Mr. Jones (Increased salary)	For Ms. Smith (Retirement plan)	Realized by Mr. Jones (28% tax)	Realized by Ms. Smith (No tax)	Mr. Jones Personal Fund (Taxed)	Ms. Smith Retirement Fund (Not taxed)
5	$10,000	$10,000	$ 7,200	$10,000	$ 8,354	$ 12,672
10	20,000	20,000	14,400	20,000	19,018	31,290
15	30,000	30,000	21,600	30,000	32,626	58,648
20	40,000	40,000	28,800	40,000	49,996	98,846
25	50,000	50,000	36,000	50,000	72,163	157,908
30	60,000	60,000	43,200	60,000	100,456	244,692

If $2,000 is paid to Jones as an increase in salary, it is immediately reduced to $1,440 due to the 28 percent effective personal income tax rate. If this money is invested at 8 percent, the investment earnings also are subject to a 28 percent personal income tax, and thus reduced to an effective return of approximately 5¾ percent.

In contrast to Jones, Smith pays no current tax on the $2,000 pension contribution made on her behalf and earnings on this contribution also accumulate free of taxes until retirement. (See Ill. 10.2.)

As you can see, Smith incurs no tax liability under a qualified retirement plan before retirement. However, the salary increase to Jones and interest earned are both taxed continuously as they are received or credited. Smith's benefits at the time of retirement are subject to tax as benefits are received.

■ TYPES OF QUALIFIED PLANS

Before considering the general qualification requirements of qualified plans, let's briefly consider the different types of plans. Basically, such plans may be classified into two major categories: (1) *defined contribution plans* and (2) *defined benefit plans*. (See Ill. 10.3.)

Defined Contribution Plans

A *defined contribution plan* is one that provides for an individual account for each participant and for benefits based solely on the amount contributed to the account plus any income, expenses, gains and losses and any forfeitures of accounts of other participants that may be allocated to that person's account. There are three types of defined contribution plans: profit-sharing, money-purchase pension and stock bonus plans. Only the first two types will be covered in this chapter.

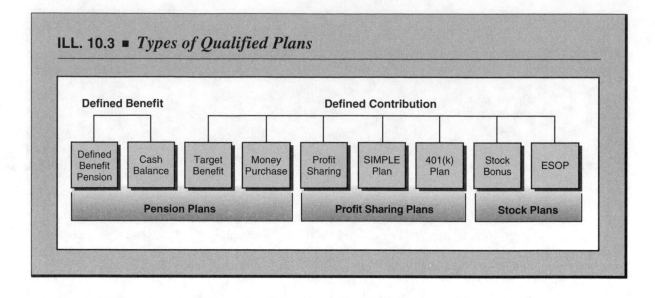

ILL. 10.3 ■ *Types of Qualified Plans*

A *profit-sharing plan* is one that is established and maintained by an employer to provide for the participation in profits by employees or their beneficiaries. However, contributions are not necessarily limited to profits. Often, a 401(k) plan is part of a qualified profit-sharing plan. On the other hand, a *money-purchase pension plan* is a formal pension plan in which a specific annual contribution is made and in which employee benefits are directly related to the size of contributions and length of service. Participants in one of these defined contribution plans are limited to annual allocations of 25 percent of compensation or $30,000 (indexed), whichever is less. However, no more than $170,000 (in 2000, and subject to annual adjustment for inflation) of an employee's compensation may be taken into account for purposes of determining contributions or benefits under a qualified retirement plan.

In all cases, a defined contribution plan is characterized by provisions that cover amounts going into the plan currently and/or the current allocation of the plan's funds.

The Money-Purchase Pension Plan

The *money-purchase pension plan* is one in which the employer's contribution is fixed by a predetermined formula. The amount called for by the formula cannot be based upon the profits of the company nor can the annual amount of contribution per participant exceed the limits mentioned above. Ultimate retirement benefits depend upon the length of time an employee is under the plan, investment plan performance and the amount of money contributed on his or her behalf each year. Thus, employees who are younger when the plan is set up can build full career benefits more easily than older employees.

The contribution formula of a money-purchase pension plan can be expressed in several different ways. It may call for a flat dollar amount (e.g., $4,000) to be contributed to the plan each year. It may be expressed as a percentage of payroll (e.g.,

5 percent of annual payroll). Or it may be expressed as a combination of the two. But it must not be determined by the company's profits and it must not exceed the current legal limit per employee.

The contributions to the plan are then allocated to the employee's account. These contributions are projected to retirement and the ultimate benefits are determined. The predictable contribution called for by the plan is the key to the plan's ability to provide a determinable benefit. It is this characteristic of determinable benefits that places the money-purchase plan within the category of a pension plan.

The Profit-Sharing Plan

A deferred payment *profit-sharing plan* is basically what its name implies. Under this type of plan, the employer contributes a portion of each year's company profits to a trust for future benefit of the company's employees. A deferred payment profit-sharing trust may accumulate funds for distribution to its participants after a fixed number of years of employment, the attainment of a stated age or the occurrence of some specified event such as layoff, illness, disability, retirement, death or severance of employment.

Included in the broad category of profit-sharing plans is the immediate cash or deferred arrangement (401(k)) profit-sharing plan. Before we discuss this specific category of profit-sharing plan, let's discuss the features and characteristics of profit-sharing plans in general.

Employer Profit-Sharing Contributions. An employer may make straightforward profit-sharing plan contributions. A company's contribution to a profit-sharing plan may be determined in a number of ways. It may be a fixed percentage of profits before or after taxes, a fixed percentage of profits in excess of a stated amount or a combination of any of these and other methods.

The simplest contribution formula is the flat percentage of profits formula. Under this formula the employer agrees to contribute a flat-percentage of company profits to the plan, such as 10 percent, 15 percent or 25 percent.

Another formula provides for the contribution of a percentage of profits above a minimum level. An example of this formula calls for the contribution of a stated percentage of profits above $10,000. This helps the employer to protect the company in years of low profits.

A third formula calls for an increasing contribution as profits increase. An example might be 10 percent of the first $20,000 annual profit, plus 20 percent of annual profits between $20,000 and $50,000, plus 30 percent of annual profits in excess of $50,000 and so forth. This approach can have a production incentive effect if it is properly publicized to the employees.

Finally, and perhaps most common among small employers, the employer can simply make discretionary contributions in an amount (if any) it determines each year. Employer contributions to a profit-sharing plan are not limited to the employer's current or accumulated profits.

Limitation on Contributions. The government places a few additional restrictions upon the methods of determining employer contributions to profit-sharing plans. The employer is restricted to a maximum tax-deductible contribution equal to 15 percent of the participating employees' payroll up to $170,000 (in 2000, and subject to annual adjustment for inflation) per employee for any given year. Generally, if the employer has more than one type of qualified plan, the total deductible contribution for all plans cannot exceed 25 percent of aggregate compensation of covered employees.

Allocation of Funds. A predetermined formula is necessary for allocating company contributions among the participating employees. Many plans use a simple formula where the amount allocated to each employee bears the same ratio to the company contributions as the employee's annual compensation bears to the total compensation of the participating employees. Thus if an employee is paid 10 percent of the total participating payroll (up to $170,000 per employee), 10 percent of company contributions to the profit-sharing plan will be credited to his or her account.

Another popular formula is the *unit system,* which not only gives each participant unit credits based on compensation, but also gives unit credits based upon years of service. For example, one unit may be given for each $100 of annual compensation and one unit for each year of service. Plans that use this kind of formula, or other variations from pro-rata compensation, must pass nondiscrimination tests under IRS regulations to ensure the formula does not discriminate in favor of highly compensated employees.

Distribution of Funds. The plan sets forth the manner in which funds credited to a participant's account will be distributed. This includes retirement, disability, termination of employment and payment to named beneficiaries if the employee should die.

Generally the entire amount credited to the employee's account may be paid to the participant who retires or becomes disabled, and to the beneficiaries if the participant dies. In the event of termination before retirement, the participant receives only his or her *vested interest* in the plan. To discourage career employees from leaving the company before retirement, most plans do not give employees full right to their account until a stated number of years has elapsed. Instead, their interest in the plan gradually increases until the account finally becomes fully vested. If they should quit before retirement but after the account is fully vested, their entire credited amount would be made available. If they should quit before the account is fully vested, the unvested portion would be allocated among the remaining participants.

Investments. The instrument creating the profit-sharing plan will usually have a provision controlling investment of the contributed funds. The trustees of the profit-sharing plan have the responsibility for investing these funds. Such investments are varied, but they may include preferred and common stocks, corporate and government bonds and real estate mortgages. Some profit-sharing trusts invest some or all of the participant's share in life insurance or annuity contracts because of their advantages.

New Forms of Profit-Sharing Plans

Two new forms of profit-sharing plans are gaining acceptance in the employee benefits planning arena. One is the age-based profit-sharing plan and the other is the new comparability profit-sharing plan.

Age-Based Profit-Sharing Plan

An age-based profit-sharing plan especially appeals to business owners who are older and more highly paid than most of the other employees at the business. Like a traditional profit-sharing plan, employer contributions are flexible. But an age-based plan allocates contributions under a formula based on both age and salary, giving older plan participants a higher percentage of salary than younger ones.

New Comparability Profit-Sharing Plan

The other form of profit-sharing plan, a new comparability plan, is tested under general nondiscrimination rules based on projected benefits at a uniform retirement age (such as age 65), with different contribution rates applied to separate classes of employees. Like an age-based plan, this plan is best suited to companies where there is a discernible age spread between the select group of employees the employer wants to benefit most and other employees. The allocation classes may be based on any reasonable objective business-related criteria, including job categories and nature of compensation (hourly or salary-based).

Both plans must satisfy nondiscrimination rules typically allocating at least 3 percent of compensation in each employee's account.

Cash or Deferred Arrangement or 401(k) Plans

As noted earlier, included in the category of profit-sharing plans is the *cash* or *deferred arrangement* or *401(k)* plan. These are plans that include a provision permitting employee-plan participants to make an election each year whether to take the employer's contribution as taxable cash compensation or to defer the contribution under the tax-deferral provisions of the plan. Internal Revenue Code §401(k) makes this election possible by specifically exempting the employee's right to receive cash in lieu of deferral from the *constructive receipt doctrine* under which the right to income (whether exercised or not) results in inclusion of the amount in taxable income.

Profit-sharing plans with 401(k) provisions have been increasingly popular in the past several years as employees, employers and their advisors become aware of the availability of *salary reduction* techniques that allow employees to elect to defer a portion of their current income into the plan trust. The benefit to the employee, wholly apart from any employer-matching formulas, is the tax deferral of voluntary salary deferrals, which are not subject to current income taxation.

The extremely favorable salary reduction feature under a 401(k) plan accounts for its popularity. This can be combined with the advantages to the employer of the profit-sharing plan under which contributions are not required in marginally profitable or loss years. Prior to the enactment of IRC §401(k), salary reduction agreements were only available under 403(b) plans for public school teachers and employees of certain not-for-profit organizations. (See Chapter 2.) Correspondingly, tax-exempt organizations and state and local governmental units generally are not eligible to establish 401(k) provision profit-sharing plans, with a limited grandfather exception for some existing plans.

Elective Deferral Limit

Elective employee deferrals under the 401(k) provisions are limited to $10,500 per year (in 2000, and subject to annual adjustment for inflation). If the limitation is exceeded, the excess must be repaid to the employee as taxable income.

The $10,500 adjusted limit applies on a per taxpayer basis so that the participant cannot defer more than $10,500 per year under all plans in which he or she participates (including, for example, simplified employee pensions and all other tax-qualified plans). If this limit is exceeded by deferrals to a plan, the plan must return the excess to the employee by April 15 of the following year, to avoid a double taxation of the excess. That is, these amounts will be taxed as income now and then taxed again when they are distributed in the future.

Highly Compensated Employee Limit

Since plans with 401(k) provisions could be used disproportionately by highly compensated employees and owners (who have more money to defer), special rules apply to insure that the level of deferrals made by such employees are not disproportionate to deferrals made by rank-and-file employees. Specifically, average elective deferrals for highly compensated plan participants may not exceed the greater of:

1. 125 percent of the average deferral percentage (ADP) for nonhighly compensated employees; or

2. twice the average elective deferral percentage for all other eligible employees (but not more than 2 percentage points greater than the average deferral percentage of the other employees).

The deferral percentages are first calculated separately for each employee, and then they are averaged for the highly compensated group and the nonhighly compensated group. (Identifying highly compensated employees is covered later in this chapter.)

The following table describes the ADP test for highly compensated employees. Failure to meet the test will cause highly compensated participants to be taxed on the amount by which their elective deferrals exceed the ADP limit (the Code refers to amounts in excess of the ADP limit as *excess contributions*). These excess contributions must be returned to participants in a timely manner to avoid serious consequences. If the 401(k) plan does not return these excess contributions along with accumulated investment earnings on the excess, to participants by March 15 of the following year (or where the plan uses a fiscal year, within 2½ months after the close of the plan year) the employer is subject to a 10 percent excise tax. More importantly, if the 401(k) plan does not return the excess contributions, plus accumulated investment earnings, before the end of the following plan year, the plan is subject to disqualification.

The ADP test is as follows:

If the ADP for Nonhighly Compensated Employees Is	The Maximum ADP for Highly Compensated Employees Is
1%	2.00%
2	4.00
3	5.00
4	6.00
5	7.00
6	8.00
7	9.00
8	10.00
9	11.25
10	12.50
11	13.75
12	15.00

Employer Matching Contributions

The employer may, if it wants, make "matching contributions" of a given percentage of part or all of the employee deferrals. This encourages lower-paid employees to make elective deferrals, which raises the ADP test for highly compensated employees and enables those highly compensated employees to make larger elective deferrals (as well as to receive matching contributions themselves). Matching contributions are subject to a test similar to the ADP test.

SIMPLE Plans

We will now turn our attention to a relatively new type of plan established by Congress in 1996 called savings incentive match plan for employees (SIMPLE plan) which certain employers may adopt. Under the law, an employer can structure a SIMPLE plan as either an individual retirement account (IRA) (see Chapter 2 for further information on IRAs) or a 401(k) arrangement. Congress created SIMPLE plans to encourage more small employers to establish a formal qualified plan for their employees by eliminating some of the rules normally applicable to qualified plans.

As either an IRA (SIMPLE IRA) or 401(k) arrangement (SIMPLE 401(k)), an employee can make contributions, within set limits, to his or her individual account through a salary reduction election. Under this election, the employer will transfer the amount to the employee's account. The employer in turn is required to make an annual contribution to each participating employee's account. Both the employee's and the employer's contributions are deposited into either the employee's IRA or a 401(k) trust account and grow tax deferred within the account/trust until distributed.

Eligible Employers

Not all employers qualify for a SIMPLE plan. Only employers with no more than 100 employees who received at least $5,000 of compensation from the employer in the preceding year may adopt a SIMPLE plan. To qualify, the employer must count employees working for a business under common control (whether incorporated or not) to make sure it does not exceed the 100-employee limit.

Additionally, an employer cannot create a SIMPLE plan if it already maintains another qualified plan. However, there is an exception to this rule if the other qualified plan (1) covers only employees under a collective bargaining agreement that was subject to good faith collective bargaining or (2) is maintained during the year of acquisition, disposition or similar transaction, and certain other requirements are met.

Two-Year Grace Period

Because employee counts can fluctuate with business activity, there is a two-year grace period should the employer establish a SIMPLE plan and then exceed the 100-employee limit later. If an employer no longer meets the eligibility requirements, the employer may continue to maintain the SIMPLE plan for two years after the last year it was eligible. At the end of the two-year grace period, however, the employer must discontinue the SIMPLE plan if it no longer meets the eligibility requirements.

Participation

An employer must open its SIMPLE plan to every employee who:

1. received at least $5,000 in compensation from the employer during any two of the preceding calendar years (whether or not consecutive); and

2. is reasonably expected to receive at least $5,000 in compensation during the current calendar year.

Contributions

Employee contributions are from deferred income and are limited to $6,000 annually (for 2000, and adjusted annually for inflation) for either the IRA or 401(k) type of arrangement. Employers must make annual contributions to their employees' SIMPLE accounts pursuant to one of the following formulas:

1. Matching Contribution Formula—match the employee's contribution dollar for dollar up to 3 percent of the employee's compensation. With an IRA SIMPLE plan, a lower percentage can be elected by the employer but must be communicated to the employee in advance and cannot be elected for more than two out of any five years. For the 401(k) type of SIMPLE plan, the employer cannot reduce the matching contribution to less than 3 percent.

2. Two Percent Nonelective Contribution—Regardless of whether or not eligible employees defer income into the plan, the employer would contribute

2 percent of compensation for all eligible employees. The maximum annual compensation for each employee that can be taken into account for any plan year is $170,000 (in 2000, and adjusted annually for inflation).

If the employer follows one of these two formulas and vests employees in 100 percent of the employer's contributions, the plan is not subject to any other nondiscrimination rules. Therefore, be sure to suggest a SIMPLE plan when a small employer wants a qualified plan for employees but is discouraged about creating one because of the cumbersome nondiscrimination rules.

Plan distributions follow the type of SIMPLE plan used whether it is an IRA or a 401(k) type of arrangement.

Defined Benefit Plans

A *defined benefit plan* is any plan that is not a defined contribution plan. Generally, those plans that promise a specific retirement benefit are defined benefit plans. The plan itself will contain a benefit formula for determining the correct benefit at retirement. An individual's retirement benefit is not affected by the amount of the employer's contributions, forfeitures nor investment experience. Generally, the defined benefit plan formula can be based on a fixed amount or on a percentage of the employee's annual compensation. For example, a defined benefit plan may provide a benefit of $100 a month or one equal to 2 percent of an employee's average annual wage. In either case, definitely determinable future benefits are promised. These future benefits dictate the timing and amount of current contributions. Illustration 10.4 contrasts this approach with that of the defined contribution plan where current contributions determine future benefits.

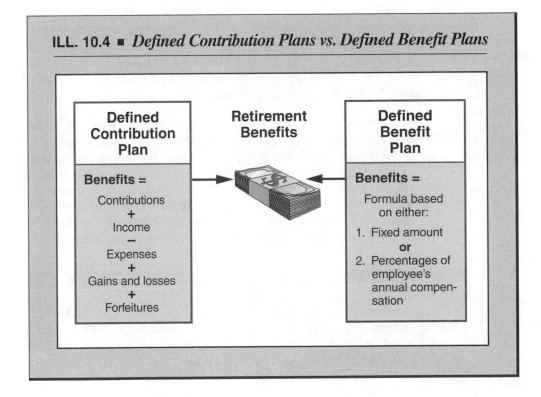

ILL. 10.4 ■ *Defined Contribution Plans vs. Defined Benefit Plans*

Defined Contribution Plan	Retirement Benefits	Defined Benefit Plan
Benefits = Contributions + Income − Expenses + Gains and losses + Forfeitures		**Benefits =** Formula based on either: 1. Fixed amount **or** 2. Percentages of employee's annual compensation

Benefits under the defined benefit pension plan are determined by a benefit formula that sets forth the retirement benefits to be received by a participant. Here, the annual amount of benefit per participant is limited to the lesser of $135,000 (in 2000, and subject to annual adjustment for inflation) or 100 percent of the participant's average annual compensation for his or her highest consecutive three years. There is also a limit of $170,000 (in 2000, and subject to annual adjustment for inflation) on compensation for contribution and benefit purposes. Generally, the employer must contribute enough to fund the promised benefits, taking into account various accounting and actuarial assumptions. Subject to such limitations, by controlling the type of benefit formula used under the plan, the employer can control the benefit distribution that is best suited for the company. The employer can choose from several formulas, including the flat amount, flat percentage of salary, unit-benefit formula or Social Security integration formulas.

Flat Amount Formula

This formula provides that all employees participating under the plan will receive a given amount of money at retirement (e.g., $50, $200 or $350 a month). This benefit is payable to all employees regardless of income during employment or length of service. This type of formula has been largely replaced by other forms that reflect the participant's income or length of service.

Flat Percentage of Salary Formula

This formula provides for benefits to be paid in direct proportion to the employee's income. Pension benefits such as 20 percent, 30 percent or 50 percent of employee's salary are provided by such a formula.

Unit-Benefit Formula

This may provide for a flat amount to be given at retirement for each year of service with the employer, such as $8 a month for each year of service with the company. Thus the employee who has accumulated 30 years of service at retirement would receive a $240 monthly pension.

A more popular version of this formula is expressed as a percentage of salary. The plan may provide for 1 percent or 2 percent of salary for each year of service with the company. For example, a plan may provide for 2 percent of salary for each year of service. An employee with 25 years of service would be entitled to 50 percent of salary as a pension benefit ($2\% \times 25$ years = 50%). Salary may be defined to be the average over the three or five highest years before retirement (which automatically adjusts the benefit for inflation during the employee's working career), or a career average salary over employee's entire period of employment.

Social Security Integration Formula

Another approach for determining benefits under a defined benefit plan takes into account Social Security benefits. Here the employer's plan contribution formula is combined with Social Security benefits and together treated as one retirement program. Since Social Security benefits (as a percentage of working compensation) are skewed toward the lower paid, these integration formulas allow plan benefits to be skewed to the higher-paid (within limits set by IRS regulations).

■ GENERAL QUALIFICATION REQUIREMENTS

There are several basic federal income tax requirements in order for a plan to obtain, and retain, tax-qualified status. In addition, there are special qualification requirements for *top-heavy plans,* which we will discuss later. While it is the responsibility of the company's attorney to make certain that a plan satisfies these requirements on a continuous basis, you will want to be familiar with them as well. The general qualification requirements are as follows:

1. *The plan must be for the exclusive benefit of the employees or their beneficiaries.* No one other than employees of the business can participate in the plan. Remember, though, that in corporate situations, shareholders who also are employees of the business may be covered under the plan. Thus, qualified plan benefits that accrue to employees and their families are available to shareholders who are bona fide employees of the corporation.

2. *The plan must be nondiscriminatory and constructed to cover the employee group as a whole.* Tax benefits may be denied to plans in which the percentage of highly compensated employees who benefit unreasonably exceeds the percentage of other employees benefiting under the plan. A plan must satisfy at least one of the three following nondiscrimination tests:

   a. *Percentage test.* The plan must benefit at least 70 percent of the employer's nonhighly compensated employees.

   b. *Ratio test.* The percentage of nonhighly compensated employees covered by the plan must be at least 70 percent of the percentage of highly compensated employees covered under the plan.

   c. *Average benefit test.* The average benefit provided to nonhighly compensated employees must be at least 70 percent of the average benefit provided to highly compensated employees in relation to each group's relative compensation. This test also considers how close the plan came to passing the ratio test, and other facts and circumstances of the employer.

   50/40 test. In addition, if the plan is to remain qualified, it must benefit the lesser of 50 employees or 40 percent or more of all employees. This requirement must be met on each day of the plan year. If this requirement is not met for one or more days during a plan year, the plan may be amended by the last day of such plan year to satisfy the test retroactively by expanding coverage, improving benefits or modifying eligibility conditions.

   In applying these tests, all businesses controlling, controlled by, or under common control with the company sponsoring the plan are considered one employer. Also, businesses that have some common ownership (short of control) with the sponsor, and which provide services to or receive services from the sponsor, may have to be treated as part of the employer for these purposes under the *affiliated service group* rules of the Internal Revenue Code.

For purposes of these tests, an employee is *highly compensated* if he or she:

a. was a 5 percent owner at any time during the current year or the preceding year; or

b. had compensation from the employer in excess of $85,000 during the preceding year, and if the employer elects, was in the top-paid group of the employer for the preceding year.

3. *The contributions to—or benefits of—the plan cannot discriminate in favor of officers, shareholders and other highly compensated employees.* The same formula must be used for all employees when computing contributions and benefits. For instance, one formula cannot be used for executives and another formula for hourly employees.

However, since contributions or benefits generally will be proportionate to the employee's salary and length of service, shareholder-executives and other key employees usually will receive greater contributions—and thus benefits—than other employees (subject to special rules and limitations if the plan is top heavy as discussed later).

4. *Certain benefits for spouses are required.* A qualified plan must provide for automatic survivor benefits for a surviving spouse of a vested plan participant who dies before reaching retirement age. A defined benefit or money-purchase pension plan must provide that, unless waived by the participant with the consent of the spouse, retirement benefits will be paid in the form of a *qualified joint and survivor annuity.*

5. *No contributions to the plan can revert to the employer.* Once a contribution is made, it is irrevocably committed for the benefit of the employees. However, this does not preclude transferring employer contributions that have already been made for the benefit of a terminating employee to the account of the remaining employees. However, an employee's right to his or her normal retirement benefit must be nonforfeitable upon the attainment of normal retirement age. Minimum vesting requirements are discussed later.

6. *Forfeitures can be reallocated to participants or used to reduce future contributions or administrative costs.* This is closely related to vesting requirements. When a qualified plan participant separates from service and receives a distribution of his or her vested interest or incurs a five-year break in service, nonvested benefits may be forfeited. In a defined benefit plan, forfeitures may not be used to increase benefits; rather, they must be used to reduce future employer contributions or to offset administrative expenses. Other plans are allowed to reallocate forfeitures to other participants. Thus, forfeitures under any defined contribution plan (including a money-purchase plan) can be either (1) reallocated to the accounts of other participants in a nondiscriminatory fashion or (2) used to reduce future employer contributions or administrative costs.

7. *The benefits under a pension plan must be definitely determinable.* This means that either the retirement benefits payable to the employee or the employer's contributions to the plan—in practically every case—must be actuarially determinable.

    If the amount of retirement benefits is the determining factor (e.g., $200 monthly), the arrangement generally is known as a defined benefit plan. If the employer's contribution is the determining factor (e.g., 5 percent of salary), the arrangement is referred to as a money-purchase pension plan.

8. *There must be a contract, trust or other legally binding arrangement that sets forth the plan in writing.* In the case of certain pension plans, for example, those funded with common stocks, there must be a written trust agreement. No trust agreement is needed when the plan is funded by group or individual annuities or retirement income insurance policies. The terms of the plan may be set forth either in the insurance or annuity contract itself, but a separate written document is preferable. One exception is the case of a comprehensive group annuity contract that embodies the plan requirements.

9. *Distributions must be made within prescribed age or time limits.* A qualified plan generally includes a provision that defines the "normal retirement age," the age at which a participant is entitled to benefits under the plan or the age after which no more contributions will be made on his or her behalf. For many plans, the age is 65. Generally, a plan does not need to make retirement distributions to a plan participant until the later of April 1 of the calendar year following the calendar year in which the participant attains age 70½ or the year in which the participant retires from the employer maintaining the plan. The rule is different for plan participants who own more than 5 percent of the sponsoring employer. Such participants cannot defer the payment of initial retirement benefits beyond age 70½ even if they have not retired from the plan sponsor. A qualified plan generally cannot force distributions on a participant before retirement age, unless the participant's entire benefit has a present value of $3,500 or less and he or she is paid that benefit.

Plan Eligibility Provisions

An employer generally has a broad range of employees in terms of age, levels of experience, length of employment, income and responsibility in the organization. Within that range, there are typically one or more key employees who are considered most valuable to the organization. Consequently, the employer may want to discriminate in favor of these individuals in the qualified plan.

Overly stringent eligibility provisions are one of several plan qualification requirements that can cause disqualification of the plan for being discriminatory. However, the laws recognize that certain restrictions on entry are reasonable and necessary for efficient plan operation and are not discriminatory per se. Specifically, employers may restrict from plan coverage individuals who:

- have less than 12 months' service (24 months if the plan calls for immediate vesting);

- are under age 21;

- are part-time or seasonal employees (working less than 1,000 hours a year); or

- are covered by an employee bargaining unit.

These individuals can also be ignored in applying the antidiscrimination coverage tests described in the preceding section.

Vesting Provisions

The term *vesting* is analogous to ownership. It refers to the manner and time period in which a plan participant achieves a nonforfeitable right to benefits under the plan. A participant who is *20 percent vested,* for example, has a right to 20 percent of the benefits; a participant who is 100 percent, or fully, vested has full rights to the plan benefits. In order to protect employees who have served long periods of time with a company and are still in danger of losing their accumulated benefits merely because they quit their jobs or are discharged, a qualified plan must provide for some schedule of vesting benefits over the employee's working career.

The law is specific about the minimum vesting requirements that must be met by a tax-qualified plan. Initially, a plan must specify that all accumulated benefits derived from an employee's own contributions are 100 percent vested and nonforfeitable. Thus, employees must always be entitled to the accumulated benefits purchased by their own contributions, whether those contributions were made as a mandatory requirement for participating in the plan, on a voluntary basis to provide additional retirement income or on a salary-reduction basis. Benefits derived from 401(k) salary deferrals must also be 100 percent vested.

The Code further stipulates that a non-top-heavy retirement plan will qualify if it meets one of two minimum vesting schedules that apply to the benefits accumulated through an employer's contributions.

Five Years—100 Percent Schedule

A plan will meet the minimum vesting requirements if the employees are provided with nonforfeitable rights to 100 percent of their accumulated benefits after a period of five years. Under this provision, an employer has the latitude of adopting a number of different vesting schedules. For example, a vesting schedule that would meet the above requirements could provide for 0 percent vesting for service between one and two years, 50 percent after three years of service and 100 percent in the employer's benefits at the end of the fourth year of employment.

Another more traditional variation of the above would provide for 0 percent vesting from one to four years and 100 percent vesting after the fifth year. This type of schedule, known as a *cliff vesting schedule,* may be best applied to retirement plans in which there is a very high degree of turnover in the early years of employment.

Three-to-Seven-Year Graded Schedule

The three-to-seven-year vesting schedule is a graded standard under which employees must be at least 20 percent vested in their accrued benefits derived from employer contributions after three years of covered service and vest by at least 20 percent increments for each additional year of service. The schedule is as follows:

Years of Service	Nonforfeitable Vested Percentage
0–2	0%
3	20
4	40
5	60
6	80
7	100

■ TOP-HEAVY RULES

In many ways, the *top-heavy rules* are similar to the previously discussed nondiscrimination rules. However, their purpose is to measure potential discrimination in accumulated benefits rather than discrimination caused by eligibility. The top-heavy rules were introduced to restrict the use of qualified plans as tax shelters for business owners. The rules for top-heavy plans are tax qualification requirements. Thus, a trust forming part of a top-heavy plan meets the qualification requirements of the law *only if* the additional requirements discussed below are met.

Most small plans (those with 10 or fewer employees) are by their nature top-heavy plans and financial services professionals typically design the plan document according to top-heavy specifications. Larger plans do not generally meet the definition of "top-heavy" and need not meet the additional restrictions. However, all plans, whether large or small, must include provisions that automatically take effect should the plan become top-heavy in actual operation.

When Is a Plan Top-Heavy?

A defined benefit plan is top-heavy if the present value of accumulated benefits for key employees under the plan exceeds 60 percent of the value for *all* participants under the plan. In the case of a defined contribution plan, the 60 percent test is applied to account balances of key employees and all plan participants, respectively. In other words, if a plan provides more than 60 percent of accrued benefits or contributions to key employees, the plan is top-heavy.

Where an employer maintains two or more plans, the plans will be aggregated for determining whether the group of plans is top-heavy (top-heavy group). The top-heavy group rules will apply to all plans of related employers under the existing controlled group and affiliated service group rules.

Who Is a Key Employee?

For the purposes of the top-heavy rules, a key employee is any plan participant who, during the current year or four preceding plan years, is:

- an officer of the employer who earns more than 50 percent of the defined benefit dollar limitation in effect for that year (in 2000, this limitation was $135,000; thus, the 50 percent compensation limit was $67,500);

- one of the 10 employees having annual compensation from the employer in excess of the defined contribution limitation ($30,000 in 2000) and owning more than a .5 percent interest and one of the 10 largest interests in the company;

- a greater-than-5 percent owner of the employer; or

- a greater-than-1 percent owner of the employer with annual compensation in excess of $150,000.

Illustration 10.5 shows how to identify a key employee.

Qualification Requirements for Top-Heavy Plans

In addition to the qualification requirements all plans must meet, top-heavy plans are subject to three additional restrictions that do not apply to non-top-heavy plans:

1. accelerated vesting;

2. minimum contributions or benefits requirements; and

3. restrictions on multiple plans.

Accelerated Vesting

For any plan year for which a plan is top-heavy, an employee-participant's right to accrued benefits must be nonforfeitable under one of the following two vesting schedules:

1. *Three-Year Cliff Vesting*—This alternative schedule is satisfied if an employee with at least three years of service has a nonforfeitable right to 100 percent of the accrued benefit derived from employer contributions.

2. *Six-Year Graded Vesting*—A plan satisfies the second alternative schedule if an employee has a nonforfeitable right to a percentage of the accrued benefit from employer contributions under the following table:

Years of Service	Nonforfeitable Vested Percentage
2	20%
3	40
4	60
5	80
6	100

ILL. 10.5 ■ *Identifying the Key Employee*

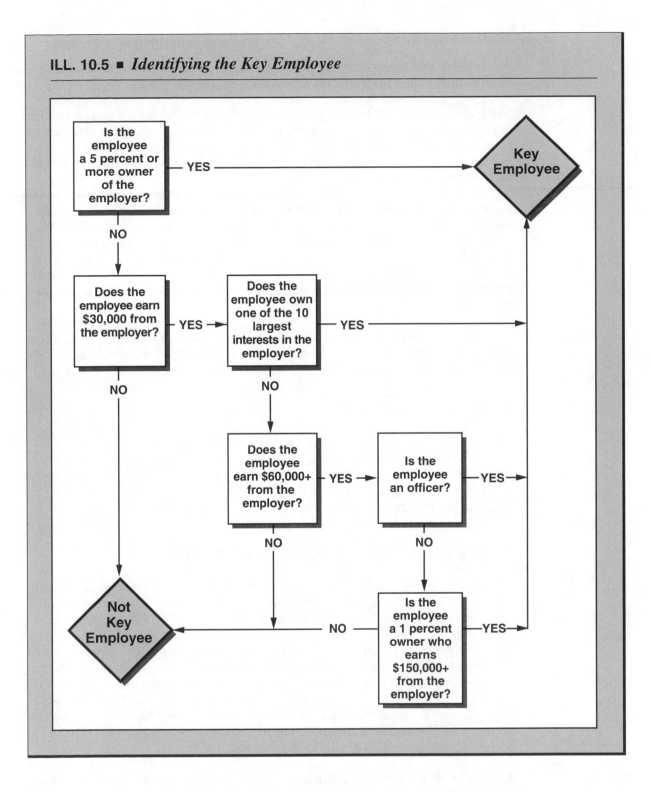

Minimum Benefits or Contributions

A top-heavy plan must also provide for minimum nonintegrated benefits and minimum nonintegrated contributions for non-key employees.

In the case of a defined benefit pension plan, for every year (maximum of 10) the plan is top-heavy, each non-key employee must accrue a benefit equal to the lesser of at least 2 percent of compensation times years of service or 20 percent of that average compensation. The compensation period is the average of the five consecutive highest years of pay.

For example, suppose Tom, a non-key employee, had five years of service. Tom earned a total of $120,000 over the last five years. Dividing the $120,000 by 5 results in an average salary of $24,000. Tom must have a minimum annual benefit of $2,400 ([24,000 × .02] × 5 years of service). If Tom continues working for the same employer and earns a total of $170,000 over the next five years, his average salary would be $34,000 and he would be entitled to an annual benefit of $6,800 ([$34,000 × .02] × 10 years of service).

In the case of a defined contribution plan, the minimum annual employer contribution must be no less than 3 percent of each non-key employee's compensation (provided the key employees receive at least 3 percent).

Restrictions on Multiple Plans

If the employer maintains both a defined benefit plan and a defined contribution plan for key employees, the aggregate amount that can be contributed for both plans is lower than would be possible if the plan were not top-heavy. If there are multiple plans that cover non-key employees, however, the employer generally need not duplicate the minimum benefits by providing the minimum benefit for both plans.

■ CONTRIBUTORY VS. NONCONTRIBUTORY PLANS

A basic decision facing the employer is whether to bear the entire cost of the contemplated plan, or whether to ask employees to share the cost. The former is called a *noncontributory plan*; the latter, a *contributory plan*.

The noncontributory plan has much in its favor. For one thing, the employer's contributions to a plan are deductible, whereas outside of the 401(k) arrangement, the employee has to first earn the money and then contribute to the plan without a tax deduction. The net cost to a corporation in the 34 percent tax bracket is only 66 cents of every dollar contributed to the pension plan. An employee in a 28 percent bracket participating with after-tax contributions has a before-tax cost of about $1.39 for each nondeductible dollar contributed.

Although plan participants cannot deduct their voluntary contributions to the plan, they do get the advantage of having interest and gains as these contributions grow tax deferred.

In addition, a noncontributory plan does away with the need for payroll deductions and other administration problems. Many employers find it simpler to assume the full cost of the plan themselves.

The employer may have strong reasons, however, for preferring a contributory plan. For instance, under this arrangement, the employees have a greater awareness of the plan. Every time they make a contribution they are reminded that the employer is also making a contribution for them. This may not be the case with a noncontributory plan where the employer's contributions are too often made without much publicity. But if a noncontributory plan is properly presented to the employees in the first place and given regular publicity, the communication problem should solve itself. Most qualified pension plans today are noncontributory.

Employer Matching Contributions and Employee Contributions

A qualified plan may allow employees to make after-tax contributions to a qualified plan, and such contributions may be either voluntary or mandatory. Mandatory employee contributions include those required as a condition of obtaining employer-derived benefits (for example, employee contributions made as a condition of obtaining employer matching contributions).

Nondiscrimination Requirements for Contributions

A qualified plan may not discriminate as to contributions or benefits in favor of officers, shareholders or highly compensated employees. Generally, this requirement is met if all participants are allowed to make contributions on the same terms and conditions. For example, voluntary employee contributions have been permitted where all participants have been eligible to make contributions and no employee was permitted to contribute more than 10 percent of compensation, determined based on cumulative contributions and cumulative compensation during the period of participation.

Employer contributions, or the benefits derived from them, must meet the usual nondiscrimination requirements applicable to qualified plans after subtracting out (under IRS guidelines) the employee contributions or the benefits derived from them. Social Security contributions by an employer generally can be considered in determining whether employer contributions constitute a uniform percentage of compensation or provide nondiscriminatory benefits.

A special nondiscrimination test is applied to the following arrangements: (1) employer matching contributions and employee contributions under qualified defined contribution plans, (2) employee contributions under defined benefit plans (to the extent allocated to a separate account for the employee) and (3) employee contributions under a qualified cost of living arrangement. This is similar to the special nondiscrimination test applicable to cash or deferred plans.

The test is satisfied if the contribution percentage for highly compensated employees does not exceed the greater of (1) 125 percent of the contribution percentage for all other eligible employees or (2) the lesser of 200 percent of the contribution percentage for all other eligible employees or such percentage plus two percentage points. The contribution percentage for a group of employees for a plan year is the average of the ratios (calculated separately for each employee of the group) of the sum of matching and employee contributions on behalf of each such employee to the employee's compensation for the year.

An employer may elect, under IRS rules, to take into account elective contributions and qualified nonelective contributions under the plan or under any other plan of the employer. Qualified nonelective contributions mean any employer contribution (other than a matching contribution) with respect to which (1) the employee may not elect to take in cash and (2) the vesting and withdrawal restrictions applicable to cash or deferred plans are satisfied (and hardship withdrawals are not permitted).

A plan will not be disqualified if excess aggregate contributions are distributed before the end of the following plan year. However, a 10 percent excise tax is imposed on the employer unless the excess is distributed within 2½ months following the close of the plan year. Such distributions are includable in the employee's gross income (without penalty) as if received during the taxable year in which the excess contribution was made.

■ DISTRIBUTIONS

The ultimate purpose of any qualified plan is to provide future retirement or savings benefits. Distributions at retirement may take one of two forms: periodic payments or a lump sum. Possible distribution benefits prior to or in addition to retirement benefits are loans for the qualified participant or rollovers into other tax-qualified accounts. Before moving on to the methods of funding the retirement plan, let's take a closer look at benefit payment provisions for qualified plans.

Retirement Benefits

Retirement benefits under a qualified pension or profit-sharing plan are paid out according to the plan's provisions. Generally, distributions from defined benefit plans are paid out as annuities but are also often offered as lump sums. Distributions from defined contribution plans are usually paid out as lump sums though some of these plans offer annuity payouts as well. In either case, the tax treatment of benefits conforms to the same rule: generally, amounts that were not previously taxed are taxable as income when distributed from a qualified plan.

Periodic Annuity Payments

If the benefits are received in the form of installment or annuity payments and if no after-tax contributions were made to the plan, then the entire amount of each payment is taxable. If the employee has a cost basis in the account, then part of each payment represents a return of previously taxed amounts and is not taxable again. The employee's cost basis equals the value of any after-tax contributions he or she made to the plan and, if the plan contains life insurance, the total of the P.S. 58 costs of the insurance.

How much is taxable is determined by applying an *exclusion ratio*. This is the ratio that the employee's cost basis represents to the total expected return. The total return is based upon the employee's life expectancy and the payout terms. For example, if the employee's cost basis is $5,000 and the total expected return is $100,000, then $\frac{1}{20}$th ($5,000 ÷ $100,000) of each payment represents a return of previously taxed income and that portion is received tax free. However, once a participant has received nontaxable income equal to the cost basis, then the full amount of future payments is taxable.

Lump-Sum Payments

Individuals who receive their benefits in a lump sum are able to take advantage of a special averaging technique to reduce tax liability. A *lump-sum distribution* is one that is received within one taxable year and represents the employee's entire account balance. In addition, the distribution must be received by reason of the employee's death, disability, attainment of age 59½ or because of the employee's separation from service. Also, for a distribution to be treated as a lump-sum distribution, the employee must have been a plan participant for five or more years.

The lump-sum distribution may then be taxed upon a five-year averaging provision. Under this rule, the lump sum is treated as if it were received over a period of five years, if the recipient so elects. Five-year averaging will no longer be available beginning in tax years after 1999. Ten-year averaging, the method generally available under prior law, may now be selected only by a participant who was age 50 before January 1, 1986. These "grandfathered" participants may also be eligible to treat the pre-1974 part of their distribution (if any) as capital gain.

Qualified Plan Loans

Loans for qualified participants from the plan are based on vested account balances. This offers a significant benefit to participants under plans that permit such loans. Not all plans do for reasons such as the additional administrative burden imposed on the employer-plan sponsor, for example, ensuring that loans are made available to qualified applicants on a nondiscriminatory basis. This discussion concerns only plans that permit such loans.

However, loans made under tax-qualified employer-sponsored plans are subject to restrictive rules governing the amount and the repayment schedule. Loans generally cannot exceed $50,000 (adjusted for current or prior outstanding loans) or one-half the participant's vested benefit, whichever is less. As long as these rules are followed, a loan will not be treated as a taxable distribution.

The rules deny the use of plan loans as *permanent* or *bridge financing* by prohibiting the use of balloon-note financing under a qualified plan. Plan loans must be repaid not less than quarterly in level payments. The law sets a maximum five-year term for plan loans, except for the purchase of a principal residence for the plan participant. Department of Labor regulations also apply to plan loans. Among other things, they allow only one-half of a participant's vested benefit to be pledged as security for the loan.

Rollovers

A person who receives a lump-sum or similar eligible distribution from a qualified plan may be able to defer taxation by transferring or rolling the distribution over into another tax-qualified account, including an IRA. The sum must be transferred into the other plan within 60 days of receipt.

The amount rolled over into the other account may consist of all or part of the distribution received. Of course, any portion that is not rolled over is subject to current taxation and withholding. The maximum amount that may be rolled over is the dollar amount (or fair market value of the property) received, reduced by employee after-tax contributions.

All qualified plans that might make distributions eligible for rollover treatment are required to give the participant the right to transfer the amount directly to another qualified plan or to an individual retirement account or annuity instead of receiving the distribution in cash. This assures the participant the opportunity to avoid withholding and defer tax. It also provides an opportunity for the practitioner to assist the participant in establishing the IRA and related retirement planning.

Penalty Taxes

A number of penalty taxes may apply to distributions from qualified plans.

10 Percent Early Withdrawal Tax

A 10 percent penalty is imposed on early withdrawals from a qualified plan. If payments are received early (i.e., before age 59½), there is, in addition to the regular income tax, a special tax equal to 10 percent of the amount of the distribution includable in gross income. However, several exceptions apply. The 10 percent penalty is waived if a distribution is made:

- because of the employee's death or disability;

- to an employee who has reached age 55, separated from service and has met the early retirement requirements of the plan;

- to an alternate payee under a qualified domestic relations order;

- to pay deductible medical expenses; and

- as part of a scheduled series of substantially equal payments over the participant's life or the joint lives of the participant and beneficiary.

50 Percent Penalty Tax

For plan participants with a 5 percent or greater ownership in the plan sponsor, distributions from a qualified plan must start no later than April 1 following the calendar year in which the participant turns 70½. And they must begin even if the participant has not retired. This role does not apply to non-owner participants.

Distributions must be at least equal to the minimum distribution amount, which basically equals the account balance divided by the recipient's life expectancy or the joint life expectancy of the participant and beneficiary, based on attained age. Under this rule, if the distribution in a year falls below the required minimum, then a 50 percent penalty tax is imposed on the difference between the required minimum and the amount distributed.

Death Benefits

Generally, benefits paid to a deceased employee's beneficiary are taxed the same as benefits received by a retired employee. However, one exception should be noted. This exception involves life insurance proceeds. Where the benefits consist of life insurance proceeds, the amount by which the proceeds exceed the cash value (or the reserve, if no cash value exists) of the policy immediately prior to the employee's death is received income tax free.

■ FUNDING THE QUALIFIED RETIREMENT PLAN

We now are ready to examine the various methods an employer may use in funding a qualified retirement plan. By funding we mean financing or accumulating the funds necessary to guarantee the benefits to be provided by the plan.

From a life insurance viewpoint, the employer has three basic approaches to funding a retirement plan: (1) the fully insured plan; (2) the combination, or split-funded plan; or (3) the noninsured, or self-administered plan.

We will take a detailed look at these three approaches later. First, let's examine the uses, characteristics and advantages of life insurance in any retirement plan. (See Ill. 10.6.)

Nontax Advantages of Life Insurance

Life insurance has proven itself as an ideally suited qualified plan funding medium for the small-sized and medium-sized business. For one thing, security is an essential part of funding a retirement plan. In addition, the business of working with life expectancy—a primary tool of the life insurance business—is an essential part of retirement planning. The knowledge and service capabilities so essential in a qualified retirement program are part of the established pattern of a life insurance company. These combined characteristics of life insurance provide clients with a truly sound funding medium.

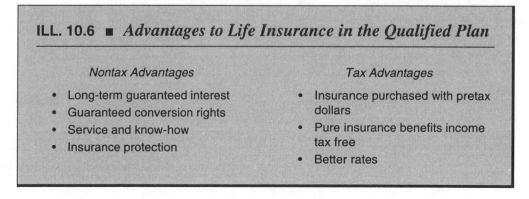

ILL. 10.6 ■ *Advantages to Life Insurance in the Qualified Plan*

Nontax Advantages	Tax Advantages
• Long-term guaranteed interest	• Insurance purchased with pretax dollars
• Guaranteed conversion rights	• Pure insurance benefits income tax free
• Service and know-how	• Better rates
• Insurance protection	

Guaranteed Conversion Rights

Only the life insurance industry can guarantee the price of future annuities. Money deposited today may be converted to retirement annuities far in the future. The "pegging" of annuity prices at today's rates is considered by many as one of the best safeguards available to a sound retirement plan.

Insurance Protection

Only a life insurance company can offer life insurance protection. There are several advantages of life insurance in qualified retirement plans. Initially, it provides a meaningful benefit for the employee now. There's no need to wait 15, 25 or 30 years until retirement to appreciate the plan. In addition, some insurance companies will offer simplified or guaranteed issue with policies issued inside of a qualified plan. Limits on face amounts and the degree of health evidence will vary by insurance company, number of plan participants to be insured and sometimes the amount of premium used to fund the insurance policies. It also is the vehicle through which the other advantages we've discussed are made available. Finally, life insurance maximizes the tax advantages of a qualified retirement plan. These tax advantages are significant enough to be examined in more detail below.

Other Nontax Advantages

The life insurance industry has the ability to provide the service and expertise required to achieve the plan's funding goals. Working with the accumulation of money in a plan which is based on the contingency of people living up to a future date is a primary function of the life insurance industry. The art of efficiently operating a qualified retirement plan is inherent to the industry's operation.

Also, life insurance is an excellent source of long-term secured interest. Virtually all administrators of retirement funds recognize the need to invest at least a portion of their holdings in secure investments. The cash values of life insurance are unchallenged in this area.

Tax Advantages of Life Insurance

Several tax advantages apply to life insurance included in a qualified retirement plan. No other funding medium offers all of these same advantages.

Insurance Purchased with Pretax Dollars

Employer contributions to a qualified retirement plan are deductible by the employer and nontaxable to the employee. With one minor exception, contributions used to purchase life insurance on the lives of the participants of a qualified plan also are nontaxable. Thus when compared to the purchase of personal policies with after-tax dollars, the true cost of the pension series policy is considerably less.

Pure Insurance Benefits Income Tax Free

The death proceeds represented by the pure insurance protection (face amount of the policy minus cash value) are income tax free to a participant's named beneficiary. This advantage is not available to other death benefits under a qualified plan. Accumulated cash paid as a death benefit is eligible for five-year averaging if available and elected by the beneficiary. A policy's cash value is treated similarly.

Better Rates

Life insurance companies do not pay federal tax on the interest earned on the reserves held under qualified retirement plans. This results in a tax savings to the insurance company that is passed on to the policyowner in a variety of ways. Most mutual companies reflect this saving in more favorable dividends. Other companies—particularly nonparticipating companies—provide reduced premium or annuity purchase rates or, in some cases, higher cash values. The competitive rates and values of pension series insurance contracts are at a maximum when compared to personally purchased policies.

Insurance Must Be Incidental

The primary purpose of a pension or profit-sharing plan must be to provide benefits at some future date. Insurance protection purchased on the life of a participant and payable to his or her beneficiary is considered an immediate benefit to the participant. However, a retirement plan may include life insurance protection on the participants provided it is *incidental* to the plan's primary purpose. To assure compliance with this requirement, the Internal Revenue Service applies the *incidental death benefit test.*

Death benefits are incidental in any type of pension or profit-sharing plan—whether insured or not—if the cost of providing the death benefit for any participant does not exceed 25 percent of the total cost of providing all benefits for that participant.

For plans funded in part through the purchase of ordinary insurance contracts, the 25 percent test is met if less than 50 percent of the employer contributions credited to the participant's account is used to purchase ordinary life insurance.

A qualified retirement plan that invests all of its funds in life insurance and annuity contracts—*a fully insured plan*—and that provides a death benefit equal to 100 times the participant's retirement benefit or the cash value of the policy, whichever is greater, will automatically satisfy the 25 percent rule. A typical retirement income insurance policy maintains this 100-times ratio or cash value death benefit. A retirement annuity contract provides a death benefit equal to a return of premiums, or the cash value of the policy, whichever is greater. Thus both contracts satisfy the incidental death benefit test.

A pension plan utilizing other than retirement income insurance or annuity contracts also must meet the incidental death benefit test. The plan cannot be funded entirely with ordinary life policies, even though the cash values will provide an annuity at retirement. This is because the death benefits under any ordinary life contract would exceed the permitted 100 to 1 ratio. Thus under such a plan the additional funds needed at retirement must be accumulated in a fund or contracts that do not provide death benefits.

It should be noted that the 25 percent rule is the ultimate test for incidental insurance, and that the 100 to 1 rule is merely a *safe harbor* rule. It has simply been determined that certain plans will satisfy the 25 percent rule in all cases if they satisfy the 100 to 1 rule.

A profit-sharing trust that purchases ordinary life insurance, for example, on the lives of the participants must meet two conditions in order for the insurance protection to be considered incidental. These are:

1. The aggregate premiums paid for the insurance on each participant's life must be less than one-half the aggregate contributions and forfeitures allocated to the participant's account at any particular time. For example, if over a five-year period a participant's total account comes to $5,000, premiums paid during that time must be less than $2,500.

2. The plan must require the trustee, at or before the employee's retirement, either: (a) to distribute the policy to the employee, (b) to convert its entire value into cash or (c) to elect a periodic-income option so that trust-owned insurance on the employee's life will not continue beyond his or her retirement.

If the plan meets the above conditions, the life insurance is deemed incidental to the main purposes of the plan—deferred distribution of profit-sharing funds.

The Cost of Pure Insurance

Employer contributions to a qualified plan are not generally taxable to the employee until they are actually distributed. However, when such contributions are used to purchase insurance on a participant's life and the benefit is payable to a beneficiary, the pure insurance protection of the policy is considered to be a current benefit and therefore the cost of this benefit is a taxable distribution to the employee.

The amount of pure insurance is determined by subtracting the cash value from the face amount of the policy. The cost of this protection is then determined by multiplying this difference by the annual renewable term rates of the insurance carrier, or by applying the P.S. 58 term rates. You will recall that the P.S. 58 table was covered in Chapter 9. Also we noted there that the P.S. 58 rates or annual renewable term rates are almost always lower than the insurance company's actual rates.

The taxable income to the employee, already nominal when compared to the employer's total contribution, will decrease as the cash value of the policy increases. For example, at age 55 the P.S. 58 term rate is $13.74 per $1,000. This amount multiplied by the pure insurance equals the taxable income to the employee. Thus if the protection in that year is $100,000, the taxable income to the employee would be only $1,374 ($13.74 × 100).

Income recognition is even lower when using the issuing insurance company's annual renewable term rate. For the 55-year-old insured example, assuming male annual renewable term rates from an insurance carrier, the rate is $1.52 per $1,000.

For $100,000 of insurance protection, the taxable income would be $152 ($1.52 × 100).

■ LIFE INSURANCE FUNDING METHODS

Now we are ready to discuss the three methods available to fund a qualified retirement plan. First, let's look at the plan where life insurance is the sole funding vehicle.

The Fully Insured Plan

In its simplest terms, the *fully insured program* is a plan that invests all contributions in life insurance, annuity contracts or a combination of the two. The insurance company receives the money deposited in the plan, accumulates it prior to retirement and distributes the benefits as they become payable.

A variety of insurance policies and annuity contracts are available for use in a fully insured plan, including individual and group coverages. However, in the small-sized and medium-sized business market, the most widely used forms of insurance under fully insured plans are retirement annuity contracts.

Retirement Annuity

A *retirement annuity contract* calls for a level premium for the year it is issued until retirement age. Its basic function is to allow for the buildup of values throughout the annuitant's working years and the orderly liquidation of these values during the retirement years.

Typically, the contract is issued in units of $10 of monthly income—payable for life—with 10 years guaranteed. A different payout may be selected, including a lump-sum distribution at retirement or severance of employment. In the event of the annuitant's death prior to retirement, the contract provides for the payment of its cash value or net premiums paid to date, whichever is greater. Here again the death benefit may be taken in a lump sum or paid in installments.

Retirement Income Insurance Policy

This policy is essentially the same as the retirement annuity contract except that it also includes an insurance element. It pays to the named beneficiary, in the event of the insured's death prior to retirement, a minimum of $1,000 of insurance for each $10 of monthly income purchased.

As the cash values of the policy increase, the insurance feature of the policy diminishes until such cash values exceed $1,000. If death occurs after that date but before retirement age, the policy's cash value is payable to the insured's named beneficiary. In this regard it is identical to a retirement annuity contract. It is not uncommon to find both types of policies used in the same plan: the retirement income policy for insurance participants and the retirement annuity contract for uninsurable participants.

The Combination-Funded Plan

The *combination-funded plan* offers services and guarantees of insurance or annuity policies, plus a more liberal investment medium.

In the small-sized and medium-sized business market, the combination-funded plan usually combines a whole life insurance policy with an auxiliary fund. Typically the auxiliary fund is invested predominantly in common stocks and other securities, which are intended to provide a hedge against inflation. At retirement, the two funds are combined to purchase the retirement benefit.

A pension plan funded by the combination approach has many of the same characteristics as one funded by retirement income policies. However, the benefits of the plan are not provided by the cash values of the life insurance policies alone but through the combination of cash values and an auxiliary investment fund.

The combination-funded profit-sharing plan provides for the purchase of life insurance with a portion of the trust fund. The amount of the fund allocated for the insurance is governed by the employer's objectives and the 50 percent limitation of the Internal Revenue Service.

The purchase of whole life insurance under a profit-sharing trust helps to round out the benefits of the plan into a sound retirement program. However, many deferred profit-sharing trusts are established on a noninsured basis. There are certain valid reasons for this, but they cannot outweigh the strong reasons for including at least a portion of the funds in life insurance. We will now discuss a couple of these reasons.

Bargain Annuity Rates

From the standpoint of retirement benefits, the purchase of life insurance guarantees the right ultimately to purchase a retirement annuity at today's prices. A whole life policy purchased today under a profit-sharing plan will include a conversion rider that guarantees the right to convert the policy's cash values plus money from the auxiliary fund into an annuity at some future date. Thus the price for annuities to be purchased 15, 20 or even 30 years in the future is provided for at a guaranteed rate set today. The danger of an employee's outliving the cash accumulation after retirement is no longer a threat since the ultimate purchase of a retirement annuity guarantees a lifetime income.

Immediate Family Protection

Life insurance provides an immediate death benefit. It takes considerable time for an employee's account under a profit-sharing plan to become large enough to protect his or her family adequately. For younger employees with family responsibilities, this is the time when the need for protection is greatest and ability to buy is most limited. The absence of an immediate death benefit in the profit-sharing plan is a serious handicap to them.

A portion of their account invested in life insurance is used, either in full or in part, to fund the retirement plan. We now turn our attention to plans where life insurance is not used at all. You should be aware of such plans primarily from the standpoint of competition. One example is the self-administered plan.

The Self-Administered Plan

A *self-administered plan* is an arrangement, where contributions are deposited with a trustee, usually a bank or trust company, that invests the money, accumulates the earnings and pays benefits directly to the participating employee. The plan operates under a trust agreement between the employer and the trustee. The written agreement sets forth the terms under which the trust fund will be created and administered. This type of plan is used primarily with large groups of employees.

Under the self-administered trust, the annual contributions are usually determined by actuarial computations, taking into consideration the age, sex, years of service, compensation and benefits of each participant. A self-administered trust is usually designed to pay only pensions but it also may provide that a deceased employee's family will be entitled to an incidental death benefit.

At first glance, the self-administered plan may seem to be the least expensive way of funding retirement plans. It should be pointed out, however, that self-administered plans must meet annual actuarial, legal and trust fees, administrative expenses and other charges. These costs can be quite substantial.

Under a self-administered plan, the integrity of principal and the rate of income depend for better or for worse upon investment experience. If more employees than anticipated live to retirement, the employer eventually must make up the difference.

On the other hand, actuarial risks are eliminated or reduced if the fund is at least partially insured. Any longevity exceeding what is expected among retired employees will be borne by the insurance company and not the employer.

■ SELLING THE QUALIFIED PLAN

Selling qualified retirement plans involves helping the employer recognize the value of having a retirement plan in the first place and funding it with insurance or annuities.

Sales Points in a Qualified Plan

Let's briefly review the general sales points of a qualified pension or profit-sharing plan and then the specific advantages of an insured plan. First, the general advantages:

1. It stabilizes employment and reduces turnover. The retirement plan becomes an important factor when a valuable employee considers competitive job offers.

2. It attracts and holds the caliber of personnel that makes for a more productive organization.

3. It increases efficiency of operations through the orderly retirement of older personnel, thus giving younger and more active employees the opportunity to move up in income and responsibilities.

4. It helps relieve employees of financial fears. A retirement plan tends to free their minds of basic financial worries, makes them more secure in their jobs and creates a base upon which they can build their own financial programs. This helps to create a group of employees who can give full concentration to their jobs.

5. It improves the company's public image. The company is placed in a more favorable light with customers, creditors, lending institutions and the public in general.

6. It provides the participants with what amounts to a tax-deferred increase in salary through the company's contributions to the plan.

7. It protects the employee's Social Security benefits at retirement. Pension or profit-sharing income permits the employee to actually retire rather than be forced to seek other employment and endanger his or her Social Security income because of the law's outside earnings limitation.

8. Employer contributions to the plan are tax deductible for federal income tax purposes within prescribed annual limitations, thus reducing the company's cost by the amount of its tax bracket. The federal government, recognizing the social desirability of contributions to retirement plans, indirectly shares in the cost of the plan.

9. Employer contributions for retirement benefits are not currently taxable to the participants. This permits the employees—including shareholder-employees, high-salaried executives and other key employees (provided special qualification requirements and limitations are met)—to store dollars for retirement on a tax-deferred basis.

10. The pension or profit-sharing fund accumulates without current payment of federal income tax, enabling it to grow to a substantially greater size than a plan that is taxed currently.

11. Payment of federal income tax by employees is postponed until retirement when the participant's taxable income is usually lower.

These 11 reasons provide you with a sales story that is extremely forceful. However, the pension and profit-sharing story becomes even stronger when you add the advantages of partially or fully funding the plan with life insurance annuities.

1. Future values are guaranteed in advance and are not subject to speculative hazards.

2. Investment and reinvestment problems for the employer and employees are eliminated entirely.

3. Actuarial risks are eliminated in fully insured plans. Under noninsured plans, any longevity exceeding what is expected among retired employees bears

heavily upon the employer. Actuarial error under a noninsured plan may require an increase in the employer's contributions. This is particularly critical for the smaller employer that cannot rely on the "law of large numbers."

4. The plan can be administered more simply and economically, with a minimum of supervision.

5. Only through an insured plan can retirement benefits be made payable on a guaranteed lifetime basis.

6. Guaranteed death benefits can be made available through the plan and be coordinated with the employee's personal life insurance program.

To sum up these points, an insured plan is one that is complete in every feature. All financial risks are assumed by the insurance company and payment of the benefits is guaranteed by the insurance company.

After the employer is convinced to look at a qualified plan, the next likely step will be to collect an employee census and provide the information to an insurance company or third-party qualified plan administrator. Using the employee data, including salary and age, a computer-generated proposal will be prepared showing a plan compatible with the employer's business objectives.

■ SUMMARY

This chapter has attempted to acquaint you with qualified plans in a summary fashion. Because of their powerful tax incentives, namely an income tax deduction for the employer and the employee in the case of 401(k) arrangements, tax-deferred growth and tax-favored distributions, qualified plans are subject to many government-imposed rules and regulations. Even so, these plans are strong tools for attracting and retaining employees while also offering retirement benefits for owner-employees.

Your ability to understand the basics of qualified plans will help you in many insurance sales situations, whether working with businesses that might be considering installing or improving an existing plan or with individuals looking to maximize the benefits of their employers' qualified plans. While this chapter cannot make you a qualified plan expert, you should now feel comfortable in discussing how these plans can benefit businesses and individuals.

■ CHAPTER 10 QUESTIONS FOR REVIEW

1. Which of the following is NOT among the benefits of a qualified employer plan?
   A. Deductible employer contributions
   B. Tax-free benefits at retirement
   C. No current taxation to the employee
   D. Tax-free growth of retirement fund

2. A qualified employer plan that promises a specific retirement benefit is which of the following?

A. Defined benefit
B. Defined contribution
C. Stock bonus
D. Profit-sharing

3. Under the three-to-seven-year vesting schedule, a participant must be vested in what percentage of accrued benefits after three years?

A. 100 percent
B. 60 percent
C. 20 percent
D. 0 percent

4. In a money-purchase plan, the limit on contributions for plan participants is the lesser of $30,000 or what percentage of compensation?

A. 10 percent
B. 25 percent
C. 50 percent
D. 75 percent

5. Which of the following statements regarding life insurance in a qualified plan is CORRECT?

A. It must be incidental to the plan's primary purpose.
B. It must be term insurance.
C. It must be part of a fully insured plan.
D. It must be owned by the employer.

6. Which of the following is NOT a profit-sharing type of plan?

A. Age-based
B. Cash balance
C. New comparability
D. 401(k) plan

7. Which of the following is NOT a characteristic of a 401(k) plan?

A. Employee deferrals of salary
B. Profit-sharing plan type of contributions from the sponsoring employer
C. A guaranteed monthly benefit at retirement
D. Individual accounts

8. In 2000, what was the maximum amount of salary a participant could defer in a 401(k) plan?

   A. Unlimited

   B. $5,000

   C. $10,500

   D. 10 percent of pay not to exceed $30,000

9. Employer contributions for a SIMPLE plan can be made to which of the following?

   A. Employee's IRA

   B. 401(k) trust

   C. Both A and B

   D. Neither A nor B

10. Life insurance proceeds paid from a qualified plan to a beneficiary upon death of the insured participant are

    A. income tax free to the extent the death benefits exceed the policy cash value

    B. subject to income tax but there is a credit for years of plan participation

    C. fully subject to income tax

    D. income tax free both for cash value and the pure insurance amount

Section Four

**Transfer Planning
for Individuals and
Business Entities**

11

Estate Planning

U p to this point in your study, you have covered a lot of ground centered on the important role life insurance plays in solving the problems and needs of business owners, their firms and their employees. Now it is time to shift the emphasis a bit. In this chapter and the next, you will be directing your attention to the problems confronting individuals both in and out of the business world. You will be studying the factors involved in building, conserving and distributing an *estate*. This chapter begins with a study of the factors that lead to estate shrinkage, shifts to a look at the basics of the federal estate tax and moves on to an introduction of estate planning tools and techniques. The next chapter will discuss the solution to estate shrinkage—life insurance.

■ ■ ■ ■ ■

■ WHAT IS ESTATE PLANNING?

When given a choice, most people choose to transfer their assets to their loved ones and favorite charities. Although everyone has this choice, few make it and, unfortunately, a significant part of their estate assets may never reach their intended beneficiaries.

Without efficient estate planning, a large portion of assets could be needlessly lost to administrative expenses, fees, taxes and probate costs. And, the larger the estate, the more of its value may be lost. Estate taxes alone can reduce the value of an estate by 50 percent, 55 percent or 60 percent!

The potential shrinkage may be a surprise to those who have not properly planned their estates because some people may have no idea of the value of their estates. They either do not know what is includable in the estate or how to calculate its current value.

As you might have guessed, one way in which an estate owner can achieve maximum beneficial use of his or her wealth and assure that it is passed on intact to heirs is through life insurance. Before we address the uses of life insurance for estate planning, it is important to understand what happens to an estate if no adequate plans are laid prior to death. Without proper planning, an estate—no matter what its size—is subject to *shrinkage.* By the term *estate shrinkage,* we mean the amount by which the value of an estate is depleted in the process of being transferred to the heirs after the death of the estate owner.

Regardless of the estate's size, it is subject to shrinkage when the estate owner dies. However, shrinkage can be controlled by a sound approach to estate planning that you, as financial advisor, can initiate. Estate planning is a field where the prospects are plentiful, the sales are large and the rewards for you are great—both financially and professionally.

■ OBSTACLES TO ESTATE TRANSFER

Contrary to popular belief, estate transfer is a privilege and not a right. Both federal and state governments have imposed conditions upon its exercise. As a result of these conditions, the process of estate transfer is neither simple nor direct.

Misconceptions held by the general public regarding estate transfer and the administration process can be traced to a number of factors. First is the lack of probate experience. Most people have had little actual exposure to estate administration and settlement. The majority of those have experience only as heirs.

Second is the problem of motivation. Many individuals tend to avoid thoughts of death and therefore put off consideration of the estate administration process and all of its ramifications. This is especially true when the estate is their own.

Third is the related problem of the attitude that not much can be done about taxes and other problems associated with death. As a result, problems may be ignored. As you will see, this can lead to financial tragedy for the heirs of the deceased.

Need for Liquidity

Settling an estate, regardless of its size, requires an outlay of cash. As we already noted, most people are unaware that the process of estate transfer is a complicated affair that is usually accompanied by a multiplicity of estate settlement costs. As a result, few estates have sufficient liquidity to assure a smooth transfer to the heirs. Estates created by ingenuity and hard work may be shrunk drastically and unnecessarily through a lack of careful planning by the creators.

An adequate source of *liquid funds*—cash or other assets that can be transformed quickly into cash—is an accepted prerequisite in running any successful business. By the same token, the successful settlement of an estate also depends upon an adequate and available supply of liquid funds.

Through proper planning, estate shrinkage can be minimized. In formulating an estate plan, however, the estate owner's responsibility does not end after planning measures that will minimize the estate's eventual need for cash. It is also necessary to make sure that sufficient funds will be available to the representative to pay those estate costs that remain. (See Ill. 11.1.) If this is not done, the problem compounds itself. Valuable assets in the estate may have to be sacrificed to raise the necessary cash, or a business interest may have to be liquidated or sold in an unfavorable

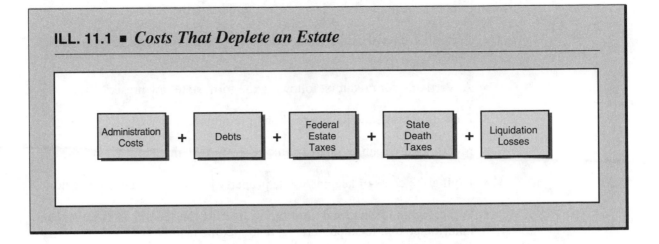

ILL. 11.1 ■ *Costs That Deplete an Estate*

market to pay the estate bills. Without adequate liquidity, unnecessary and severe shrinkage may be experienced despite an otherwise well-planned estate.

Estate Settlement Costs

There are many factors that contribute to estate shrinkage. These factors are collectively known as *estate settlement costs* and include the following:

Administration costs. These include funeral expenses, probate expenses and fees for the executor or administrator and attorney.

Debts. Current bills and cumulative liabilities that ordinarily would have been paid out of the estate owner's current income must now be paid from estate assets.

Federal estate taxes. The federal government levies a tax against the estate before it is transferred to the heirs.

State death taxes. The state government may impose one or more death taxes.

Liquidation losses. Such losses inevitably accompany the forced sale and liquidation of estate assets in the effort to get the necessary cash with which to meet the listed cash estate liabilities.

Let's take a closer look at each of these settlement costs.

Funeral and Administration Costs

One of the first duties of the estate representative is to pay the expenses of the decedent's funeral. The amount of cash needed for this purpose can be substantial.

The other duties of the representative in settling the estate are numerous. Because many of the duties are legal matters, it is usually necessary for the representative to hire an attorney. This, of course, requires additional cash.

Among the representative's most important duties are the following:

- Probating the will, filing an inventory of estate assets and paying probate court costs

- Advertising for creditors, following the form state law prescribes

- Providing bond and paying the bond premium

- Meeting the expenses related to the contesting of any claim against the estate

- Paying the costs of keeping estate property in repair and good condition

- Preparing and filing final tax returns covering the federal estate tax, state inheritance tax, local property tax and income tax

- Placing the estate in a form that will permit its distribution, either as required under the state's laws of descent or as prescribed in the will of the deceased

Even if nothing unusual develops in the handling of the estate, considerable cost may be incurred. If, however, the estate is complicated by issues such as property located in other states or a contested will, then the administration costs will mount accordingly.

For the larger estates, the nontax costs may be relatively small when compared to state and federal taxes. But for the smaller estates, probate and administration expenses often exceed the outlay required for taxes and usually represent a sizable proportion of the total shrinkage.

The following table shows a breakdown of the degree of estate shrinkage that can be expected from administration costs for estates of various sizes. It is based on information disclosed by a large number of federal estate tax returns.

Estimated Administration Costs

Size of Gross Estate	Administration Expense	Percent of Shrinkage
$ 50,000	$ 2,300	4.6%
75,000	3,450	4.6
100,000	4,600	4.6
150,000	6,900	4.6
200,000	9,200	4.6
250,000	11,500	4.6
300,000	13,800	4.6
400,000	18,400	4.6
500,000	22,500	4.5
750,000	33,000	4.4
1,000,000	43,000	4.3
2,000,000	84,000	4.2
3,000,000	126,000	4.2
5,000,000	215,000	4.3

As you can see, administration expenses take a hefty chunk out of the estate before it reaches the heirs. This is especially true in the smaller estates where administration costs frequently constitute the larger source of estate shrinkage.

The figures in the table are only averages and must be adjusted in light of circumstances pertaining to each individual estate and degree of planning. Thus, estate liquidity is needed first to meet these costs.

Debts

The second type of estate costs that must be paid are debts incurred during life. In his or her will, the estate owner usually directs that "all my just debts be paid." Whether or not this provision is included, the law *requires* payment of all debts at death. Items included under debts chargeable against the estate are:

- expenses of last illness;

- outstanding current bills; and

- unpaid mortgages and other installment and long-term obligations (unless by law, or by direction in the will, payable by the heirs).

In other words debts generally embrace the many things an individual has purchased but has not yet paid for at death. In addition, certain tax liabilities—other than estate and inheritance taxes—enter prominently into the debt picture. The tax liabilities are:

- *Personal property and real estate taxes.* In most states these taxes are assessed in one year and payable in the next. Death usually occurs at a time when one year's property taxes are due and chargeable against the estate.

- *Unpaid federal income taxes.* In spite of our withholding system, large sums still may be due at the time of death.

- *Unpaid state income taxes.* The unpaid tax will apply to income earned from the closing date of the last return until the time of death—possibly a full year's income.

The following table illustrates the effect that debts can have on estate shrinkage. By comparing the table on debts with the table on administration expenses, it is apparent that they both follow somewhat the same pattern. In smaller estates particularly, debts take a healthy bite out of the estate before it makes its way to the heirs. As with administration expenses, these debts must be paid promptly. Debts are the second reason why estate liquidity is essential.

Average Estate Debts

Size of Gross Estate	Total Debts	Percent of Shrinkage
$ 50,000	$ 2,900	5.8%
75,000	4,300	5.7
100,000	5,600	5.6
150,000	8,250	5.5
200,000	10,600	5.3
250,000	13,000	5.2
300,000	15,600	5.2
400,000	20,400	5.1
500,000	25,000	5.0
750,000	35,250	4.7
1,000,000	45,000	4.5
2,000,000	82,000	4.1
3,000,000	120,000	4.0
5,000,000	185,000	3.7

The Federal Estate Tax

The federal estate tax is a graduated tax with rates beginning at 18 percent and climbing to 55 percent. It is popularly thought of as a tax affecting only people at the very top income levels. While it is true that recent tax reform laws have provided relief to many middle and upper-middle estate owners, the estate tax can still be a factor to many large estates. We will take a closer look at the basics of the federal estate tax shortly.

State Death Taxes

The federal government is not alone in making tax claims against estates. Every state (and the District of Columbia) imposes some kind of death tax.

State death taxes take three forms: an *estate tax,* an *inheritance tax* and a *credit estate tax.* A state estate tax is levied against an individual's right to transfer property at death and is imposed on the estate as a whole. A state inheritance tax is imposed on the succession of individual shares left to different beneficiaries—it is a tax on the right to receive property at death. A credit estate tax is based on the credit allowed under the federal estate tax for state death taxes paid, an amount which many states impose as a tax. Individual states may levy any or all of these death taxes and all states do impose some kind of death tax.

State death taxes are often overlooked in considering estate settlement costs. Yet, in many cases, a state credit estate or inheritance tax is levied even if an estate is too small to incur federal tax.

From our discussion thus far, it is obvious that every estate—from the smallest to the largest—is subject to some degree of shrinkage from administration costs, debts, the federal estate tax, state death taxes or a combination of these factors. If liquid funds—or assets that can be quickly converted to cash at their fair market value—are available to meet all the costs of estate settlement, estate shrinkage will suffer only to the extent of these costs. Adequate liquidity is seldom available because most estate owners are unaware of the costs created by their deaths. This brings about the most insidious form of estate shrinkage—forced liquidation.

Forced Liquidation

Since settlement costs must be paid in cash within a limited time, the representative without the necessary funds usually is forced to liquidate estate property to raise the needed funds. In previous chapters, we saw the consequences of forced liquidation in connection with business interests. As we pointed out there, converting nonliquid property into cash is usually done through a forced sale that brings substantially less than the property's real value.

In the case of estates, the problem of forced liquidation arises because the estate liabilities must be paid in cash. For example, the representative and the attorney must be paid in cash. Similarly, the other charges against the estate such as the last illness and funeral expenses and all taxes due as the result of death must be paid in cash from the estate assets.

There is no alternative if the estate does not have the cash on hand: estate assets must be liquidated. When liquidation is necessary under pressure of time, severe loss is the normal consequence.

Liquidation Costs

In the matter of liquidation costs, the smaller estate usually fares worse than does the larger estate, because estate settlement expenses constitute a larger percentage of the average small estate than of the larger estate. In addition, the assets in the smaller estate are often limited in number. So if a quick sale is necessary, sharp liquidation losses may be involved. Even more important in the case of the smaller estate is that there is little for the family in the first place and any shrinkage is keenly felt. Heavy losses can be sustained in a million dollar estate and the beneficiaries still receive inheritances of a substantial amount. However, it takes only a little shrinkage in a $50,000 to $100,000 estate to create a substantial impact.

In the case of the larger estate, some portion of the cash demands can be met out of current estate income, since a portion of the estate is often invested in income-producing property.

It should be emphasized that the charges against the estate are cash demands, that these creditors are the preferred creditors and that, though their demands may substantially reduce the estate before the spouse and children receive even a dollar, the demands must still be met.

Causes of Loss

As we have said, the exact scope of the losses suffered as a result of forced liquidation cannot be anticipated. There are two reasons for this.

In the first place we do not know the time of death. It may occur either in a period of recession or a period of prosperity.

Even though death occurs in a period of general prosperity, it does not necessarily follow that the estate will suffer little or no loss from liquidation. Even in prosperous times, not all lines of business share equally in the prosperity. The estate may be holding investments in property or enterprises that, although general business conditions may be good, are currently at a low ebb.

If death should occur in a period of recession and there is no cash reserve on hand to protect the estate, the usual experience is tragic—the sale of estate assets at almost auction block prices.

In addition, the character of the property may change before death occurs. As the nature of the property owned will probably change from time to time as long as the estate owner lives, the liquidity of the estate will also continue to change.

If the estate consists in large part of government bonds and other highly liquid assets—such as stocks with a wide and active market—there may be a minimum of loss. But the usual estate is made up of a miscellaneous type of properties and securities, some real estate, an odd lot of bonds, business interests and a mixed collection of stock.

Then there is the additional problem of liquidating such property for estate settlement. When such property is sold, the survivors may incur a federal income tax liability on the sale, if it has gained in value since it was first obtained. The extent of the income tax liability cannot be determined in advance, since there is no way of knowing what the value of the property will be at the precise time it must be liquidated for estate settlement costs.

It is impossible to predict in advance the experience of any given estate as far as liquidation losses are concerned. We can say that unless ample cash is present so that forced liquidation is unnecessary, some loss is virtually inevitable. The best method of providing the cash is, as we shall see in the next chapter, through the use of life insurance. Before considering how life insurance and other estate planning tools and techniques can help to minimize estate shrinkage, let's take a closer look at the federal estate tax.

▪ FEDERAL ESTATE TAX

The federal government imposes an estate tax on all property a U.S. citizen owns worldwide at his or her death. Recent changes in the tax law have reduced much of the impact of the federal estate tax, especially at the death of the first spouse to die. But while this tax burden has been eased considerably for many, it has not been completely eliminated. The estate tax still exists and for many it will still create problems.

Let's look at what property gets taxed and for how much.

ILL. 11.2 ■ *Estate Quick View*

Personal Residence $ _____

Real Estate   _____

Checking/Savings   _____

Stocks & Bonds   _____

Retirement Plans   _____

Insurance Proceeds   _____

IRAs   _____

Annuities   _____

Business Value   _____

Automobiles   _____

Jewelry   _____

Collectibles   _____

Furnishings   _____

Other   _____

Estimated Gross Estate $ _____

Calculating the Federal Estate Tax

The federal estate tax is imposed on the transfer of property owned by the decedent. It is levied on the transfer, not on the property itself. However, the tax is measured by the value of the property transferred.

There are four basic steps in calculating the federal estate tax:

1. Determine the value of property included in the gross estate for estate tax purposes. (See Ill. 11.2.)

ILL. 11.3 ■ *The Federal Estate Tax*

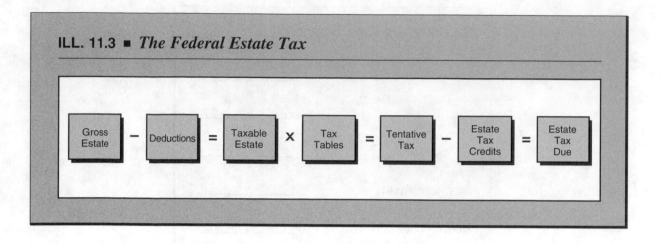

2. Subtract allowable deductions, such as amounts involved in paying final expenses and administration costs, the value of certain charitable gifts and the amount qualifying for the estate tax marital deduction.

3. Find the tentative tax from the appropriate tax table.

4. Subtract the unified estate and gift tax credit plus all other allowable credits from the tentative tax. The result is the federal estate tax payable.

Now let's look at each of these steps in greater detail. (See Ill. 11.3.)

The Gross Estate

The gross estate includes the value of all the decedent's property, real or personal, tangible or intangible, wherever located. In addition to such things as money, securities, real estate and personal and business assets, this includes property in which the decedent has a joint ownership interest, transferred property where the decedent has retained a life estate or a reversionary interest, property in which the decedent has retained certain powers of appointment and, in many cases, life insurance. Also included in the gross estate are gifts of life insurance, certain retained interests and aggregate gift taxes on such gifts, if the decedent made such transfers within three years of death.

It's important to note here that the value of the property is a value imposed strictly for the purpose of determining the ultimate estate tax payable. There are special rules for valuing certain real property connected with a family farm or business as well as for property owned jointly by a husband and wife.

It is also important to remember that virtually all types of property transferred at death are subject to the federal estate tax, including jointly held property and life insurance.

ILL. 11.4 ■ *Estate Planning Terms and Definitions*

Estate taxation and estate planning involve a number of terms with which you may be unfamiliar. Following are several of these terms, with their definitions, which will assist you in your study of this and the following chapter.

Joint Ownership—Joint ownership is ownership of property by two or more individuals. Joint ownership can take one of three forms: joint tenancy with right of survivorship, tenancy by the entirety and tenancy in common.

Joint Tenancy with Right of Survivorship—Joint tenancy with right of survivorship is a form of co-ownership where each joint tenant is considered to be an owner of the entire property subject to the rights of the other joint tenants. All joint tenants have equal rights and obligations with respect to the property. A joint tenant is free to sell his or her interest in the property without the consent of the other joint tenants, however, this severs the joint tenancy.

A key element is the *right of survivorship* under which the survivor(s) take(s) title and possession of the entire property upon the death of a joint tenant. Jointly held property is not transferable by will. That is, it passes to the surviving joint tenants by operation of law. Beneficiaries and heirs of a deceased joint tenant have no rights in the jointly held property unless they too are joint tenants.

Tenancy by the Entirety—A tenancy by the entirety is similar to a joint tenancy with right of survivorship except that it is limited to co-ownership of property held by a husband and wife. Neither husband nor wife may sell his or her interest in the property unilaterally to a third party during lifetime without the consent of the spouse. A sale of property owned by tenants by the entirety is accomplished only when both agree to the sale. Some states have abolished the tenancy by the entirety form of ownership. Therefore, it is wise to review your state law before advising clients regarding the rights and obligations of each form of co-ownership.

Tenancy in Common—Tenants in common are considered to own an undivided share of the same property. The ownership interest by each tenant may not be the same share as the other co-tenants. For example, shares in the property may be divided according to the percentage each tenant contributed to the purchase price. Each tenant is free to sell or make a gift of his or her interest in the property without the consent of the other co-tenants, unless there is an agreement to the contrary. Since tenants in common have no right of survivorship, the interest of a tenant in common passes at death to the decedent's heirs under intestacy laws or through provisions in a will. This form of ownership is frequently used in a business relationship.

Life Estate—A life estate is an interest held by a donee for his or her lifetime only (or for a period measured by another person's lifetime). The donee does not inherit the property at the donor's death. The donee merely has use of the asset for life, after which time the title to the property passes to another.

Power of Appointment—A power of appointment, which can be general or limited, is the right (received from the owner of the property) to make a gift or otherwise transfer property titled or vested in another person. A *general power of appointment* enables an individual to dispose of real or personal property for his or her own use or for the use of a third party. A *limited power*, by contrast, restricts the right of transfer in some manner, for example, to someone other than the person holding the power.

Reversionary Interest—A reversionary interest occurs where, for example, real or personal property forming the basis for a life estate reverts back to the grantor at the death of the person having the life estate. For estate tax purposes, a reversionary interest is not included in the gross estate of the deceased grantor if the property could have vested in a beneficiary during the decedent's lifetime by exercise of a general power of appointment immediately before the decedent's death. Where the decedent held a reversionary interest at death, the entire value of the property may be includable in the gross estate depending upon the value of the decedent's interest.

Deductions from the Gross Estate

Federal law permits certain deductions that reduce the gross estate. Among them are:

Final Expenses. Funeral costs, debts and certain other final expenses.

Administration Costs. These include such things as attorney and representative fees, court costs and other costs involved in effecting a smooth transfer of the estate property to the heirs.

Marital Deduction. Once the adjusted gross estate—the gross estate less final expenses and administration costs—is determined, the federal estate tax marital deduction can further reduce the amount that ultimately will be taxed.

The marital deduction, provided in §2056 of the Internal Revenue Code, is a deduction for property that passes from a decedent to the surviving spouse. The marital deduction is unlimited, but only certain property interests qualify for this deduction.

Charitable Deduction. The value of all property transferred for charitable or public purposes is also deductible in arriving at the taxable estate. The charitable deduction may be taken without limitation.

A charitable organization is defined in the Internal Revenue Code quite specifically, but generally, it means a qualified organization devoted to education, scientific and religious purposes, among others. Thus if a person leaves property to a church or school, for example, the value of the property is deductible in arriving at the decedent's taxable estate. Note, however, that bequests to individuals—no matter how needy or deserving—cannot qualify for the charitable deduction.

The Taxable Estate

After all of the deductions are taken, the resulting figure represents the taxable estate. Let's look at an example.

The Taxable Estate

Gross Estate	$750,000
Expenses and Costs	−68,000
Adjusted Gross Estate	$682,000
Marital Deduction (½ adjusted gross estate)*	−341,000
	$341,000
Charitable Deduction	−25,000
Taxable Estate	$316,000

*This example assumes that one-half of the deceased's estate is passing to the surviving spouse. The marital deduction could be as much as the entire adjusted gross estate if all the estate property passes to the spouse.

Once the taxable estate is determined, the next step is to find the tentative tax from published government tables. There are a number of software programs available that will calculate and illustrate the administrative costs and taxes an estate will likely pay at the death of an individual or at the second death of a married couple.

The Unified Federal Estate and Gift Tax

Under current law, there is a unified estate and gift tax imposed on the transfer of property or assets. In other words, the same tax rates apply whether an asset is transferred as a lifetime gift, or is included in the owner's taxable estate. However, each individual may transfer a certain amount of his or her assets to someone other than a spouse—the so-called "applicable exemption amount"—during lifetime or at death—without incurring any gift and/or estate taxes—this is known as the "unified credit."

The estate tax rates are graduated and they range from 37 percent for taxable estates over $650,000 (the 1999 exemption amount—see the applicable exemption amount) to 55 percent for taxable estates over $3,000,000. (See Ill. 11.7.) Also, there is a 5 percent surcharge that is effective for taxable estates over $10,000,000. It applies to the amount exceeding $10,000,000 and up to an upper limit (or threshold). The surcharge effectively phases out the benefits of the graduated tax rates and the unified credit. For estates over the threshold (see below), the maximum 55 percent rate applies to the entire amount. The applicable exemption equivalent, the unified credit and the threshold amount are:

Tax Year	Exemption	Unified Credit	Threshold
1999	$ 650,000	$211,300	$21,410,000
2000–2001	$ 675,000	$220,550	$21,595,000
2002–2003	$ 700,000	$229,800	$21,780,000
2004	$ 850,000	$287,300	$22,930,000
2005	$ 950,000	$326,300	$23,710,000
2006+	$1,000,000	$345,800	$24,100,000

Other Credits and Deductions

Other direct credits may also apply—such as credits for state and foreign death taxes paid—but we cannot cover all of them in detail here. However, let's look at an example of the application of the unified tax credit.

Assume an estate owner dies in 2000, leaving the $316,000 taxable estate in our preceding example. The tentative tax from the rate schedule is $93,240. The unified credit is $220,550 in 2000 (the equivalent of exempting $675,000 of property). Since the credit exceeds the tentative tax, no tax is due on the estate. This, however, does not result in a refund, even though the credit exceeds the tentative tax.

Let's assume another estate owner dies in 2000, leaving a taxable estate of $1,100,000. The tentative tax from the rate schedule is $386,800. Subtracting the unified credit of $220,550 from that amount results in federal estate tax due of $166,250.

ILL. 11.5 ■ *Joint Ownership*

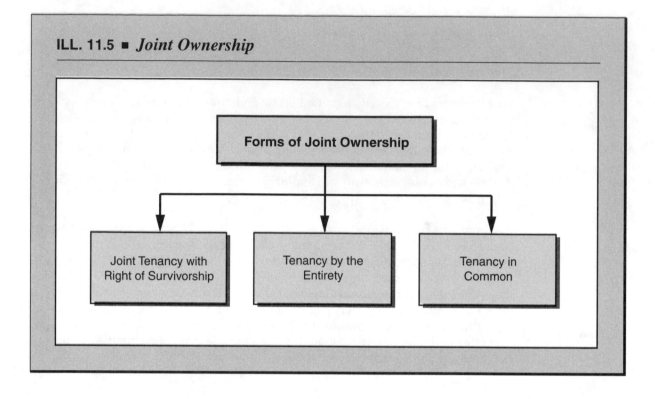

Now that we have a basic understanding of estate taxes in general, we are ready to look at a case study involving estate taxes and then examine some estate planning tools and techniques.

Case Study: Use of the Marital Deduction

As discussed previously, the federal estate tax allows an unlimited deduction for property passing to a surviving spouse. In other words, the value of all qualifying property that passes from a decedent to his or her spouse may be deducted from the decedent's gross estate, thereby lowering (or eliminating) the value that will be taxed.

This unlimited deduction is initially attractive, especially at the first death. Effectively, all of a decedent's property can pass to a surviving spouse, resulting in no taxable estate and no estate taxes. But what about the second death? Remember that a widow who receives everything at the death of a spouse has no marital deduction to use at her death (unless she remarries). Because of progressive estate tax rates, the total tax bill when the widow dies may be higher than the taxes would have been for the two estates separately, if a portion of the first estate had not gone to the surviving spouse.

For example, at the time of his death in 1995, Harold, a successful businessman, had accumulated an estate valued at $1,800,000. In his will he directed that his entire estate pass to his wife, Helen, after all settlement costs had been paid. Settlement costs amounted to 10 percent of the estate, leaving $1,620,000 to pass to Helen. The

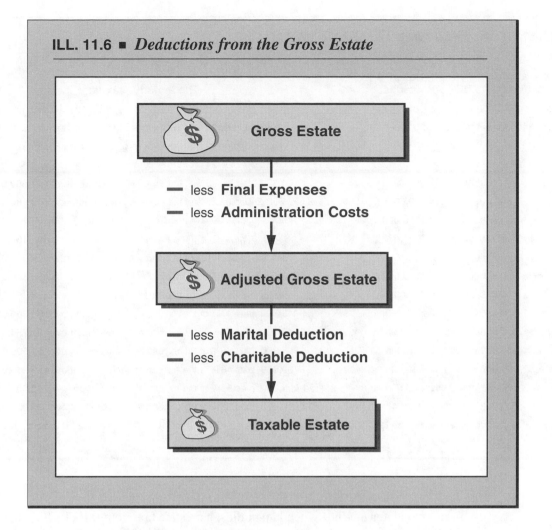

ILL. 11.6 ■ *Deductions from the Gross Estate*

Gross Estate

— less **Final Expenses**
— less **Administration Costs**

Adjusted Gross Estate

— less **Marital Deduction**
— less **Charitable Deduction**

Taxable Estate

entire $1,620,000 qualified for the marital deduction; consequently, Harold's taxable estate was $0 and no estate taxes were owed.

Four years later, Helen dies in 1999, leaving her marital share of the estate to her two sons. Settlement costs were $162,000, or 10 percent of her gross estate, which leaves a taxable estate of $1,458,000. The tentative estate tax on this amount is $537,740. The unified credit of $211,300 is applied to the tentative tax, resulting in an estate tax of $326,440.

Now let's assume another scenario in which Harold, before his death, had the benefit of legal counsel who explained that utilizing the unlimited marital deduction for the first estate may wind up costing more in the long run. Consequently, Harold revised his will and directed that, once all settlement costs had been paid, one-half of his estate would pass to his wife; the remainder would go to his two sons. Upon his death in 1995, his representative paid the $180,000 in settlement expenses, leaving an adjusted gross estate of $1,620,000. Half of that amount, or $810,000, passed to Helen under the marital deduction, leaving a taxable estate of $810,000. The tentative tax on this amount is $271,700, to which the 1995 unified credit of $192,800 is applied. Thus Harold's estate was taxed $78,900.

ILL. 11.7 ■ *Estate and Gift Tax Rates*

If the amount to which the tentative tax to be computed is:	The tentative tax is:*
Not over $10,000.	18% of such amount
Over $10,000 but not over $20,000	$1,800, plus 20% of the excess of such amount over $10,000
Over $20,000 but not over $40,000	$3,800, plus 22% of the excess of such amount over $20,000
Over $40,000 but not over $60,000	$8,200, plus 24% of the excess of such amount over $40,000
Over $60,000 but not over $80,000	$13,000, plus 26% of the excess of such amount over $60,000
Over $80,000 but not over $100,000	$18,200, plus 28% of the excess of such amount over $80,000
Over $100,000 but not over $150,000	$23,800, plus 30% of the excess of such amount over $100,000
Over $150,000 but not over $250,000	$38,800, plus 32% of the excess of such amount over $150,000
Over $250,000 but not over $500,000	$70,800, plus 34% of the excess of such amount over $250,000
Over $500,000 but not over $750,000	$155,800, plus 37% of the excess of such amount over $500,000
Over $750,000 but not over $1,000,000	$248,300, plus 39% of the excess of such amount over $750,000
Over $1,000,000 but not over $1,250,000	$345,800, plus 41% of the excess of such amount over $1,000,000
Over $1,250,000 but not over $1,500,000	$448,300, plus 43% of the excess of such amount over $1,250,000
Over $1,500,000 but not over $2,000,000	$555,800, plus 45% of the excess of such amount over $1,500,000
Over $2,000,000 but not over $2,500,000	$780,800, plus 49% of the excess of such amount over $2,000,000
Over $2,500,000 but not over $3,000,000	$1,025,800, plus 53% of the excess of such amount over $2,500,000
Over $3,000,000	$1,290,800, plus 55% of the excess of such amount over $3,000,000

*A 5 percent surtax is applied to the tentative tax on amounts transferred between $10,000,000 and $21,040,000. This surtax is added to phase out the benefit of the unified credit and graduated rates for transfers exceeding $10,000,000.

Four years later in 1999 when Helen dies, her estate tax picture looks like this: her $810,000 marital share creates settlement costs of $81,000, which leaves a taxable estate of $729,000. The tentative tax is $240,530, against which the unified credit amount of $211,300 is applied. The estate tax at Helen's death is $29,230.

In the first scenario, Harold utilized the full marital deduction at his death. The resulting estate taxes were $0 on his estate and $326,440 on Helen's estate.

In the second scenario, Harold passed half of his estate to his wife, applied the unified credit to the other half of his estate, and his estate paid $78,900 in estate taxes. At her death, Helen's estate paid $29,230 in estate taxes. The two taxes combined, $108,130, are less than the single tax Harold's estate paid in the first scenario, when a full marital deduction was used.

The point of this example is to emphasize that the marital deduction must be used carefully. (See Ill. 11.8.)

Qualified Family-Owned Business Interest (QFOBI) Deduction

Another deduction to consider, if the estate includes a business or business interests that meet certain requirements, is the qualified family-owned business interest

---

ILL. 11.8 ▪ *The Case of Harold and Helen*

Harold's Estate in 1995

	Scenario #1: (Full Marital Deduction)	Scenario #2: (50% Marital Deduction)
Gross Estate	$1,800,000	$1,800,000
Expenses, etc. (10%)	− 180,000	− 180,000
Adjusted Gross Estate	$1,620,000	$1,620,000
Marital Deduction	−1,620,000	− 810,000
Taxable Estate	$ 0	$ 810,000
Tentative Tax	$ 0	$ 271,700
Unified Credit	$ 0	− 192,800
Tax at Harold's Death	$ 0	$ 78,900

Helen's Estate in 1999

Gross Estate	$1,620,000	$ 810,000
Expenses, etc. (10%)	− 162,000	− 81,000
Adjusted Gross Estate	$1,458,000	$ 729,000
Tentative Tax	$ 537,740	$ 240,530
Unified Credit	− 211,300	− 211,300
Tax at Helen's Death	$ 326,440	$ 29,230
Total Tax (both deaths)	$ 326,440	$ 108,130

(QFOBI) deduction. There are certain requirements the estate must meet to qualify for this deduction. However, complete discussion of these requirements is beyond the scope of this book.

Here briefly is how it works. Under current law, the executor of an estate is given the right to elect a maximum QFOBI deduction of $675,000 from the gross estate—regardless of the year of death. But the total amount excluded and exempted from estate taxes—that is, the QFOBI deduction combined with the applicable exemption cannot exceed $1,300,000. In other words, if the maximum $675,000 deduction is claimed, the applicable exemption amount is limited to $625,000—regardless of the year of death.

For example, if an estate owner dies in 2002 with a gross estate of $4,000,000 of which only $500,000 consists of a QFOBI, the estate can elect a $500,000 QFOBI deduction and will have an applicable exclusion amount of $700,000 (the exemption amount available in 2002). The total amount of assets shielded from estate taxes is $1,200,000 (the sum of $500,000 and $700,000). On the other hand, if the QFOBI were valued at $1,000,000, the same estate could claim a maximum QFOBI deduction of $675,000, and the applicable exemption would be reduced to $625,000 for a total of $1,300,000.

For an estate claiming the QFOBI deduction, the unified credit cannot be obtained from tax reference materials. Instead, it must be calculated separately—depending upon the amount of the QFOBI deduction claimed—to determine the estate tax liability.

■ ESTATE PLANNING TOOLS AND TECHNIQUES

As we'll discuss later, life insurance can play a critical role in estate planning, but there are a number of other things that are essential to truly achieve the goal of minimizing estate shrinkage and maximizing readily available cash to meet desired goals. Four such estate planning tools and techniques are wills, trusts, lifetime gifts and the marital deduction. The principal device that must be considered first is a *will*.

The Need for a Will

The importance of a will cannot be overstated. Procrastination in drafting a will is all too common. While many clients know they should have a will drawn up or their existing will revised, it is human nature not to want to face the reality of death. Nevertheless, the importance of a will to the client's heirs and dependents must be emphasized.

For those persons who die without a will (a situation known as *intestacy*), the state will impose its intestacy laws which set forth how property is to be divided among various classes of dependents, heirs and family members. The problem with state intestacy laws is that they make no special provision for bequests other than to

---

ILL. 11.9 ■ *The Need for a Will*

With a Will	Without a Will
The will dictates who receives estate assets.	State laws determine who receives assets.
The will dictates how and when beneficiaries receive their inheritance.	State law makes such determinations.
The will appoints the manager (executor) of the estate.	The court appoints an administrator of its choosing.
The will nominates guardians for minor children.	The court appoints guardians.
There can be a reduction in taxes and administrative expenses.	Costs and taxes are typically greater.
The will can make bequests to charities.	Favorite charities will get nothing.
The will can create various trusts.	No such flexibility.

statutory classes. If the client wishes, for example, to make a charitable donation (or to disinherit a lineal descendent), such a specific direction is possible only with a properly executed will.

Where as part of your information gathering, you ask clients if they have a will, they may ask why they need one. The disadvantages of intestacy include (and by no means are limited to) the following:

- Special bequests at death are not possible without a will.

- Unequal division of gifts among classes is not possible without specific will provisions (the laws of intestacy presume that members of a class, children of the deceased, for example, are to be treated equally).

- The courts will appoint the estate manager (executor) rather than having it named in the will.

- If minor children are involved, the court will name their guardian rather than having it named in the will.

- Estate expenses can be saved since the will can direct the executor to determine inventory, pay creditors in a timely fashion, etc.

- Charitable bequests are not possible at death without a will.

- Estate planning to take advantage of testamentary trusts (for example, a protective or spendthrift trust for a minor child) is impossible without a will.

Now let's consider another estate planning vehicle often used in conjunction with a will to help achieve an individual's wishes, namely trusts.

Trusts in Estate Planning

Most estate owners start out their adult life with a very small estate and work hard to accumulate assets. Over a period of time, hard work, success and inflation push the net worth of the estate owner into a high estate tax bracket. At this point, the simple will that was adequate in meeting the needs of the estate during early adulthood becomes obsolete. The estate owner needs to understand the concept of *trusts* and how they can be used in the estate.

A trust is essentially an arrangement in which property is held by a person or corporation (*trustee*) for the benefit of others (*beneficiaries*). The *grantor* (person who transfers the property to the trustee) gives legal title to the trustee, subject to the terms set forth in a trust agreement. Beneficiaries have equitable title to the trust property. Trusts may be either revocable or irrevocable and may be created either during the lifetime of the grantor (*inter vivos trusts*) or after the death of the grantor (*testamentary trusts*).

Why People Use Trusts

People use trusts in estate planning for four main reasons. First, trusts can achieve *income tax and estate tax savings.* The trust is a separate taxpayer for tax purposes and this combined with the fact that beneficiaries may be in lower tax brackets than the grantor could produce income savings in some cases. With respect to the estate tax, the trust property can escape taxation at the beneficiary's death, even though the beneficiary had significant interests in and powers over the trust (e.g., the right to all trust income, certain powers to withdraw trust principal and others).

The second motive behind the creation of trusts is to provide *professional asset management.* This is particularly true when the beneficiaries are minors, elderly persons or bereaved widows and widowers. These persons may not have the experience, mental competence, legal capacity or emotional stability to manage property for their own benefit. The trust is a very convenient device to provide for these persons.

The third motive, and one that should not be underestimated, is that a trust allows the grantor to *keep strings attached,* or as attorneys sometimes put it, "to reach out

---

ILL. 11.10 ■ *Trust Terms and Definitions*

The subject of trusts requires using many legal terms and phrases that may be unfamiliar. Following are several common trust terms with their definitions to assist you in your study.

Corpus—Meaning "body." Used in connection with trusts to describe the trust principal or trust estate, constituting the body of the trust. It is also called the trust *res* or the trust property.

Grantor—The term we will use to describe the person creating and establishing a trust.

Funded Trust—A term used in connection with life insurance trusts when the grantor-insured not only transfers his or her insurance to a trustee, but also delivers property to the trustee from which such insurance can be maintained either from earnings or corpus.

Irrevocable Trust—A trust is irrevocable if the creator of the trust does not reserve the right to revoke or terminate it at his or her pleasure.

Living Trust—A living trust is simply one created to take effect during the lifetime of the grantor, as distinguished from a testamentary trust, which does not become operative until death. A living trust is also called and *inter vivos* trust.

Revocable Trust—A trust under which the grantor retains the right to revoke the agreement during lifetime and personally recover the property or retains the right to change or terminate the trust.

Testamentary Trust—One that is created by will and does not take effect until the testator's death, as distinguished from a living trust.

Testator—A term used to describe the person creating and establishing a testamentary trust.

Trustee—Cotrustee—The person to whom the legal title to property is entrusted for the use and benefit of someone else. Two or more persons serving jointly are cotrustees.

Trust Estate—Trust Fund—The property turned over by the grantor and held by the trustee; same as corpus. When the trust covers real estate and other kinds of tangible property securities, it is more accurate to use the term *trust estate,* whereas the term *trust fund* is proper when the trust covers only money. The distinction is, nevertheless, seldom observed, and the two terms are commonly used without distinction.

Unfunded Trust—A term connected with life insurance trusts, in which the grantor-insured assigns his or her insurance to the trustee but the insured pays premiums from his or her own funds and the trustee has no substantial duties prior to the insured's death.

from the grave." The trust allows a grantor to restrict the use of property by the beneficiary in a way that could not be accomplished with an outright gift or bequest. The grantor can do this by the specific terms of the trust or by vesting discretion over trust distributions in the trustee.

The fourth motive is *privacy.* A living trust agreement is a discrete contract between two parties, much like a life insurance policy. A will, on the other hand, is private only until the testator's death; at that point it is filed in the local probate court and becomes a matter of public record.

Advantages of Trusts

Listed below are some of the significant advantages generally attributable to the trust structure as a medium for the living gift.

1. The trust may eliminate the necessity for guardianships in the case of minor or disabled beneficiaries. The guardianship is often an expensive and cumbersome device.

2. It may provide life estates in the trust income for elderly beneficiaries, with gifts of the principal to others at the death of such beneficiaries, thus making possible the elimination of successive death taxes.

3. It may provide (subject to certain limitations) for the accumulation of income by the trustee until the beneficiary reaches a certain age, when the principal is to be turned over to the beneficiary. In this way, control over the property and income may be withheld until the beneficiary attains a maturity of age and judgment.

4. Though the trust must be absolute and irrevocable if estate and income tax and other savings are to be available, many contingencies can be provided for in the directions to the trustee concerning distribution of the income and principal of the trust.

5. The trust gift permits flexibility not possible in the direct gift. Various circumstances can be provided for that may arise in the future and that might make it desirable to alter the plans for distribution of the property. And the trustee can be granted discretion in the solution of many problems.

6. The use and enjoyment of the property by the beneficiaries can be subjected to appropriate restrictions and limitations; spendthrift provisions, protecting the property from dissipation by the beneficiary and from absorption by his or her creditors, can ordinarily be incorporated in the trust.

7. The trust can qualify for the gift tax and estate tax marital deductions, provided it complies with the statutory requirements in connection with terminable interests.

ILL. 11.11 ■ *The Basic Trust*

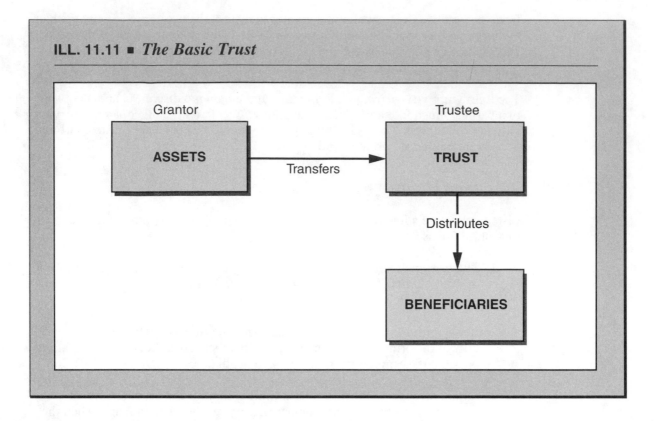

A Q-TIP Trust and the Marital Deduction

A Q-TIP trust (qualified terminable interest property trust) is a testamentary trust created by means of a will and taking effect upon the date of death. Effectively, it creates a life income interest for a surviving spouse with direction that the trust principal may not be used for anyone other than the surviving spouse during the survivor's lifetime. A Q-TIP trust permits a donor to elect to have a spouse's life income interest in the trust qualify for the marital deduction, even though the life income interest would normally have been subject to estate tax.

Why would a representative elect unlimited marital deduction treatment for Q-TIP assets? Each case will differ and several factors enter into the decision, including concern about the spouse remarrying or whether the overall tax savings are sufficient to make the election. In cases where the election only defers the estate tax until the second death and may increase the aggregate estate tax (for example, where the survivor has a larger estate than the first spouse to die) it may be advantageous not to make the Q-TIP trust election on the federal estate tax return.

The best of both worlds is possible under a Q-TIP trust by providing a lifetime income to a surviving spouse with irrevocable directions to dispose of the remainder, for example, to children or grandchildren.

The By-Pass Trust

The most basic tax planning trust may be the "by-pass" trust, which is commonly used in conjunction with a trust(s) that qualifies (or qualify) for the marital deduction. It can be established during an estate owner's lifetime and funded at his or her death. Alternatively, it can be created by a testamentary trust contained in the decedent's will provision. It gets its name because assets can be transferred—up to the applicable exemption amount (discussed earlier)—at death into this trust for the benefit of heirs (typically, children) and by-pass estate taxes. This is because the effective unified credit can be applied against the estate taxes due on the transferred assets.

If married, both spouses can each utilize the unified credit to transfer estate assets— free of estate taxes—to their children. To take full advantage of the unified credit, the couple must have a proper estate plan in effect. Without a proper estate plan, the amount that husband and wife can pass free of estate taxes to their heirs could be greatly reduced or totally eliminated.

Example: Assuming death occurs when the applicable exemption amount is $1,000,000 (in 2006 or later), up to that amount of assets may be transferred to the by-pass trust estate tax free. Although the net income generated from this trust can be paid to the surviving spouse during his or her lifetime—and the trust assets can also be used for his or her health care, education or support—the property remaining in this trust at the second spouse's death will not be includable in his or her estate

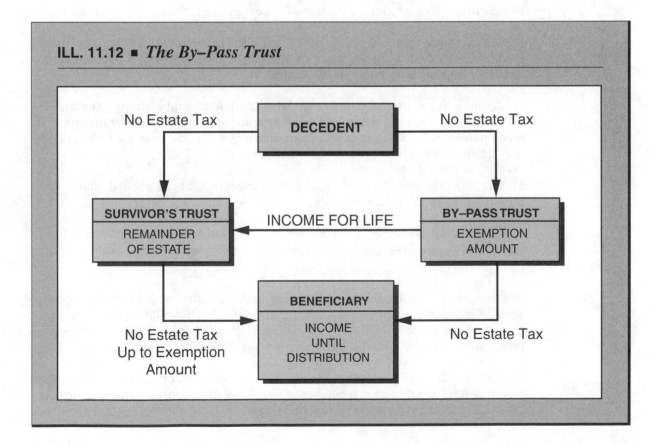

ILL. 11.12 ■ *The By–Pass Trust*

and will be received by the children estate tax free. Additionally, $1,000,000 of the spouse's estate assets may also be passed to the children. If properly planned, a total of $2,000,000 can be transferred to the children free of estate taxes.

Lifetime Gifts

As paradoxical as it sounds, an often overlooked way for an estate owner to control the shrinkage of his or her estate is through the use of lifetime gifts. Except in very limited situations in which the three-year rule applies to a direct gift, the grantor's estate is not taxed on any appreciation in the property's value that occurs in the hands of the donee.

In the past, gifts often shifted income from the high bracket donor to lower bracket children, with the result that total family income remained the same but total family taxes were reduced. However, this tax benefit no longer exists. Net unearned income of a minor child *under the age of 14* is now taxed to the child at the top rate of the parents (in 1999, approximately $1,400 of such income was taxed at a lower bracket rate—with the amounts adjusted in the future for inflation) regardless of the source of the assets resulting in the income.

Today, lifetime gifts also can result in reduced probate and estate administration expenses, because property given away during life generally is not included in the probate estate.

There are numerous advantages of a lifetime gift that are not related to estate expenses and taxes. In certain instances, these advantages may be more important to the prospective donor than the expected cost savings.

First, a gift is not open to public scrutiny unless the parties involved choose to make it so. This is unlike property passed by will, since a will becomes a public record available for anyone who wants to examine it.

A lifetime gift can give children financial independence and maturity. And, most importantly, the grantor gets to see this independence during his or her lifetime. To many parents who desire to see their children enjoy the best possible in life, this may be an overwhelming reason for the lifetime gift.

Further, the grantor is relieved of the management of the property and, thus, likewise relieved of the related worries.

It is impossible to enumerate all the motives that could possibly induce an individual to make a gift. We have, therefore, limited our discussion to the reasons that are most predominant.

In some cases, a living gift is inappropriate, either because of the size of the prospective grantor's estate, his or her age or the nature of the estate assets. It is important, therefore, that the estate planning advisor determine from the prospect's family and financial circumstances whether large gifts are advisable or not.

As you can see, a gift made during the lifetime of the grantor is a valuable estate planning device. Of course, a number of very important considerations must be taken into account whenever an individual contemplates making a gift. One

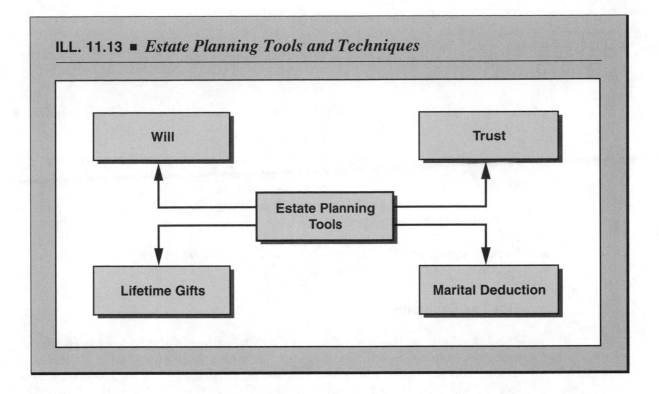

ILL. 11.13 ■ *Estate Planning Tools and Techniques*

Will

Trust

Estate Planning Tools

Lifetime Gifts

Marital Deduction

consideration affects nearly all others in one way or another—the federal gift tax. Since this tax permeates the entire subject of gifts, let's take a closer look at the federal gift tax.

■ THE FEDERAL GIFT TAX

The federal gift tax, like the federal estate tax, is a tax imposed upon the right and privilege of transferring property to another. While the estate tax reaches those transfers that take place when a property owner dies, the gift tax reaches transfers that take place during the property owner's lifetime.

Despite the imposition of the gift tax, there are still certain advantages to making gifts. Since life insurance policies are often used as gifts, you will need to be aware of the gift tax ramifications. To understand these, let's first take a look at the general provisions of the gift tax law. We will later examine the gift tax treatment of life insurance.

Calculating the Gift Tax

As mentioned earlier, a lifetime gift incurs a federal gift tax at generally the same rate as the federal estate tax. The unified rate schedules, included earlier, show the tentative tax relating both to taxable estates and taxable gifts. As with the estate tax, the unified credit is applied directly to reduce the tentative gift tax shown in the appropriate schedule. (See Ill. 11.7.)

The amount of gift tax payable in a specific taxable period is determined by a four-step process:

1. Total *all* of the donor's lifetime taxable gifts, including prior gifts and current gifts.

2. Apply the unified rate schedule to the total taxable gifts to reach the tentative tax.

3. Subtract the taxes payable on the lifetime transfers made for past taxable periods, based on the unified rate schedule.

4. Subtract the unified estate and gift tax credit. The result is the gift tax payable in the current period.

Even though current tax law applies virtually the same rates to taxable gifts as to taxable estates, there still are advantages in making lifetime transfers.

Gift Tax Exclusion

The federal gift tax law is not aimed at the usual exchange of gifts associated with birthdays, holidays and similar occasions. Therefore, the law permits the grantor to make this type of gift without tax by excluding the first $10,000 (in 2000 and subject to annual adjustment for inflation) of outright gifts in any one year to any one recipient.

Note that this annual $10,000 exclusion applies to gifts made to *each* recipient, per donee, no matter how many are included in the grantor's plans each year. Moreover, it is available year after year. This means that an individual could give $10,000 each to an unlimited number of recipients each year without incurring any gift tax liability.

We should also note that the exclusion is applied to each donee individually, and if a donee receives less than $10,000, the exclusion is limited to the actual amount of the gift. So if A gives $9,000 to X and $11,000 to Y, A can exclude only $19,000 ($9,000 for X and $10,000 for Y) and would have $1,000 in taxable gifts for the year.

The annual exclusion is available only where the gift is a gift of a *present interest* in property. This means that the donee must have possession or enjoyment of the property immediately rather than at some future date. The exclusion is not available in connection with gifts of *future interests* in property. This term covers any interest in property that does not pass into the donee's possession or enjoyment until some future date.

The "Gift-Splitting" Privilege

The gift tax law contains a provision allowing married couples to *split* their gifts. Thus where a married individual makes a gift of personal property to someone other than a spouse, it may be regarded as made one-half by each spouse. This privilege of "splitting" a gift when made to a third party is extended only to property given away by a husband or wife. If the property was owned by the husband, for instance, his gift tax return will show the total gift, and then subtract one-half as a gift made by his spouse. This, in effect, gives the taxpayer the advantage of doubling the annual exclusion. Therefore, a married individual can make gifts of $20,000 per year to any one beneficiary without incurring any gift tax liability if the spouse consents to splitting the gift. Keep in mind that gift-splitting is *not automatic* and requires an affirmative election by the spouses on their federal gift tax return.

Gift Tax Deduction

Like the federal estate tax marital deduction, the gift tax marital deduction permits tax-free transfers between spouses without limit as to amount. Also, the gift tax law permits full deduction of gifts to qualified charities just as the federal estate tax law does. Such charitable organizations are generally of the same type as those mentioned previously in our discussion of the estate tax charitable deduction. Gifts to private individuals can never qualify for the charitable deduction.

Lifetime gifts to charities may qualify for current income tax deductions and gifts of highly-appreciated, long-term, capital assets may provide income tax deductions at full market value without recognition of capital gains at the time of the gift.

If properly structured, a split-interest gift, such as a charitable remainder trust, may create an immediate charitable deduction, eliminate capital gains taxation, and provide a lifetime income for the donor and his or her spouse. While discussion of these arrangements is beyond the scope of this book, keep in mind there are a variety of split interest gifts available with various income, gift and estate tax consequences.

Effect of Gifts on Federal Estate Tax

There are certain areas where the federal gift tax rules have an effect on determining the taxation of estates at the death of the owners.

The relationship of the federal gift tax to the federal estate tax is a complex subject that cannot be covered in depth in our discussion here. For purposes of this course, the basic things to keep in mind are generally how the federal income, estate and gift tax provisions work with one another.

As you now know, each taxpayer has a unified lifetime estate and gift tax credit of $220,500 in 2000. This lifetime credit may be used to offset taxable gifts made during one's lifetime, and, to the extent unused while alive, the remaining credit at death may be used to reduce federal estate tax (if any). Thus, taxable gifts made during one's lifetime may have the gift tax offset by lifetime utilization of the unified credit, to the extent those *inter vivos* gifts are taxable.

■ SUMMARY

This concludes our discussion of estate planning, the problems in estate transfers, the federal estate tax, estate planning tools and techniques and the federal gift tax. Our objective has been to provide some insight into the many problems that face the estate owner. Some of these are common sense problems that can be solved with a common sense approach, once an understanding of the problem has been attained.

Many, however, are of a specialized nature that can only be solved with proper legal and fiscal counsel.

The attorney, the accountant and the trust officer are essential members of the *estate planning team.* When the problems encountered require legal or accounting knowledge, such problems should be referred to the estate owner's advisors. But the practitioner enjoys a unique position on the estate planning team. The practitioner alone can arouse the estate owner's interest in the problems of estate transfer and shrinkage, discuss them frankly and motivate the owner to take action toward their solution.

■ CHAPTER 11 QUESTIONS FOR REVIEW

1. Estate settlement costs include all of the following EXCEPT

   A. state and federal death taxes

   B. debts

   C. administration costs

   D. marital deductions

2. Administration costs generally account for a larger percentage of shrinkage in what size estate?

   A. Smaller

   B. Larger

   C. The percentage is approximately the same regardless of estate size.

   D. Administration costs do not contribute to shrinkage.

3. What is the major reason an estate faces liquidation losses during the settlement process?

   A. Small size of the federal estate tax unified credit

   B. Requirement that estate liabilities be paid in cash

   C. Amount of debt that most decedents have

   D. Progressive nature of federal estate tax rates

4. Generally speaking, what is the principal estate planning device available to property owners?

   A. Marital deduction

   B. Revocable trust

   C. Gift tax exclusion

   D. Will

5. In 2000, the estate and gift tax unified credit equals

   A. $220,500

   B. $600,000

   C. 18 percent of the gross estate

   D. 55 percent of the gross estate

6. Which of the following is NOT a trust-related term?

   A. Forced

   B. Testamentary

   C. Corpus

   D. Grantor

7. Which of the following is a benefit to having a will?

   A. It will eliminate the ability for creditors to make a claim against the estate.

   B. It will avoid having assets go through probate court.

   C. It will likely increase estate taxes than if no will had been created.

   D. It can allow specific charitable bequests.

8. Which of the following is NOT a deduction when calculating the portion of the estate that will be subject to estate taxes?

   A. Marital

   B. Charitable

   C. Amounts owed by the decedent

   D. Bequests to named individuals

9. Estate taxes can go as high as what percentage of an estate?

   A. 3 percent

   B. 10 percent

   C. 60 percent

   D. 100 percent

10. Which of the following would NOT be a part of a person's gross estate?

   A. His or her IRA

   B. Personal residence

   C. Personal property such as jewelry

   D. Stock given five years ago to an adult child

12

Estate Liquidity

o matter how efficiently estate planning is done, it cannot completely eliminate estate shrinkage. That leaves us with the problem of finding the liquidity needed to pay the costs that cannot be avoided. Without sufficient liquidity, a distress sale of assets or the like will add to the estate shrinkage.

This chapter first gives an overview of the methods that are generally available. Then we'll zero in on life insurance and its many advantages as a source of liquidity for estate settlement costs. You'll see why it is the only plan under which the very event—death—that creates the need also creates the liquidity fund to satisfy that need in full.

■ ■ ■ ■ ■

■ SOURCES OF ESTATE LIQUIDITY

Let's begin by making clear what we mean by the term *estate liquidity*. Estate liquidity refers to the availability of property in the estate that can be readily converted into cash. Examples are cash itself, savings accounts, bonds, marketable securities and life insurance. Liquidity involves a number of considerations including such things as taxes, probate expenses and other administration costs.

The problem of coming up with the cash for estate liquidity can be solved in one of only four ways. The first method is for the representative to *sell* enough of the estate assets to meet the cash needs. As we emphasized in the last chapter, this method means that assets often must be liquidated in forced sales. We are already familiar with the disastrous results that can arise out of this situation.

As we have seen, the most liquid property in the estate will probably be allocated to pay taxes, administration costs and other cash needs. The family will inherit the assets of poorer quality and the assets that are most difficult to convert into cash.

The second method is for the representative to *borrow* the necessary cash. The first drawback of this plan is that there is no guarantee the representative will be able to borrow a sufficient amount. Even if the representative is able to obtain a large enough loan to pay all of the cash obligations of the estate, the family eventually must repay the loan with interest. In other words, borrowing doesn't solve the problem; it only postpones dealing with it. In the long run, this method of obtaining the needed cash may be more expensive than a forced sale.

The third method is to *keep sufficient cash* or liquid investments on hand to meet the cash needs of the estate. This method would be like keeping $100,000 in the bank to replace a home if it burns. The average person does not follow this plan but allows the risk to be carried by the fire insurance company and pays premiums to protect against the possibility of a $100,000 loss. Obviously, this is a sensible procedure to protect a property owner against the risk of fire; the same approach can be employed by an estate owner to protect against estate shrinkage. This brings us to the final method.

The fourth—and by far the best—way to create estate liquidity is to provide an adequate amount of *life insurance*. To illustrate this, contrast the results of the life insurance plan with the other three methods above:

- Under the first method, the estate is depleted by the amount of the assets that must be sold.

- Under the second method, the estate goes into debt and must not only repay the loan but also interest on the loan.

- Under the third method, the obligations of the estate are paid for with 100-cent dollars.

- Under the life insurance plan, the obligations are met out of current income, with the premium deposits amounting to only 2 percent to 4 percent of the principal sum per year.

■ THE LIFE INSURANCE PLAN

The life insurance plan has many advantages. The more important are enumerated below. These are the points you should emphasize when selling life insurance for estate liquidity purposes.

First, it avoids the losses that can result from the forced sale of estate assets.

Second, it enables the estate to meet its liabilities without borrowing. Rather than place the burden on the heirs to pay interest on the shrinkage costs and to pay the principal sum, the client pays the interest personally while he or she is alive. The principal never becomes due.

Third, it promotes the effective transfer of the estate. With the estate free of encumbrances, the representative can more easily carry out the plans as the owner would have desired.

Fourth, it makes it unnecessary to keep a large amount in cash or low-yield bonds. The insurance plan takes a small amount of today's current income and at death leaves the estate's cash and securities untouched.

Fifth, by simplifying estate transfers, it reduces administration costs. This saving may substantially offset the cost of the insurance.

Sixth, it permits the payment of estate obligations on the installment plan. Just as income and property taxes are paid in installments year-by-year, the life insurance plan makes it possible to pay death costs in the same way.

Seventh, the life insurance plan can pay the cost *for* the estate instead of *from* the estate. As we will discuss later, current tax law allows the insured to remove life insurance proceeds from the taxable estate if certain conditions are met. Clearly, for the estate owner with a potential estate tax problem, this provision of the law is important. It adds an even stronger argument for using life insurance as a source of estate liquidity because under this method none of the proceeds go to the government.

Finally, the life insurance plan is the least expensive solution to the problem. Estate dollars are needed to meet estate liabilities and estate dollars can be purchased at less cost under the life insurance plan than under any other plan. Let's take a closer look at this.

Cost of the Insured Plan

Cost is an important consideration in any estate liquidity plan. All other factors being equal, the most economical method is obviously the preferred method. There are two practical points that make life insurance the most economical method.

1. *Future Delivery of Needed Dollars.* First, estate costs do not occur until death and it is not until death that liquidity is needed. Consequently, the liquidity plan should be one that reserves dollars today for future delivery at death. In this regard, the advantages of the life insurance plan are unmatched.

2. *Bargain Dollars.* Second, life insurance is purchased with *bargain dollars.* By purchasing annual premium life insurance, the estate owner can effectively liquidate all estate costs at death for a few cents annually on the dollar.

Life insurance, in virtually every case, is the most economical way to provide the cash required to pay estate liabilities. By using annual premium life insurance, the estate owner can liquidate the tax bill at death—and meet all other estate debts—for a few cents annually on the dollar. Especially in the early years of a policy, life insurance provides greater returns in estate dollars for every current dollar contributed than any other plan or kind of property. The dollars necessary to meet estate liabilities can be purchased for pennies—two to four cents per year for each dollar of guaranteed death benefits.

Illustration 12.1 indicates a representative price at which life insurance dollars can be purchased at different ages. The cost is, of course, simply the total premiums paid per dollar of face value of insurance available for meeting estate transfer liabilities.

Here, indeed, is a demonstration of the economy of life insurance in meeting estate costs. Under any other plan, each dollar used to pay taxes and other charges consumes a full dollar of the estate assets. For example, a $10,000 tax bill takes $10,000 out of the estate and away from the family. Furthermore, where the tax bill is to be paid with cash from the sale of estate assets, it may take much more out of the estate. The specific amount depends on the liquidation loss arising from the forced sale of estate assets. But under the life insurance plan, the tax bill can be met by paying a few cents annually on each dollar—$200 to $400 per year in premiums, instead of $10,000 in cash assets.

Referring to Ill. 12.1—which shows the cost of a nonparticipating ordinary life policy—we see that even after the contract has been in force for many years, the total premium cost will still be less than the face value. Only if the estate owner is advanced in years will the total premiums over the life expectancy ever exceed the face value of the insurance. Consequently, in almost every instance, life insurance will pay the tax bill *for* the estate at a cost far less than the bill itself.

■ USES OF THE LIFE INSURANCE PLAN

We have examined the important role that life insurance plays in meeting estate settlement costs, and the many advantages that the life insurance plan has over other methods of acquiring cash for this purpose.

Now we are ready to discuss several methods of using life insurance for estate liquidity focusing specifically on how the proceeds are paid out. A plan that is ideal under one set of circumstances may not be well suited to a different set of facts. Each client has a unique set of problems that must be carefully examined and analyzed on an individual basis.

Proceeds Payable to the Estate

The simplest and most direct method of arranging life insurance for estate liquidity is to make insurance proceeds payable to the estate. Such an arrangement is advantageous in modest estates where shrinkage is minimal. However, this approach makes the proceeds includable in the insured's gross estate for federal estate tax purposes. In larger estates, this results in a substantial increase in death tax liability. Let's look at the advantages and disadvantages of such an arrangement.

Advantages of Estate as Beneficiary

Life insurance proceeds payable directly to the estate provide the representative with cash to meet the estate settlement costs promptly, making possible an early distribution of the net estate to the heirs. This is one advantage to making the estate the beneficiary.

However, when proceeds are paid to the estate, they are includable in the insured's gross estate for federal estate tax purposes and, in most states, they are subject to state death taxes as well. In smaller estates, the tax considerations are generally not significant. In most cases, no federal estate tax will be due after utilizing the unified lifetime estate and gift tax credit. State death tax rates and administration expenses will usually be relatively low unless there are special administration problems. The additional life insurance required for estate settlement in these smaller estates will add little to existing tax burdens.

ILL. 12.1 ■ *The Cost of Estate Dollars Under the Life Insurance Plan*

Cost Per Dollar of Insurance*
If Death Occurs During

At Age	1st Year	2nd Year	5th Year	10th Year	15th Year	20th Year
40	2.4¢	4.7¢	11.8¢	24¢	35¢	47¢
45	2.9¢	5.7¢	14.3¢	29¢	43¢	57¢
50	3.5¢	6.9¢	17.4¢	35¢	52¢	69¢
55	4.3¢	8.6¢	21.5¢	43¢	64¢	86¢
60	5.4¢	10.9¢	27.2¢	54¢	82¢	
65	7.0¢	14.1¢	35.2¢	70¢		

* These figures are based on nonparticipating ordinary life rates. By using net premiums, one can approximate these figures in any company. Of course, adjustments must be made for each company's individual rate structure, but the figures above indicate the possibilities in this presentation of the insurance plan's cost

NOTE: These figures are simply actual premiums paid and do not reflect cash values.

Disadvantages of Estate as Beneficiary

There is one significant disadvantage in having the insurance payable to the estate, whether the estate is large or small. Where insurance is payable to the estate, the cash value of the policy may be subject to claims by the insured's creditors during his or her lifetime. The significance of this fact will depend, of course, upon individual circumstances and state law.

In the larger estate, there may be a substantial increase in the federal estate tax, state death taxes and administration expenses with the designation of the insured's estate as beneficiary. The extent to which the proceeds will increase the estate tax depends, of course, upon the size of the estate and whether or not the marital deduction is taken.

Proceeds Payable to the Estate and the Marital Deduction

As we learned in the previous chapter, when there is a surviving spouse, the marital deduction is available. The marital deduction is initially an attractive estate planning device to save on estate taxes. The value of all qualifying property that passes from a decedent to his or her estate and ultimately to the surviving spouse may be deducted from the decedent's gross estate, thereby lowering or eliminating the value that will be taxed. Insurance proceeds payable to the estate are includable in the gross estate, thus increasing the size of the estate, but they are eligible, as part of the estate, for the marital deduction. The marital deduction can be used to effectively pass all of a decedent's property from the estate to a surviving spouse, resulting in no taxable estate and no estate taxes.

Should the surviving spouse take advantage of the 100 percent marital deduction? The answer depends upon the size of the estate and many other variables that we covered in the previous chapter. You will remember that the unified lifetime estate and gift tax credit exempts from federal estate tax all taxable estates valued at $600,000 or less. It is only those estates that exceed that lifetime unified credit amount that require careful analysis before applying the full marital deduction. In some cases, using the marital deduction for the entire estate will be the best option and in other cases it will be better to use the marital deduction for only a portion of the estate. The calculations we described in the previous chapter should help you in making that decision.

Proceeds Payable to Named Beneficiary

If one person (usually the estate owner's spouse) will be the sole or primary beneficiary of the policy, it usually is expected that the beneficiary will make the proceeds available to the estate representative through a loan or by purchasing assets from the estate. This usually avoids forced liquidation losses. However, the beneficiary is under no compulsion to make the proceeds available. Such flexibility may be an advantage or a disadvantage, depending upon the individual situation.

Advantages of Named Beneficiary Plan

The proceeds of life insurance payable to a named beneficiary—even if they're subject to estate tax—are *not* part of the insured's general estate for administration purposes. Since many expenses of administration are directly related to the value of the estate assets, savings may result.

Another advantage of the named beneficiary arrangement is that, since the insurance proceeds pass outside of the general estate, they generally are not subject to claims of the insured's creditors. In some states, however, the exemption is granted only if the named beneficiary is the surviving spouse or children. However, since these are normally the beneficiaries of insurance purchased for estate liquidity, the proceeds under this plan are usually exempt.

Yet another advantage to having the insurance payable to a named beneficiary is that in many states the proceeds are entirely free from death taxes. In other states, the proceeds payable to named beneficiaries are exempt if they do not exceed the special exemption allowed under state law.

If the total insurance proceeds are within the exempt amounts, the insured can even retain ownership rights and control over the policy during his or her lifetime. This is desirable in a smaller estate where the insurance fund may also be the main source of retirement funds for the insured.

Remember that if the insured retains ownership rights and control over the policy, the proceeds will be in the insured's estate for estate tax purposes. Of course, if the surviving spouse is the beneficiary, the proceeds will be eligible for the marital deduction. This assumes that the spouse survives the insured, and that the marital deduction is used. Although the added life insurance increases the adjusted gross estate, it can also increase the maximum allowable marital deduction.

Disadvantages of Named Beneficiary Plan

When life insurance for estate settlement purposes is arranged with a family member as beneficiary, it is anticipated that he or she will make the proceeds available to the estate representative for that purpose. Usually the beneficiary purchases assets from the estate or makes a loan to the estate; however, the beneficiary cannot be compelled to do this and may well decide to keep the insurance proceeds. This can defeat the purpose for which the insurance was purchased.

Practical Suggestions

If a named beneficiary is to receive life insurance proceeds for the purpose of paying estate settlement charges, keep these things in mind:

1. The policy should be payable in cash to the named beneficiary or payable on an interest option with privilege of withdrawal of the proceeds in whole or in part at any time. The funds will then be available at once for meeting death taxes and other estate liabilities. Furthermore, the proceeds should be payable to the insured's estate if the beneficiary predeceases the insured or dies shortly thereafter.

2. It is not ordinarily desirable to name a minor as beneficiary. If the beneficiary is still a minor when the insured dies, the insurance proceeds will come under the control of a court-appointed guardian whose conduct will be under close scrutiny by the probate court. In most, if not all, jurisdictions, it is doubtful whether the court would approve the use of the proceeds for estate settlement purposes. If the client still wants to name a minor as beneficiary, a life insurance trust arrangement—discussed later—may solve the problem.

3. The named beneficiary should be advised of the plan and must understand why these policies are being made payable to him or her and the purpose of the arrangement.

4. The beneficiary must not be obligated in any way to use the proceeds to discharge obligations of the estate. The policy must simply provide the named beneficiary with the necessary cash, but with full discretion as to how the cash may be used. The beneficiary may be advised that the insurance is designed to provide the funds with which to meet estate liabilities. If the beneficiary is required to use the proceeds for this purpose, they may be subject to federal and state death taxes regardless of the beneficiary designation.

5. Because the use of the proceeds necessarily rests in the discretion of the named beneficiary, there is no absolute certainty that those proceeds will be applied to the purpose for which the insurance has been purchased. So use of this plan should depend on the circumstances of the particular estate and the character and relationship of the beneficiary.

Proceeds Payable to Revocable Life Insurance Trust

As mentioned in the preceding chapter, a trust may be either a living trust or a testamentary trust. And a living trust may be either revocable or irrevocable. A living (or *inter vivos*) trust is simply one that is definitely and expressly created by the grantor during his or her lifetime and becomes operative prior to his or her death. It is distinguished from a testamentary trust, which is created by and as a part of the grantor's will and does not become operative until the grantor's death. A lifetime gift of property in trust (as opposed to a direct gift) is, of course, given through the living trust.

Where life insurance proceeds are paid to a revocable trust, the plan is such that the grantor creates a life insurance trust and designates the trustee as beneficiary of enough life insurance to meet any possible cash demands in the estate. The insurance proceeds may be made available to the estate by provisions authorizing the trustee to purchase estate assets from or make loans to the representative. The grantor's will should contain provisions authorizing the representative to make sales to or obtain loans from the trustee of the insurance trust.

Advantages of the Revocable Trust Plan

The revocable trust is a trust that the grantor can terminate at any time he or she desires. This, in itself, is the major advantage of the revocable trust over a direct gift or an irrevocable trust. For while use and control of the property is lost to the grantor forever under either the direct gift or irrevocable trust, such is not necessarily the case with the revocable trust. Under the revocable trust, if the economic needs of the grantor change or if other circumstances make it desirable for the grantor to retain the use and control of the property, the grantor can simply end the trust.

Another important advantage of the revocable trust is that the property placed in the trust is not subject to probate and distribution as part of the estate under the intestacy laws or under the will. This fact carries with it several advantages:

1. The usual costs of probate and estate settlement are avoided and eliminated with respect to the property in the trust.

2. The trust continues in operation uninterrupted by the grantor's death. The trustee continues to hold and administer the trust under the plan set up by the grantor. Thus, the delays that are inherent in probate procedure are avoided. Notices to creditors and so on are unnecessary. The trust income becomes immediately payable to whichever persons the grantor has named. And distribution of the principal can be effected promptly, if such distribution is called for.

3. The revocable trust provides greater certainty of ultimate distribution according to the desires of the grantor. A possibility always remains that the distributive plan set up under the will may fail to function. A will may be attacked as invalid for a variety of reasons, including the incompetence of the testator or duress in its execution. While a living trust might also be attacked on these same grounds, such attacks are seldom successful. The fact that the transaction was completed by the grantor during his or her lifetime, and was in operation for some period of time prior to death, makes it difficult

to prove that the trust represented other than the real intentions of the grantor.

4. The revocable trust may also prove useful in cases in which property is located in a number of states, and the grantor wants to avoid probate in each of those states (as would be the case if the property passed into the probate estate).

5. The grantor in effect preadministers the estate. One outstanding advantage of the revocable trust over a will, for example, lies in the opportunity that the trust gives to the grantor to watch the estate plan work during his or her lifetime. A person can provide an income for a spouse, children or other dependents, with full power to make whatever adjustments appear desirable.

After reading this impressive list of the advantages, it might seem that the revocable trust is the answer to all estate planning problems. However, it is not totally without its disadvantages.

Disadvantages of the Revocable Trust Plan

The revocable trust does have some disadvantages when compared to either the direct gift or the irrevocable trust. Primarily, these disadvantages concern the income tax and estate tax advantages that can be realized by the direct gift or the irrevocable trust. Generally, when determining which route to follow, the grantor must weigh the advantage of keeping some measure of control over the property against the loss of these tax savings.

Property in a revocable trust is includable in the grantor's gross estate. Thus, the grantor will realize no estate tax savings if he or she transfers property into a revocable trust. Likewise, the grantor will not enjoy any income tax savings if the trust is revocable. The income of a revocable trust will be taxed as if the grantor still owns the property funding the trust.

When the gift is made by way of trust, certain fees usually will have to be paid in connection with the administration of the trust and the management of trust property. Primarily, this expense will consist of the fee charged by the trustee.

This cost of trust administration will obviously serve in a minor way to offset the savings that can result from keeping the property out of the probate estate. Although the expenses are usually not a major factor, they are something that should be taken into account when a gift in trust is contemplated.

Insurance payable to a revocable trust will be included in the estate owner's estate. However, if there is a surviving spouse and the trust is properly arranged, the proceeds of the insurance paid into the trust can qualify for the marital deduction. This will shelter some or all of the proceeds from the tax. In other words, life insurance payable to a trust will normally be treated the same as if the spouse were named as beneficiary. Moreover, the proceeds are guaranteed to be available for the payment of costs.

■ ELIMINATING FEDERAL ESTATE TAXES

In large estates, the insurance fund itself may increase the burden of taxes and other settlement costs. As mentioned previously, one solution to this problem is to remove the insurance from the insured's estate. However, removing it from the estate for administrative purposes does not necessarily eliminate federal estate taxes. Here, we will discuss two methods to eliminate federal estate taxes on the insurance fund. Both methods involve paying the insurance proceeds to an owner-beneficiary other than the insured.

One method involves making the proceeds payable to an individual other than the insured—for example, the spouse or an adult child. The other uses an irrevocable trust as the beneficiary. For maximum estate tax savings under either method, the beneficiary also must possess all incidents of ownership in the policy.

Individual Owner-Beneficiary

This plan simply calls for the insurance on the estate owner's life to be owned by and payable to an individual other than the insured. As noted above, the beneficiary must possess all incidents of ownership in the policy for maximum estate tax savings.

Advantages of Individual Owner-Beneficiary

The primary advantage is it achieves estate liquidity without incurring additional estate taxes. In addition, the insurance proceeds will not be a part of the probate estate. Thus, they will not cause additional estate administration charges, nor will they be subject to the claims of the insured's creditors.

However, the very cornerstone of this plan—unconditional ownership in the policy in someone other than the insured—gives rise to some unfavorable possibilities.

Disadvantages of Individual Owner-Beneficiary

The insurance may not necessarily be used for the intended purpose. To avoid estate taxes, the owner-beneficiary must not be obligated to use the proceeds to meet estate obligations. If the owner-beneficiary is the insured's spouse or adult child, this danger is usually minimized. However, there can be no guarantee that the proceeds will be used for estate liquidity purposes.

There also may be gift tax consequences. If the policy is taken out by the owner-beneficiary or if the insured takes it out and then gives it away immediately, there would be little or no gift tax initially. However, succeeding annual premium payments made by the insured may incur a gift tax, depending upon the size of the premium payments.

If the owner-beneficiary dies before the insured, the value of the policy, normally its cash value, will be included in the owner's estate for estate tax purposes. Whether, in fact, they will be subject to tax depends upon the size and character of the owner-beneficiary's estate.

The policy proceeds normally will be included in the insured's estate if the policy's ownership was transferred by the insured to another person within three years of the insured's death or if the insured retained any incidents of ownership.

Irrevocable Trust as Owner-Beneficiary

Most of the advantages of the previous arrangement can be retained—and some of its drawbacks eliminated—by substituting an irrevocable trust in place of an individual owner-beneficiary.

Under this arrangement, the estate owner creates an irrevocable trust and names it owner-beneficiary of the insurance on his or her life. It may be either a new policy or an already existing contract. The trustee, as in the case of the revocable trust, will have discretionary power to purchase assets from—or make loans to—the estate of the insured to meet estate liquidity needs.

Advantages of Irrevocable Life Insurance Trust (ILIT) as Owner-Beneficiary

The primary advantage of this arrangement is the guarantee of the cash fund. Contrary to the previous plan, the availability of the cash is not dependent upon the continued life of a policy beneficiary.

As in the previous plan, the insurance proceeds will not be a part of the general estate, so they are not subject to administration costs nor are they available to the insured's creditors.

Properly arranged, the life insurance proceeds will not be subject either to federal estate tax or state death taxes. It is important that the policy be owned by the trustee, with the insured retaining no incidents of ownership. Furthermore, as in the previous arrangement, the trustee must be under no obligation to make the proceeds available for the estate liabilities.

Disadvantages of Irrevocable Trust as Owner-Beneficiary

With an irrevocable trust, the grantor must give up completely and forever all control over the property placed in the trust. Even if he or she should need the property, it will not be available once it is placed in an irrevocable trust.

Both the irrevocable trust and the revocable trust possess the same characteristics with the above exception. Generally, the cost of creating the trust as well as administering it offset savings that can result from keeping the property out of the probate estate. Thus, although the expenses are usually not a major factor, they should be taken into account when a trust is contemplated.

Our purpose in this section has been to acquaint you with the many advantages of life insurance as a source of estate liquidity. However, before leaving this chapter, we should cover in more depth the estate and gift taxation of life insurance.

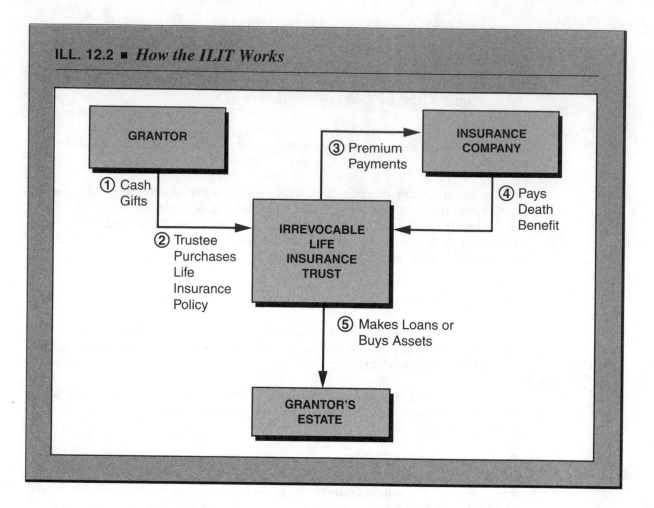

ILL. 12.2 ■ *How the ILIT Works*

■ TAXATION OF LIFE INSURANCE PROCEEDS

With respect to estate taxation of life insurance proceeds, the basic rule is that the value of the proceeds is included in the insured's gross estate if either:

- The proceeds are payable to the decedent's estate, whether directly or indirectly.

- The decedent possessed any "incidents of ownership" in the policy at the time of death.

- In addition, the *value* of a life insurance policy will be included in the insured's gross estate if the policy was transferred or gifted within three years of death.

We must consider these three situations separately.

Proceeds Payable to the Estate

The entire amount of life insurance proceeds payable either (1) to the estate outright, (2) to the representative or (3) for the benefit of the estate must be included in the gross estate as proceeds "payable to the estate."

What Constitutes Payment to the Estate?

Insurance payable to the insured's estate is included in the gross estate for federal tax purposes whether the policies are payable directly to the representative of the insured, or *indirectly* to some other person for the benefit of the estate. Thus, even where policies are made payable to a trustee or other individual beneficiary (as distinguished from the estate or the representative), the proceeds are considered receivable by the estate and fully taxable if the beneficiary is under a legally binding obligation to use them to pay a loan or other estate obligations, such as funeral and burial expenses.

Where insurance is payable to the estate, it is immaterial when the policy was taken out, who paid the premiums on the policy or even who owned the policy.

Where a policy is payable to a named beneficiary under a binding agreement that he or she will use the proceeds to satisfy a debt or other legal obligation of the insured, or where a creditor holds a policy as collateral security for the insured's debt, the estate is deemed to receive the amount actually used in liquidating its debts or obligations. The same result holds where the proceeds are earmarked to pay death taxes. However, it should be pointed out that the amount of the loan or other obligation paid out of these proceeds, together with interest to date of death, is deductible as a debt of the estate.

Proceeds as Community Property

In community property states, the proceeds of life insurance payable to the decedent's estate are split so that one-half belongs to the decedent's spouse and the other half is considered receivable by the representative. Consequently, only half of the proceeds are includable in the decedent's gross estate. However, if the policy is the separate property of the spouse, it is not included in the decedent's gross estate.

Incidents of Ownership

Where insurance proceeds are not payable to the estate, but rather to a named beneficiary, their value may still be included in the decedent's estate if, at the time of death, the decedent had any *incidents of ownership* in the policy. Basically, incidents of ownership are rights and they include the right to:

- change the beneficiary of the policy;

- surrender the policy for its cash value;

- borrow on the policy; and

- pledge or assign the policy as security for a loan.

If a person takes out a policy and names a spouse or child as beneficiary, but retains any rights in the policy, the proceeds of the policy are includable in his or her gross estate. To keep the proceeds out of the gross estate, the insured would have to transfer *all* incidents of ownership in the policy to some other person (who is not legally obligated to use the proceeds for the benefit of the insured's estate).

Transfers of Life Insurance Within Three Years of Death

As a general rule, gifts or transfers of property within three years of death are not includable in a decedent's gross estate. There are a few exceptions to this rule, one being the transfer or gift of life insurance. The transfer of a life insurance policy to a third party within three years of an insured's death will cause the inclusion of the policy's value in the insured's gross estate. The same is true for gifts of life insurance. A gift of a life insurance policy within three years of death will bring the policy back into his or her gross estate for estate tax purposes.

Where the decedent pays all premiums on a life insurance policy taken out in another's name within three years of death, the decedent is considered to have purchased the policy and transferred it and the proceeds are includable in the decedent's gross estate.

Because this rule only applies to transfers within three years of death, it still is worthwhile for the estate owner to consider such a transfer to reduce estate taxes. Even if the property is included in the estate, certain reductions described in our discussion of the federal gift tax will apply.

Life Insurance Owned by the Decedent on the Lives of Others

To conclude our discussion of the estate tax treatment of life insurance, we will look briefly at policies of life insurance the decedent owned on the lives of *other* individuals.

Let's assume a wife owns a life insurance policy on her husband at the time of her death. Since it is property owned by the decedent at the time of her death, the value of the policy, of course, is includable in her gross estate. In this case, however, the value includable is not the face amount of the policy, since the policy has not matured. Rather, the value will be either the policy's *replacement cost* or its *interpolated terminal reserve value,* depending upon the type of policy involved. A discussion of both of these methods of valuation is included in our gift tax discussion, next.

■ GIFTS OF LIFE INSURANCE

As was stated earlier, life insurance is often the subject of gifts. In fact, as you are probably aware, a life insurance policy is especially well suited for gifts. The general subject of gifts of life insurance includes gifts of the policy itself, gifts of premium payments and gifts of policy proceeds. We will deal with each of these individually, since the valuation of each differs. Keep in mind during the discussion that the $10,000 annual exclusion (discussed in Chapter 11) for gifts of present interests also applies to gifts of life insurance.

Gift of Life Insurance Contract

If an insured purchases a life insurance policy with the proceeds payable to a beneficiary other than the insured or the estate, and retains no interest in the policy whatsoever, the insured has made a gift of the policy. Likewise, an insured who irrevocably assigns all of his or her rights in an existing policy has also made a gift of the policy.

New Policy

If a grantor takes out a new policy (either annual premium or single premium) and immediately gives it to a donee, or has it issued initially in the name of a donee, the value of the gift equals the gross premium that the grantor has paid. If the policy is an annual premium contract and the grantor continues to make premium payments, each premium that he or she pays thereafter will be a gift in that amount.

> *Example: If A purchases a life insurance policy for an annual premium of $4,000 in 2000 and immediately gives it to B, the value of the gift is $4,000. If A then makes the $4,000 premium payment due in 2001, A has made another gift in the same amount.*

Existing Paid-up Policy

If a grantor gives a donee a single premium or paid-up life insurance policy that was issued in a prior year, the value of the gift equals the *replacement cost* of the policy. The replacement cost of a policy is equal to the single premium that an insurance company would charge for a comparable contract issued at the insured's attained age.

> *Example: C gives a paid-up life insurance policy issued in 1970 to B in 2000. A quotation would have to be obtained from the insurance company as to what a substantially identical policy on the insured's life would cost (single premium) at his attained age in 1991.*

Existing Annual Premium Policy

If a grantor gives a donee a life insurance policy issued in a previous year on which premiums remain to be paid, the replacement cost of the policy may be difficult to ascertain. Thus the government regulations provide that the value of the gift equals what is known as the policy's *interpolated terminal reserve.* This is an amount equal to the policy reserve interpolated to the date of the gift, *plus* the value of unearned premiums and any accumulated dividends, *less* any indebtedness creating a lien against the policy. The reserve value, not the cash surrender value, is considered, although the difference will be negligible except in the early years of the policy. The following example illustrates the computation of the policy's interpolated terminal reserve.

> *Example: A gift is made four months after the premium due date for a whole life insurance policy issued nine years and four months earlier. The insured was*

35 years of age at the date of issue. The gross annual premium is $2,811. The computation follows.

Terminal reserve at end of tenth year	$14,601.00
Terminal reserve at end of ninth year	−12,965.00
Increase	$ 1,636.00
One-third of such increase (the gift having been made four months following the last preceding premium due date) is	$ 545.33
Terminal reserve at end of ninth year	+12,965.00
Interpolated terminal reserve at date of gift	$13,510.33
Two-thirds of gross premium ($2,811)	+1,874.00
Value of the gift	$15,384.33

Gifts of Insurance Premiums

When an individual makes premium payments on a life insurance policy that he or she neither owns nor is the insured, the individual has made a taxable gift to the policyowner in an amount equal to the premium paid. So if A makes a premium payment on a policy owned by B, and under which C is the insured, A has made a gift to B in the amount of the premium payment.

On the other hand, premiums paid by an insured are gifts only if the insured has no incidents of ownership in the policy and the proceeds of the policy are payable to a beneficiary other than his or her estate. Finally, premiums paid by a sole beneficiary of a policy who also owns the policy are not taxable gifts.

Gift of Insurance Proceeds

Under normal circumstances there will be no gift when life insurance proceeds are paid to a beneficiary. However, in some extraordinary instances there may be a taxable gift.

Where a third person (neither the insured nor the beneficiary) owns a life insurance policy, a gift of the proceeds may occur when, at the insured's death, payment is made to a revocable beneficiary. The amount of the gift equals the full amount of the insurance proceeds.

W owns a policy of life insurance on her husband's life, with their children named as revocable beneficiaries. W will be deemed to have made a gift to the children in the full amount of the proceeds when they are paid at her husband's death. This is an example of a situation where there is no real intent to make a gift in the literal sense—but where there is, nevertheless, a *taxable* gift.

A gift of endowment insurance proceeds likewise occurs when, upon the maturity of an endowment insurance policy, the proceeds are paid to a revocable beneficiary of the policy other than the owner.

■ **SUMMARY**

Our purpose has been to acquaint you with the many advantages of life insurance as a source of estate liquidity. We have shown that there are several ways in which the life insurance plan can be implemented. The various owner-beneficiary arrangements discussed illustrate the flexibility of life insurance and how it can be tailored to the prospect's specific needs. While the material here is basic, it should provide a firm foundation from which to operate and upon which to build in the future.

■ **CHAPTER 12 QUESTIONS FOR REVIEW**

1. What is the federal estate tax treatment of life insurance proceeds paid to the insured's gross estate?

   A. Excluded

   B. Excluded unless the insured had incidents of ownership

   C. Included

   D. Included but deductible in full

2. Which of the following is an advantage of having a life insurance policy payable to a named beneficiary?

   A. Never part of the gross estate

   B. Part of the estate for administration purposes

   C. Usually not subject to claims of the insured's creditors

   D. Beneficiary must use proceeds to pay estate costs.

3. What is the federal estate tax treatment of life insurance proceeds payable to a revocable trust?

   A. Excluded

   B. Excluded unless insured had incidents of ownership

   C. Included

   D. Included but fully deductible

4. What is the amount of the gift tax annual exclusion?

   A. $10,000

   B. $20,000, unless the gift is split

   C. $30,000

   D. $192,800

5. The gift value of an existing paid-up policy is measured by which of the following policy figures?

   A. Total premiums paid

   B. First year's total premiums

   C. Terminal reserve value

   D. Replacement cost

6. Which of the following is NOT a method to provide for estate liquidity?

   A. Sell estate assets

   B. Keep sufficient cash on hand

   C. Do not file an estate tax return

   D. Provide an adequate amount of life insurance

7. Life insurance in an irrevocable trust has all of the following advantages EXCEPT

   A. policy proceeds will not be subject to estate administrative expenses

   B. policy proceeds are not available to creditors of the insured

   C. policy proceeds are not included in the insured's estate

   D. the trust is required to use the insurance proceeds for estate taxes

8. All of the following are incidents or ownership EXCEPT the ability to

   A. pay premiums on the policy as a gift to the owner

   B. surrender the policy for its cash value

   C. change the beneficiary of the policy

   D. pledge the policy as security for a loan

..... Answer Key to Chapter Review Questions

CHAPTER 1

1. C
2. B
3. C
4. C
5. D
6. A
7. A
8. A
9. A
10. D

CHAPTER 2

1. D
2. C
3. C
4. C
5. C
6. A
7. D
8. D
9. A
10. B

CHAPTER 3

1. C
2. B
3. D
4. B
5. B
6. B
7. A
8. A
9. A
10. C

CHAPTER 4

1. A
2. B
3. D
4. A
5. A
6. C
7. D
8. D
9. C
10. D

CHAPTER 5

1. D
2. D
3. C
4. C
5. A
6. B
7. D

CHAPTER 6

1. B
2. D
3. B
4. A
5. C
6. B
7. C
8. A
9. D
10. C

CHAPTER 7

1. D
2. B
3. C
4. D
5. A
6. D
7. D
8. D

CHAPTER 8

1. C
2. A
3. D
4. D
5. A
6. C
7. C
8. C

CHAPTER 9

1. C
2. C
3. D
4. B
5. A
6. C
7. C
8. C

CHAPTER 10

1. B
2. A
3. C
4. C
5. A
6. B
7. C
8. C
9. C
10. A

CHAPTER 11

1. D
2. A
3. B
4. D
5. A
6. A
7. D
8. D
9. C
10. D

CHAPTER 12

1. C
2. C
3. C
4. A
5. D
6. C
7. D
8. C

Survey of Advanced Sales, 7th Edition

Comprehensive Test

(This test is for your use only,
unless your trainer or manager gives you further instructions.)

Important: This test has not been approved for insurance continuing education credit and cannot be used for that purpose. If you need insurance continuing education credit for this course, a different exam is required. Contact Dearborn at 1-800-423-4723.

_____
Name

_____
Date

_____
Company

Survey of Advanced Sales, 7th Edition

Answer Sheet

1. _____   16. _____

2. _____   17. _____

3. _____   18. _____

4. _____   19. _____

5. _____   20. _____

6. _____   21. _____

7. _____   22. _____

8. _____   23. _____

9. _____   24. _____

10. _____   25. _____

11. _____

12. _____

13. _____

14. _____

15. _____

Survey of Advanced Sales
7th Edition

1. The estate gift tax rate that currently applies on taxable transfers over $3 million is

   A. 39 percent
   B. 42 percent
   C. 53 percent
   D. 55 percent

2. Which of the following statements correctly describes the tax treatment of life insurance proceeds paid to a beneficiary under a settlement option?

   A. The entire proceeds are tax free to the recipient.
   B. The beneficiary must report a portion of each payment as a capital gain.
   C. The interest amount of each payment is taxed as ordinary income.
   D. The payments are tax free until an amount equal to the policy's basis has been distributed.

3. What type of inflation is MOST effectively controlled by proper application of monetary and fiscal policy?

   A. Demand-push
   B. Demand-pull
   C. Cost-push
   D. Cost-pull

4. All of the following are advantages of SEPs EXCEPT

   A. contributions by the employer are tax deductible as ordinary and necessary business expenses
   B. SEPs are simple to establish
   C. earnings accumulate tax free to the participant
   D. SEP maintenance is easy because contribution amounts are the same for all participants

5. Whom of the following is NOT a key employee for the purpose of the top-heavy test?

   A. Officer of the employer who earns more than the 50 percent compensation limit
   B. A 3 percent owner of the employer with annual compensation of $100,000
   C. A 10 percent owner of the employer
   D. One of the 10 employees having annual compensation from the employer in excess of the defined contribution limit and owning more than a .5 percent interest and one of the 10 largest interests in the company

6. Section 303 of the Internal Revenue Code allows an estate to sell stock back to the corporation to generate liquidity for payment of death taxes and funeral and administrative expenses and treat the cash received from the sale as

   A. a capital gain
   B. ordinary income
   C. a tax credit
   D. a tax deduction

7. All of the schedules listed below will meet minimum vesting requirements for tax qualified plans EXCEPT

   A. 100 percent vesting after 7 years, 20 percent vesting per year beginning after 3 years of service.
   B. 100 percent vesting after 4 years, 50 percent vesting after 3 years of service
   C. 100 percent vesting after 5 years, no vesting for 1 to 4 years of service
   D. 100 percent vesting after 7 years, no vesting for 1 to 6 years of service

8. Under the typical disability income rider to a life insurance policy, how long must the disability exist before payments begin?

   A. Seven days
   B. One month
   C. Six months
   D. One year

9. In a limited partnership, limited partners

   A. contribute capital but have no control over the management of the business
   B. control the management of the business and contribute capital
   C. must sell their personal assets to satisfy the partnership's debts
   D. are limited by law in the amount of capital they can contribute to the partnership

10. The type of buy-sell arrangement in which the corporation owns, pays for and is beneficiary of all policies that insure the arrangement is known as a(n)

    A. cross-purchase plan
    B. entity plan
    C. reorganization plan
    D. stock redemption plan

11. Premiums paid on a key executive life insurance policy are

    A. not deductible for income tax purposes
    B. deductible up to $5,000 per year
    C. deductible up to 15 percent of the employee's salary
    D. completely deductible for income tax purposes

12. Which of the following is generally NOT used to fund a deferred compensation plan?

    A. Treasury bond
    B. Deferred annuity contract
    C. Life insurance contract
    D. Mutual fund

13. Which of the following statements regarding revocable trusts is NOT correct?

    A. The trust allows avoidance of typical probate and estate settlement costs.
    B. The grantor can discontinue the trust at any time.
    C. Property in a revocable trust is not includable in the grantor's gross estate.
    D. If properly arranged, proceeds of insurance paid into a revocable trust can qualify for the marital deduction.

14. In defining contribution and benefit limits for a SEP, the maximum amount of compensation that can be taken into account is

    A. $100,000
    B. $160,000
    C. $200,000
    D. $260,000

15. All of the following statements about Keogh plans are correct EXCEPT

    A. a Keogh plan is top heavy if more than 60 percent of value of benefits belongs to key employees
    B. owner-employees covered under Keogh plans must apply for a DOL exemption to borrow from the plan
    C. a spouse may participate in a Keogh plan only if he or she is on the payroll as disclosed on form W-3
    D. all Keogh plans, regardless of funding options utilized, must be established as trusts

16. Which of the following plans is NOT a defined contribution plan?

    A. Profit-sharing plan
    B. Money purchase plan
    C. Defined benefit pension plan
    D. Stock bonus plan

17. The consequence of a 401(k) plan's failure to pass ADP testing limits is

    A. plan disqualification
    B. plan termination
    C. taxation of plan benefits exceeding limits to highly compensated employees
    D. 10 percent excise tax if excess deferrals with accumulated earnings are not returned by the close of the plan year

18. Which of the following statements concerning policy ownership under split dollar plans is correct?

    A. If the collateral assignment method is used, the employer owns the policy and names the beneficiary.
    B. Corporate-owned policies allow an interest deduction on policy loans on the first $100,000 of protection only.
    C. Under the endorsement methods, the employer is beneficiary of the greater of the cash value or cumulative contributions.
    D. Under the endorsement method the beneficiary cannot be changed by the employer without the employee's consent.

19. Which form of business organization is MOST prevalent today?

    A. Sole proprietorship
    B. General partnership
    C. Limited partnership
    D. Corporation

20. All of the following are deductions allowed by federal law to reduce the gross estate EXCEPT

    A. administrative costs
    B. charitable deduction
    C. marital deduction
    D. inheritance tax deduction

21. All of the following rights are considered incidents of ownership in a life insurance policy EXCEPT the right to

    A. change beneficiaries
    B. pay premiums
    C. surrender the policy for its cash value
    D. assign the policy to a third party

22. A credit estate tax is a

    A. state tax on the right to receive property on death
    B. federal tax on the right to receive property on death
    C. federal tax on early withdrawals from the estate
    D. state tax based on the credit allowed under the federal estate tax for state death taxes paid

23. Early withdrawals from a qualified plan are subject to a penalty tax of

    A. 5 percent
    B. 10 percent
    C. 15 percent
    D. 50 percent

24. The purchase or redemption of a disabled shareholder's stock should be provided for in a formal, written agreement and should contain all of the following general provisions EXCEPT a(an)

    A. employee continuation plan
    B. valuation formula
    C. open-ended time period during which benefits are paid
    D. funding provision

25. Which of the following investments may NOT be used to fund an IRA?

    A. Real estate investment trust
    B. Life insurance contract
    C. Mutual fund
    D. Variable annuity